DAILY LIFE DURING

THE REFORMATION

Recent Titles in
The Greenwood Press Daily Life Through History Series

DAILY LIFE DURING

THE REFORMATION

JAMES M. ANDERSON

The Greenwood Press Daily Life Through History Series

 GREENWOOD

AN IMPRINT OF ABC-CLIO, LLC
Santa Barbara, California • Denver, Colorado • Oxford, England

Library of Congress Cataloging-in-Publication Data

Anderson, James Maxwell, 1933–
    Daily life during the Reformation / James M. Anderson.
        p. cm. — (Greenwood Press daily life through history series)
    Includes bibliographical references and index.
        ISBN 978–0–313–36322–1 (hardcopy : alk. paper) — ISBN 978–0–313–36323–8
(ebook)
1. Reformation. 2. Europe—History—16th century. 3. Europe—History—
17th century. 4. Europe—Religious life and customs. 5. Europe—Social life and
customs. I. Title.
BR305.3.A53 2011
940.2′3—dc22   2010036285

ISBN: 978–0–313–36322–1
EISBN: 978–0–313–36323–8

15 14 13 12 11   1 2 3 4 5

This book is also available on the World Wide Web as an eBook.
Visit www.abc-clio.com for details.

Greenwood
An Imprint of ABC-CLIO, LLC

ABC-CLIO, LLC
130 Cremona Drive, P.O. Box 1911
Santa Barbara, California 93116-1911

This book is printed on acid-free paper ∞

Manufactured in the United States of America

Copyright Acknowledgments

Quotations from Markham are courtesy of McGill-Queens University Press.

Table from Ladurie courtesy of Perry Cartright, University of Chicago Press.

I have drawn extensively on materials published at the time including Fynes Morrison, Rien Poortvliet, and Gervase Markham, and have attempted to gain permission for use wherever possible.

This book is affectionately dedicated to my wife, Sherry, to Corri, Siwan, and Patrick, and to Viv and Remi.

CONTENTS

PREFACE

Dramatic changes and profound upheaval affecting all aspects of society took place in Europe during the sixteenth and first half of the seventeenth centuries. This was the time of the transition from medieval society to early modern times—a period of discovery and colonization of new continents, new trade routes, wars with the Turkish Empire, and internal and territorial conflicts. It was also an age of forced migration, rampaging mercenary armies, the flowering of the Renaissance and of Humanistic philosophy. Printing presses disseminated new ideas and partisan propaganda to all levels of society along with the shattering social discord of the Protestant Reformation.

Issuing forth in Germany, the Reformation spread throughout Europe as men and women were affected in their relationships with one another and their perception of God, religion, and nature.

Impacted to a greater or lesser degree by this movement, all the countries of Europe underwent turbulent times. Least affected were Spain and Italy—remaining staunchly Catholic—while most Germanic- speaking regions (Germany, Holland, England, and Scandinavia) opted for the Reformed Church. Still others, such as France, Austria, Switzerland, the Czech lands, and Poland, went through periods of turmoil, some more than others, before the religious issues were settled.

During the centuries leading up to the Protestant Reformation there were unsuccessful attempts to extirpate Church corruption and to restore the doctrines and practices to conform to the Bible. This inspired further efforts that called for a return to a simple, unpretentious, purer religious body as it had been in the beginning. These reformers and their followers were devout Catholics who found fault with what they considered the specious doctrines and malpractices within the Roman Church, and with the wealth, arrogance, and vanity rampant among high-ranking clerics.

Sixteenth-century reformers asserted that the way to serve God was through freedom from the unnatural limitations imposed by the asceticism and restraints of the Catholic Church. This philosophy, splitting the Church, caused many to reject the ancient and medieval conceptions of Christianity.

Those who left the Catholic Church came to be known as Protestants (protesters), a term that went under many names: Huguenots in France, Lutherans in Germany, Calvinists in Switzerland, Puritans in England, and Anabaptists in various other places. This movement, a schism in the Catholic church, fractured Christian unity, inflaming widespread conflicts for over a century.

Religious intolerance accompanied the split in western Christendom, justified by both Catholic and Protestant supporters. Protestant leaders claimed they were restoring the pure faith as found in the Bible. For them, the pope was the devil incarnate. For Catholics, reformers were heretics inspired by satanic forces.

Economic, social, and political change, along with bloody religious confrontations, endured until the Peace of Westphalia at the conclusion of the Thirty Years, War in 1648.

The nineteen chapters that follow present an account of the religious furor that engulfed Europe. While numerous books deal with the Reformation, few focus on the circumstances of ordinary people caught up in the often bitter disputes and angry confusion that ruled their actions. Included for further reference are a chronological list of events, a glossary of terms and three appendices comprising the holy sacraments that provoked major contention within the Catholic Church, as well as a list of monarchs and popes mentioned in the book along with their dates, and the text of a document embodying the hopes and aspirations of the German peasants.

ACKNOWLEDGMENTS

I would like to acknowledge the following friends, family, and colleagues for their expertise, assistance, and hospitality.

Dorothy Beaver, McGill-Queens University Press
Anja Brandenburger
Richard Dalon
Dr. Patrick Francois University of British Columbia
Dr. and Mrs. Stanley Goldstein, Sion, Switzerland
Dr. Isabelle Graessle, Director, Museum of the Reformation, Geneva
Dr. and Mrs. Risto Harma
Barbara Hodgins
Dr. Ulla Johansen
Katherine Kalsbeek, Rare Books Library, University of British Columbia
Jill and Paul Killinger
Dr. and Mme Jean Larroque, Anglet
Fernando and Maribel Lopez
Dr. Bernard Mohan
Sñra. Concepción Ocampos Fuentes, Prado Museum, Madrid
Sñra. Isabel Ortega, Biblioteca Nacional, Madrid
Joanne Pisano, McGill-Queens University Press
Michel Queyrane
Dr. Richard Ring

Dr. Rodney Roche
Dr. Jurgen Untermann
Jennifer Wentworth, University of Toronto, Reference Section,
    Robarts Library

Special thanks go to my daughter, Dr. Siwan Anderson, of the University of British Columbia, for much time spent on bringing her father up-to-date with Internet usage.

The insight of my editor, Mariah Gumpert, as to what makes a good, readable text, has been invaluable. My heartfelt thanks go to her.

Finally, my deepest gratitude goes to Sherry Anderson for untold hours spent working side by side with me on this manuscript. Her persistent questioning was not always appreciated, but usually justified.

CHRONOLOGY OF EVENTS

1483   Birth of Martin Luther, Eisleben, Saxony.

1498   Savonarola burned at the stake in Florence, for heresy.

1505   Luther enters Augustinian monastery in Erfurt.

1509   John Calvin is born in Picardy. Henry VIII becomes king of England.

1512   Luther awarded doctorate degree at Wittenberg.

1515   François I becomes king of France.

1517   Luther nails his 95 theses on the church door at Wittenberg.

1519   Ulrich Zwingli initiates the Swiss Reformation in Zurich. Charles I of Spain succeeds Maximilian as Holy Roman Emperor, Charles V.

1520   Papal bull gives Luther 60 days to recant. Luther burns papal bull.

1521   Diet of Worms. Luther is excommunicated by the pope and made an outlaw by Charles V. War breaks out between Charles V and François I. First Protestant Communion celebrated at Wittenberg.

1522   Luther introduces German liturgy in Wittenberg.

1524 Erasmus publishes *On Freedom of the Will*. Beginning of Peasant Wars in southern Germany. Failure of Nürnberg Diet to condemn Luther as ordered in Edict of Worms.

1525 Start of Anabaptist movement in Zurich. Luther marries Katherine von Bora. François I defeated by Charles V at Pavia. Death of Elector Frederick the Wise. Council of Nürnberg accepted Luther's reforms. Scottish parliament bans Lutheranism.

1526 Tyndale completes printing of the English version of the New Testament. Burning of Lutheran books presided over by Cardinal Wolsey. First Diet of Speyer.

1527 Second war between Charles V and François I.

Imperial troops sack Rome. Zwingli's views on the Lord's Supper challenged by Luther. First Protestant university founded in Marburg. Paracelsus lectures on his new medicine at the University of Basel.

1528 Reformation established in Bern.

1529 Reformation officially established in Basel. Luther's followers are first called Protestants at second Diet of Speyer and death penalty for Anabaptists is restored. Tyrolean Anabaptists flee homeland for Moravia. Turks besiege Vienna.

1530 Lutheran doctrine (the Augsburg Confession) set out by Melanchthon at Diet of Augsburg, called by Charles V. First translation of Bible into French by Jacques Lefèvre d'Etaples. Protestants form Schmalkaldic League against Emperor Charles V.

1531 Zwingli killed in battle against the Catholic League.

1532 Resignation of Sir Thomas More over Henry VIII's divorce.

1532 English clergy bow to the will of Henry VIII. Calvin begins Protestant movement in France. Religious toleration guaranteed by Diet of Regensburg and Peace of Nürnberg.

1533 Thomas Cranmer becomes Archbishop of Canterbury and ends celibacy among Anglican clerics. Ulrich von Hutter joins Moravian church that becomes known as Hutterites. Henry VIII is excommunicated by Pope Clement VII for marrying Anne Boleyn.

1534 Act of Supremacy: Henry VIII declared supreme head of Church of England. Protestant placard campaign in Paris. Treaty of Augsburg allies François I with the Protestant princes against Charles V. Luther completes translation of Bible into German. Ignatius Loyola founds Society of Jesus. Strassburg expels Anabaptists.

1535 Tyndale arrested in Antwerp and imprisoned near Brussels. Sections of the Old Testament not completed by Tyndale translated by Myles Coverdale who also publishes the first entire Bible in English—the Coverdale Bible. Thomas More beheaded. Uprising of Anabaptists at Münster squashed. Emperor forms Catholic Defense League.

1536 Anne Boleyn beheaded. Dissolution of English monasteries begins. William Tyndale is martyred for heresy.

1537 Denmark and Norway become Lutheran. Erasmus dies. Birth of Edward VI.

1538 French Protestant church founded at Strassburg.

1540 Pope recognizes Society of Jesus (Jesuits).

1541 John Calvin establishes theocracy in Geneva.

1542 Inquisition in Rome initiated by Pope Paul III.

1543 François I attacks Charles V in Netherlands and northern Spain. Luther writes *On the Jews and Their Lies*. Copernicus proves the earth revolves around the sun.

1544 François I promises his support to Charles V against the Protestants.

1545 Council of Trent to reform Catholic Church, begins. Protestants massacred in 22 French towns.

1546 Death of Martin Luther.

1547 Henry VIII dies and is succeeded by Edward VI. Henri II becomes king of France. Schmalkaldic League defeated by imperial forces.

1548 First Huguenot congregation established at Canterbury.

1549 In England uniform Protestant service introduced using the Book of Common Prayer. Renewed war between England and France.

1552 Henri II of France begins war again against Charles V.

1553 Death of Edward VI. Mary becomes Queen of England and restores the Catholic faith. Execution in Geneva of Servetus, Spanish theologian and physician, as a heretic.

1554 Cardinal Pole (Mary's Archbishop of Canterbury) attempts to reestablish monasticism in England but fails when most monks, nuns, and friars reject the practice of celibacy.

1555 Charles V signs Peace of Augsburg that says each German prince may determine the religious affiliation of the territory he governs. First Protestant Church in Paris.

1556   Charles V abdicates and his brother Ferdinand becomes Holy
        Roman Emperor. Habsburgs split into Austrian and Spanish
        branches. Felipe II succeeds to throne of Spain and takes control of
        Flanders. Archbishop Thomas Cranmer is put to death by burning.

1557   Geneva New Testament published.

1558   Accession of Elizabeth I who restores Protestantism in England.

1559   Holding of first national synod of the Reformed Churches of
        France. Accession of François II of France. John Knox leads Refor-
        mation in Scotland.

1560   Conspiracy of Amboise. Failure of Protestants' attempt to kidnap
        the king of France. Publication of Geneva Bible (both Old and
        New Testaments). First Bible printed with verse divisions.

1561   Property of anyone in France who attends any public religious ser-
        vice other than Roman Catholic will now be seized and the owner
        imprisoned, as ordered by Royal Edict. Mary Stuart becomes
        queen of Scotland.

1562   New religion recognized as legal in France by Royal edict of Saint-
        Germain. Massacre of Protestants at Vassy by the duke of Guise
        sparks off first civil war in France that would continue intermit-
        tently until 1598.

1563   Assassination of the duke of Guise. Establishment of the Anglican
        Church completed by the Thirty-Nine Articles.

1564   John Calvin dies in Geneva. The term "Puritan" first used.

1566   War between Spain and Protestant United Provinces.

1567   Mary, Queen of Scots forced to abdicate and thrown into prison.
        Spanish army under the duke of Alba moves into Netherlands to
        suppress revolt.

1568   Escape to England of Mary, Queen of Scots who then is impris-
        oned by Elizabeth I. War between Netherlands and Spain begins.

1569   Death of Condé. Peace of St. Germain terminates third war of reli-
        gion in France.

1572   Henri of Navarre and Marguerite of Valois married. St. Bartholo-
        mew's Day. Admiral Coligny murdered. Fourth Civil War begins
        in France.

1574   Death of Charles IX. Accession of Henri III. Truce with Huguenots
        in France.

1576   Formation of the Catholic League under the Guise faction. Fifth French civil war ended. Spanish sack Antwerp.

1577   Alliance between England and Netherlands.

1579   Southern Netherlands united by Union of Utrecht under duke of Parma, governor for Felipe II.

1581   Oath of Abjuration: Independence from Spain proclaimed by the United Provinces.

1584   Assassination of William of Orange. Death of duke of Anjou. Henri of Navarre now heir to the French throne. Cardinal de Bourbon proclaimed heir apparent by duke of Guise. The Guises and Felipe II sign Treaty of Joinville.

1585   Henri III capitulates to the Catholic League and the Guises. Treaty of Nemours. Start of the War of the Three Henri's. England sends aid to Netherlands rebelling against Spanish rule; Commencement of Anglo-Spanish War.

1586   Mary, Queen of Scots involved in conspiracy against Elizabeth I.

1587   Mary, Queen of Scots executed.

1588   Day of the Barricades. Spanish Armada attacks England. Both the duke of Guise and the Cardinal of Guise killed at Blois.

1589   Henri III slain. Henri of Navarre becomes Henri IV of France. Death of Catherine de Medici.

1590   Battle of Ivry. Siege of Paris.

1593   Henri IV becomes Roman Catholic.

1594   Crowning of Henri IV at Chartres.

1595   France declares war on Spain.

1598   Peace of Vervins. Death of Felipe II. French Protestants awarded civil and religious freedom by Edict of Nantes. End of Franco-Spanish War.

1601   Elizabethan Poor Law orders the parishes to provide for the needy.

1604   James I outlaws Jesuits; peace made between England and Spain.

1607   Proposals for confederation between England and Scotland rejected by Parliament.

1608   Johannes Lippershey invents telescope.

1609 Kepler *Astronomica Nova*. Twelve Years' Truce in the 'Eighty Years' War (1568–1648) agreed to by The Netherlands and Spain.

1610 Henri IV of France assassinated.

1611 King James Bible is completed. English and Scottish Protestants move to Ulster.

1618 Thirty Years' War begins when Bohemians revolt against the Habsburgs.

1620 Pilgrims arrive at Plymouth Rock, Massachusetts.

1621 Spain's truce with the Protestant northern Netherlands ends and war resumes.

1624 France, Holland, England, Sweden, Denmark, Savoy, and Venice ally against the Habsburgs.

1625 Charles I ascends the throne of England.

1626 Siege of La Rochelle begins.

1627 Charles I of England declares support for French Huguenots. English fleet sent to La Rochelle to help Huguenots fails.

1628 La Rochelle falls to French troops.

1629 Parliament dissolved by Charles I who assumespower himself.

1630 Peace made between England, France, and Spain.

1631 First newspaper published in Paris.

1633 Galileo suspected of heresy.

1635 War on Spain declared by Louis XIII of France.

1636 War continues between France and the Holy Roman Empire.

1640 Short Parliament dissolved for refusing to grant money and summoned by Charles I. The Long Parliament begins. Portugal gains independence from Spain.

1641 Irish Catholics revolt; massacre of approximately 30,000 Protestants.

1642 Civil War in England begins. Death of Richelieu.

1643 Louis XIV guarantees Edict of Nantes. Sweden invades Denmark.

1644 Habsburgs defeated by French, Swedish and Dutch.

1647 Protestantism established officially in England.

1648 Treaty of Westphalia ends Thirty Years' War.

1

HISTORICAL OVERVIEW OF THE REFORMATION

Prior to the Reformation, Europeans believed in God, Christ, saints, and the Bible as interpreted by the Catholic Church. Any criticism of Catholic views or tradition, any questioning of its dogma, could elicit dire consequences. Nevertheless, some men dared to question.

EARLIER DISSENTERS

In the 1300s, John Wycliffe, in England, denounced corruption in the Catholic Church and questioned its orthodoxy and compatibility with the Bible. He was posthumously declared a heretic, and by order of the pope his bones were disinterred, burned, and thrown into the river.

Later in the century, Jan Hus, in Bohemia, placed emphasis on the word of the Bible as the sole religious authority. Offered safe conduct to Constanz to explain his views, he was betrayed and burned there at the stake. Giralamo Savonarola, from Florence, an Italian Dominican monk, also spoke out for reform of the Church in the fifteenth century, denouncing the prevalent corruption and immorality. He and two disciples, still professing their adherence to Catholicism, were hanged and burned.

The loudest and most energetic opponents of Church abuse were mostly northern Europeans, such as Erasmus of Rotterdam, who reflected the spirit of humanism and had a great influence on reformers. At the beginning of the sixteenth century, he condemned the failings of the Church and society as well as the religious practices of the ecclesiastical hierarchy that had lost all resemblance to the apostles they were supposed to represent. Nonetheless, Erasmus remained true to the Catholic faith.

Some European monarchs, tired of seeing their wealth drained away by the Vatican, succeeded in their demands for the right to make their own ecclesiastical appointments, but they still resented the flow of wealth from their states to Rome in the form of *annates*, Peter's Pence, indulgence sales, Church court fines (Church courts shared judicial power with state courts), income from benefices, fees for bestowing the pallium on bishops, and perhaps even the money citizens paid to the priest for the many Masses they often had performed for the sake of loved ones languishing in purgatory.

They also enviously eyed Church lands and could see the waste of money tied up in vast Church and monastic holdings that could be freed for expansion. The peasants, too, who shouldered most of the financial burdens, expressed similar sentiments in occasional riots.

MARTIN LUTHER

An Augustinian monk, Martin Luther, born in 1483 at Eisleben, Saxony, in eastern Germany, also found fault with the Church's policies.

Luther was infuriated by a fellow Catholic, Johann Tetzel, a Dominican friar who preached to the people that the purchase of a letter of indulgence from the pope would ascertain the forgiveness of sins and lessen the time they or their ancestors would spend in the fires of purgatory. A good salesman, Tetzel vividly described the torments in purgatory with unrestrained imagination.

On October 31, 1517, Luther, now a professor at the University of Wittenberg, nailed 95 theses to the door of the Wittenberg Castle church, intending for these points, critical of the Church and the pope, to be subjects of academic debate. The most controversial points centered on the selling of indulgences and the Church's policy on purgatory. He was not trying to create a new religious movement.

Luther sent a copy of the theses to Archbishop Albrecht of Mainz, Tetzel's superior, requesting the Archbishop put a stop to Tetzel's high-pressure sales of indulgences. He also sent copies to friends. There were direct references to reform in the document: thesis 86, for example, referring to money collected from indulgences supposed to help fund the construction of Saint Peter's Cathedral in Rome, asked "Why does not the pope, whose wealth is to-day greater than the riches of the richest, build just this one church of St. Peter with his own money, rather than with the money of poor believers?"[1]

Luther directs the posting of his 95 Theses, protesting against the sale of indulgences, to the door of the Castle Church in Wittenberg, Germany, 1830. (Library of Congress.)

Archbishop Albrecht, who held three benefices (contrary to canon law), acted as chief commissary for the disposal of money from indulgences. Pope Leo X had granted him a dispensation for the sum of 24,000 ducats that Albrecht raised by borrowing from private bankers. To pay off his debt, half of the income from indulgences was to go to Albrecht and his bankers and the other half to the pope. How much Luther knew of the secret and shady deals at the Vatican may never be known. The fall in revenues worried Albrecht, and he reported Luther's interference and questionable orthodoxy to the pope who at first considered the theses the work of a drunken German. Luther wrote to the pope that faith alone, not priests, was the way to salvation. Such an opinion was anathema to the Catholic Church and resulted in his condemnation.

In August 1518, Luther was summoned to Rome to be examined on his teachings, but his territorial ruler, Elector Frederick III of Saxony, knowing the journey would not be safe, intervened on his behalf and supported Luther's wish to have an inquiry conducted in Germany since he felt it was his responsibility to ensure his subject was treated fairly. After seeing what had befallen Jan Hus, who could be sure of what would happen in Rome?

The pope agreed to Frederick's demands because he needed German financial support for a military campaign against the Ottoman Empire, whose forces were poised to march on central Europe, and because Frederick was one of the seven electors who would choose the successor of the ailing Emperor Maximilian. The Papacy had a crucial interest in the outcome of this election, hoping for a dedicated Roman Catholic.

Luther was summoned to the southern German city of Augsburg to appear before an imperial Diet in October 1518, where he met with Cardinal Cajetan, who demanded that the monk repudiate his beliefs. Luther refused, and nothing was accomplished.

By the end of the same year, Luther came to some new conclusions regarding the Christian notion of salvation. In the view of the Church, good works were pleasing to God and aided in the process leading to salvation. Luther rejected this, asserting that people can contribute nothing to their salvation, which is fully a work of divine grace. His insight that faith alone provided the road to salvation came to him while meditating on the words of Saint Paul.[2] For Luther, neither indulgences nor good works played any part in this. Man could not buy his way into Heaven.

The controversy prompted Johann Eck, a Catholic theologian, to set up a public debate with Luther in Leipzig in July 1519. Eck attacked Luther, and the debate over Church authority grew fierce. Eck demanded to know how God could let the Church go astray. Luther responded by pointing out that the Greek Orthodox Church did not acknowledge Rome; hence it had already gone astray. Luther was then charged with taking the point of view of the heretics, Wycliffe and Hus. He also demanded to know if Luther considered the Council of Constanz (which had condemned Hus) had made a bad judgment, and Luther affirmed that councils could err, a heretical statement in itself.

Arguments on other matters such as purgatory and penance continued for several more days. Convinced that through Christ alone lay the road to redemption; Luther asserted that he recognized only the sole authority of scripture. After Luther departed Leipzig, a war of books and pamphlets by both factions ensued.

Luther's writings in 1520 included his belief in the priesthood of all believers, and he tried to convince secular rulers to use their God-given authority to rid the Church of immoral prelates including popes, cardinals, and bishops.

Attacks on the holy sacraments followed. A Papal Bull, issued by Pope Leo X on June 15, 1520, gave Luther 60 days to repent.

On December 10, 1520, sympathetic Wittenberg students lit a bonfire burning up books of canon law as well as others written by Luther's enemies. Luther himself threw a copy of the pope's Bull into the flames. Another Papal Bull issued on January 3, 1521 excommunicated Luther

Luther burning the Papal Bull of excommunication with vignettes of Luther's life and portraits of other reformers including Hus, Savonarola, Wycliffe, Melanchton, Gustav Adolf, and Bernard of Saxe-Weimer. Lithograph. H. Schile, c. 1874. (Library of Congress.)

and gave orders to burn all his writings. The aging Holy Roman emperor, Maximilian I, had meanwhile died in 1519, and Charles V, a rigid Catholic, was now at the helm of the Empire.

EDICT OF WORMS

In April 1521, Charles V was persuaded by the Elector Frederick III, to allow Luther to defend his writings at the Diet of Worms. Bearing a safe conduct pass, Luther was escorted to the city by Franz von Sickingen, a German knight. Traveling in a small covered wagon, Luther arrived at Worms on April 16, 1521, where he was greeted heartily by many of the town's people. Luther was escorted to the Bishop's palace where, as the crowds gathered, he was requested to recant. The following day he stated that unless he was convinced by scripture, he did not accept the authority of the popes and councils. He would recant nothing. Luther was dismissed but not arrested because of his letter of safe conduct that allowed him 21 days to reach home.

Both the Church and the emperor had failed to convince Luther to disavow his teachings at Worms. The princes who supported him hoped that forthcoming events would significantly weaken the political and economic power of Rome over Germany.

After Luther departed, Charles V imposed an imperial act making Luther an outlaw; he could be killed on sight by anyone without danger of punishment.

On the journey home, Elector Friedrich III had Luther whisked away by his soldiers to his secluded Wartburg castle, to guarantee Luther's safety and to allow him to disappear for awhile. Rumors about his death spread. Meanwhile, colleagues who favored the new beliefs began to organize. While Luther remained at Wartburg Castle, Andreas Karlstadt, a reformer in Wittenberg who had won over the city council to his views, performed the first reformed Communion service on Christmas Day 1521. He did not elevate the Eucharist during Communion, he wore secular clothing during the service, and he made no references to sacrifice from the traditional Mass. He spoke aloud, rather than whispering the words of Communion in German rather than Latin. Rejecting confession as a prerequisite for Communion, he allowed the communicants to take the bread and wine themselves instead of it being given to them. In January 1522, the Wittenberg city council authorized the removal of imagery from churches, affirming the changes introduced by Karlstadt. Roman Catholic efforts to eliminate the new preachers of the Reformation were unsuccessful and within two years after the Edict of Worms, it was widely recognized that the movement for reform was too strong to be suppressed. Luther returned to Wittenberg the first week of March 1522, where his teachings aroused popular protests among Catholics that threatened to undermine law and order. Luther detested civil disobedience and managed to control the course of reform in Wittenberg.

The new Pope, Adrian VI, sent his nuncio to the Nürnberg Diet of 1522 to insist that the Edict of Worms be executed and action be taken promptly against Luther. This demand was coupled with a promise of thorough reform in the Roman hierarchy and admitted the partial guilt of the Vatican in the decline of the Church.

After the Edict of Worms, the inducement to reform turned from simply a religious struggle into both legal and political conflicts, and reformers themselves had their large egos and petty jealousies. Luther fell out with Karlstadt for a time and started to campaign against him, denying his right to publish and preach without Luther's authorization.

Crucial decisions about who would preach in local churches, Catholic or reformer, were now often made in the city councils or higher echelons of secular government. By 1523, various influential reformers appeared on the scene such as Thomas Münzer, an itinerant preacher, Ulrich

Zwingli in Zürich, and Martin Bucer in Strassburg, all advocating more radical reforms of Church and society.

Although the Catholic Church prohibited common people from reading the Bible, biblical phrases and ideas stuck in their minds after attending evangelical sermons and listening to religious ideas that were considered heretical. The overworked and heavily taxed laborers of the cities, small farmers, landless peasants, impoverished journeymen, beggars, the debt-ridden small masters, the impecunious knights, and the unemployed mercenary soldiers all responded to Luther's criticism of the authority of the Roman Church and found consolation and incentive to action in the notion of divine justice available to everyone.

Catholic priests countered with the notion that God had created the earthly hierarchy of classes from peasant to king, and it was against His will to try and change it.

Gaining support in towns and cities in central Europe, the Reformation reached remote villages where peasants had a difficult time knowing whom to listen to and what to believe. They were told to give up fasting during Lent, to abandon their saints and images, that their priests should marry, that faith alone was sufficient to attain heaven, and that the idea of purgatory and indulgences was a sham. They were now also told they could divorce from an unhappy marriage and even remarry. Peasants' lives were in turmoil. Listen to the priest or the evangelists?

PEASANTS WAR

As in other parts of Europe, the peasants in the Holy Roman Empire lived a miserable life supporting the Church and the nobility with their toil, sweat, and taxes, while their restrictions were many.

They could not hunt or fish to supplement their meager diet or collect firewood for warmth, as the land, the forest, and the game in it were the property of the landowner. The peasant would be forced to watch his crops destroyed by wild animals or by nobles hunting on horseback in his fields. If he wished to marry, he needed the lord's permission and would pay a tax for the right. When the peasant died, the lord of the manor was entitled to his best animals and tools. The justice system, staffed by clergy, wealthy townsmen, and patricians would take the side of the upper classes when a problem arose. There were complaints and rebellions in local areas, but to make their strength felt, peasants needed to organize.

In the summer of 1524, peasants in southwestern Germany participated in uprisings partly inspired by Luther's pronouncements and reforms. Concerned also with economic and political grievances, many refused to pay their tithes. By the spring of 1525, the rebellion had spread into central Germany, and supported by the reformer Münzer, they published a proclamation known as the 12 Articles of the Peasants. (See Appendix III).[3]

In the first, relatively nonviolent period of the uprising, the grievances were directed more against the clergy, particularly monasteries and cathedral chapters, than against the aristocracy. But soon political and economic protests against serfdom, labor services, and landlords' exploitation of forests, waters, and common meadows would become linked with demands by villagers to administer their own tithes and to choose pastors who would preach the Word of God without manmade additions that benefited only the Church.

It had been a large ideological step for most peasants to accept the ideas of the reformers, who questioned the authority of the Church. It was not much further to go to challenge the power of landowners, both secular and ecclesiastical. On one estate, it was said that the wife of a count began a rebellion by insisting that their tenants gather wild strawberries for her on a religious holiday.

United in large numbers and carrying the only weapons they had— scythes, axes, pitchforks, hoes, and clubs—the peasants set up camps and formed what they called the Christian Brotherhood. The leaders held a parliament in the small town of Memmingen in March 1525. From here, notice of their actions and demands were sent to the Catholic Swabian League and to the emperor explaining that the action taken was in accordance with the gospel and with divine justice. The league stalled for time while it amassed an army, making promises it did not intend to keep, to consider peasant grievances.

By this time, the entire country around Ulm was in a state of insurrection led by Hans Müller, a former soldier of fortune. A black, red, and yellow flag was stitched together under which, on Saint Bartholomew's Day, August 24, 1524, 1,200 peasants marched to Waldshut under cover of a Church ale that was being held in the town. They fraternized with the inhabitants of the little town, and the first Evangelical Brotherhood came into existence. Members were asked to contribute a coin weekly to facilitate the expenses of secret dispatches that were distributed throughout Germany, inciting a general uprising, their message stating there should be no lord other than the emperor to whom proper tribute should be rendered, and all castles and monasteries should be destroyed together with their charters and their jurisdictions.

The inevitable conflict occurred primarily in southern, western, and central regions of the German lands, and affected, to a lesser degree, Switzerland and Austria.

As the peasant movement spread, Truchsess, the commanding general of the Swabian League, gathered forces and kept the enemy under surveillance, sometimes negotiating, sometimes threatening. But as winter approached, little was done on either side. The peasant bands sacked some monasteries while Austrian authorities at Ensisheim, in Alsace, the seat of Habsburg power in the west, gathered forces, burned homesteads and seized livestock. As peasant momentum grew, nobles deserted their castles for towns whose loyalty and defensive walls offered more personal safety. As many as 300 clergy, some of them disguised and with the tonsure covered, fled to Überlingen, a safe haven, on Lake Constanz.

On January 20, an informal meeting took place between Truchsess and representatives of the Austrian Habsburg power on the one side and delegates from the disaffected population on the other. Truchsess succeeded in convincing some of those present to go home. Others mistrusted his promises. Even while their farms and villages were going to ruin, they refused to disperse and return to the old oppressive system.

On February 14, having gathered a large mercenary force, Truchsess sent the peasant bands an ultimatum, accompanied with the threat to pursue them without mercy if they failed to accept his conditions. The whole of central Europe now anticipated a bloody struggle. By the beginning of April, war raged throughout Germany.

The preacher, Thomas Münzer, believed like Martin Luther that the last judgment was imminent. A popular preacher, agitator, and self-appointed leader in the peasants' revolt, Münzer had preached a sermon on July 13, 1524, at Allstedt, in which he asserted that the last days were at hand. He saw the first signs of God's final judgment in the peasants' war. For him, these rebellious subjects were God's elect carrying out His plan of apocalyptic judgment.

With vengeance on their minds on Easter Day, April 16, 1525, peasants camped at Neckarsulm on the River Neckar north of Stuttgart, learned that Count Ludwig von Helfenstein, governor of Weinsberg, along with his nobles, had left his castle and gone down into the town to persuade the citizens of Weinsberg not to join the peasant hordes, promising immediate death to all rebellious peasants who fell into his hands. **The Massacre of Weinsberg**

Those camped at Neckarsulm made haste to the vulnerable castle. Scaling the walls, they captured the countess and her children, plundered the castle, and then appeared before the town. To the count's dismay, the townspeople supported the attackers and opened the gates. The peasants seized the count, the nobles, and a cavalry unit. A nobleman called down from the church tower begging for mercy and offered them money. The rebels shot him. Then they marched the count and his retinue to a nearby field where they formed a circle around them. The count offered to give them a barrel of money if they would let him live, but he and 23 others were slaughtered and left lying naked on the ground. The peasants set the castle on fire and then marched off to Würzburg.[4]

Lack of communication and coordination between peasant forces in north, central, and southern Germany, however, and pitched battles with trained imperial soldiers cost them the war and a rapid collapse of the movement. Most battles were one-sided slaughters. The defeat of rebel forces in May, 1525, marked a major victory of the status quo.

The war was a disaster for the farmers and villagers of **Results of the** Germany. About 100,000 were killed, and large numbers **Peasants' War** were left homeless. Disease and famine abounded. Bandits ranged the roads and forests, and beggars crowded into the larger cities. Orphans, the sick, and the elderly were severed from the normal charities. Many froze or starved to death in the vast forests where numbers of them had vainly sought shelter. Rural artisans, miners, foresters, bakers—everyone suffered. Intense resistance extended mainly from late January to early June 1525, mostly in upper Swabia, the upper Rhine, Franconia, Württemberg, Alsace, Thüringia, and the Tyrol. The rebel groups numbered about 300,000 at their high point. Luther wrote two responses concerning the Twelve Articles. In the first, he expressed sympathy for the peasants and in the second, with his sense of civil order, he denounced them.

Many in the movement of 1525 thought of it as part of the Reformation and would have taken it for granted that it was appropriate to apply God's law as perceived by Luther to economic, political, and social abuses; but many felt betrayed by Luther's condemnation. Their political agenda sought to remove the Catholic clergy, and, for some, to remove the aristocracy from positions of worldly authority. They sought greater autonomy for villages and more power for urban and rural commoners in the representative assemblies of the states. There were attempts in southwestern Germany to adhere to the model of the neighboring Swiss Confederation or programs modeled on contemporary working political institutions such as peasant estates in Denmark and Sweden with representative assemblies.

At the end of the revolt, little had changed except that the population had been greatly bloodied and reduced.

JEWS

The situation for Jews in the sixteenth century was lamentable. They had been expelled from various European countries under terrible conditions and forced to seek refuge primarily in North Africa, the Ottoman Empire, and eastern Europe.

Many Jews, forced to flee the Iberian Peninsula under the fanatical, insensate Queen Isabella in 1492, settled in Holland, especially Amsterdam, where they were granted freedom of worship. In southern France, they lived mainly in the port cities of Bordeaux and Bayonne, while in the German city of Hamburg, Jews were welcomed and permitted to openly practice their faith, although, as in Frankfurt and other places, they were restricted to living in a ghetto.[5]

Although some converted Jews would play a part in the Reformation movement as teachers, printers, writers, editors, and publishers, most had no appreciable role and only suffered the consequences.

In 1553, Pope Julius III displayed his anti-Jewish disposition declaring the Talmud sacrilegious and blasphemous and placing it on the Index of Forbidden Books, and some years later Pope Pius V expelled the Jews from all papal states except Ancona.[6]

In Augsburg, they were forbidden to mix with Christians, such act being, in theory, punishable by death.[7]

The pressure was always there to convert to Christianity. Defamation of Jews as morally and socially degenerate and their isolation and abuse caused bitterness and hatred between Jew and Christian. Horror stories about Jews killing Christian infants, poisoning wells, bringing on the plague, desecrating the host by stealing wafers and burning them in the conviction that they were destroying Christ himself, and impugning the Virgin Mary, always appealed to a large audience.

Such stories circulated at all levels of society and were subjects of sermons by coarse and ignorant monks trying to stir up passions among the populace.

In Luther's early days, he seemed sympathetic to the plight of Jews, knowing that Jesus himself was a Jew; **The Jews and** and Jews who were aware of the first stirrings of the Ref- **Luther** ormation welcomed it because it was dividing their persecutors. Giving them false hopes while trying to win them over to his cause, Luther stated that they should be treated in a friendly manner, hoping that a policy of toleration would yield converts.

Failing to convert them en masse, however, he became vindictive, his anti-Jewish sentiments emerging in his article, "Concerning the Jews and their Lies," published in 1543. Here, he asserted that no Jews, heretics, Turks, heathens, false Christians, and hypocrites could be saved without embracing the congregation of the faithful. He further urged people to burn down Jewish schools and synagogues, confiscate their texts, and if this did not succeed in converting them, they should be expelled.

Jews came to realize that neither Catholic nor Protestant could be trusted. In his later years, Luther saw the Jews and Turks as allied in a conspiracy to destroy the Holy Roman Empire on orders of the devil. For him, Jews clinging obstinately to their own faith presented a rebellion against God who had already punished them with continued misery.

One of Luther's last recorded statements accused Jewish doctors of poisoning their patients and offered advice to his successors that "if the Jews refuse to be converted, we ought not to suffer them or bear with them any longer."

Despite Luther's anti-Jewish stance, members of his own circle included many who maintained a friendly approach to the Jews. One, the noted theologian Andreas Oslander, issued a pamphlet anonymously discrediting the libel and superstitious defamation.

During the sixteenth and seventeenth centuries, as the Counter-Reformation sought to strengthen Catholicism and the papacy, many of the regulations against Jews were tightened and increased.

Sixteenth-century German communities, which still permitted Jews to cohabit with Christians, also found ways to degrade them. In Frankfurt, 4,000 Jews were confined to a ghetto and treated as criminals. They could not leave except on important business, and two could not walk together. They were obliged to soften their voices so as not to offend Christian ears, and special, identifying badges with such symbols as an ass, a dragon, or garlic, had to be worn on their clothes and attached to their houses.

WOMEN OF THE REFORMATION

The average life span for women of the times was about 24 years. Lack of sanitation was the primary cause of death. Giving birth at home, with only an often-inexperienced midwife in attendance and little thought of hygiene, endangered both mother and baby and often had fatal results. Girls would be married as early as the age of 12, and five, six, or seven children were often the result—each one a potential death threat. About 12 percent of young women whose parents found it a burden to feed them and with no suitor in sight were incarcerated in convents. Upper class women of impoverished families could suffer the same fate.

While the great majority of women were illiterate peasants, strongly attached to their village priests, and reluctant or slow to change their allegiance from the Catholic to the Protestant Church, others of noble birth, educated and enlightened, as were some of the wives and friends of reformers, had a significant impact on the Reformation and helped shape the events of the time. They were able to read the scriptures for themselves and make their own judgments.

After years of convent life, for example, Katharina von Bora became intrigued by the growing reform movement. She was 18 when Martin Luther issued his 95 Theses from Wittenberg, and unhappy at the convent, she plotted with several other nuns to escape. Secretly contacting Luther, the women pleaded for his assistance. On the eve of Easter 1523, he sent someone to rescue them. The nuns escaped by hiding in a covered wagon amidst fish barrels and fled to Wittenberg.[8] Katharina eventually married Luther.

Her dedication to the welfare of her husband and to her household would have been typical of the women of the times; up before dawn, she worked into the night maintaining the animals and crops on their land, cooking, washing, gardening, and looking after the many guests who came to see her husband.[9] Similarly, wives of artisans or merchants were often partners in the business, as well as managers of affairs at home. They kept accounts and records of other business matters that might be required while their husbands concerned themselves with production or trade. Farmers' wives tended the cottage, looked after the children and the meals, milked the cows, worked in the vegetable garden, and gathered wood, along with endless other chores.

There were many thousands of outstanding women involved in the Reformation on both Catholic and Protestant sides. Some we hear of only fleetingly, while others were more prominent.

Not only were uneducated women of the Catholic faith reluctant to change. Caritas Pirckheimer, one of the most learned women in Germany, was well known for her *Journal of the Reformation*, written while she was abbess of the Convent of St. Clare. This records her struggle with the Nürnberg city council, and presents a defense of her convent life and of her Roman Catholic faith at the advent of Lutheranism when the city council tried to pressure the nuns into accepting the new reforms and renouncing their vows. She was an advocate of equal rights and the right of individuals to choose whatever style of life and faith they preferred. Her views reflected those of many Catholic women, both nuns and others, whose voices have not been heard.

Early in 1522, the Bavarian government banned Lutheranism, fearing the social unrest that would come with it. Students were more sensitive to the changing situations than most other people, as conflicting views were generally expressed in the classrooms of universities. The following year, a university student, arrested for advocating these ideas, was accused of heresy and forced to publicly recant or face the flames. Such actions discouraged student religious dissent out of fear of the authorities.

NOTES

1. Martin Luther. "Disputation of Doctor Martin Luther on the Power and Efficacy of Indulgences." Project Wittenberg, http://www.iclnet.org/pub/resources/text/wittenberg/luther/web/ninetyfive.html (accessed March 19, 2010).

2. Romans 1:17.

3. All known copies of the twelve articles were confiscated. The Saxon State library has a surviving rare copy, *Handlung, Artikel und Instructions von allen Rotten und Haufen der Bauern*. See also the following Web site that includes the twelve articles of the peasants in full, http://www.marxists.org/archive/marx/works/1850/peasant-war-germany/index.htm (accessed August 15, 2010).

4. Scott and Scribner, 158.

5. Kamen, 100.

6. Ozment (1999), 157–158.

7. Roper, 98–99.

8. For the escape from the convent, see Markwald, 41ff.

9. For more about Katharina Von Bora, see Markwald, passim.

2

THE SETTING

LANDSCAPE

The lives of many sixteenth-century Europeans were determined to a large extent by the physical topography. The land was much less densely settled than today, and there were still immense areas of woodland and marshlands. The dark, impenetrable forests of southern Germany and eastern Europe provided almost impassable barriers. Roads were primitive, often muddy trails in winter and swirling dust in summer. Those connecting major cities were usually rudimentary and dangerous, not only because of their condition but also because of brigands that lurked along the route. Distances were considered in terms of towns, lodgings, taverns, tolls, and river crossings rather than political sovereignty.

POPULATION

About 85 percent of the European population were peasants, 10 percent were middle class (merchants, tradesmen, and townsmen), and the remaining 5 percent belonged either to the nobility or the clergy with the wealth and power concentrated in their hands. Europe was still recovering from the devastating effects of the Bubonic Plague that killed a third of the population in 1348. The lethal epidemic continued to strike periodically here and there throughout the next several centuries.

The population in millions at the end of the sixteenth century has been estimated as:

Netherlands	3
England and Wales	4.5
Scotland and Ireland	2
Scandinavia	1.4
Spain and Portugal	9
Italy	13
Germany	20
France	16
Poland and Lithuania	8[1]

People everywhere were prone not only to rampant disease but also to death caused by wars, famine, and childbirth. In rural areas an average of about 50 percent of children died before the age of seven.

When times were difficult, unskilled rural laborers poured into the cities causing overcrowding, begging, and theft to the extent that many cities would not let them reside within the walls. Nor did they like the shanty towns that grew up outside, whose residents entered the gates every day to look for work or beg for alms at the doors of the churches.

SOCIAL CLASSES

Society was structured in three traditional estates: the first consisted of members of the Church who looked after souls and whose prelates lived mostly in a state of luxury. At the low end of the hierarchy, the village priest might be as poor as his parishioners. The first estate was the most powerful, owning or controlling a good third of all European land and collecting enormous revenues from taxes, dispensations, and indulgences, paying little or no taxes itself. It had its own courts to try and punish those who disagreed with its beliefs and was well known for its ability to forge documents to prove its claims. The second estate comprised the nobility that ranged from kings, princes, and dukes down to the knights—mounted men-at-arms who served the king or local princes, engaged in war and who were supposed to protect the people.

The third estate encompassed the middle and lower classes. The bourgeoisie of the towns who owned shops and businesses were often well enough off. Laborers were less fortunate, owning little and being poorly paid. Those who worked the land for a living often did not own it and ranged from a near slave of the landholder (both secular and ecclesiastic) to a free peasant who generally rented his house and land. These were the people who worked hard and supported the first two estates with their labor and taxes—the latter in money or kind.

ECONOMY

The economies of Europe differed from region to region depending on trade routes, fertility of the soil, mineral deposits, and the stability of governments and levels of taxation. Factories as we know them today did not exist. Manufactured goods were produced in shops run by the artisan owner. With the exception of printing, there were few innovations in technology, but capital was beginning to flow more freely, and the middle class was starting to rise mostly through commerce and credit provided by the growth of banks.

The vast majority of people cultivated the land, the size of which varied widely, growing mostly wheat, barley, **Agriculture** and rye as well as fruit and vegetables. A poor family might work half-a-dozen acres living at subsistence level, while the average farm in another area might be ten times larger.

When the peasant paid his rent in cash, the amount was usually fixed, and he was better off as demand and prices rose as they did in the sixteenth century, especially if he had a surplus to sell at the market. When the peasant paid in kind, the landowner prospered; when prices went up, the peasant suffered.

Most held their farms for life and upon death, the land reverted to the lord. Often, however, the farm went to the tenant's heir upon payment of a fee and sometimes under a new rental agreement. Peasants who leased the land on a short-term basis such as two, three, or ten years were worse off. In southern Germany on ecclesiastical estates, the tenant had to renew his contract every year giving the Church annual opportunities to collect contract fees and raise rents.

Still more economically deprived were sharecroppers who worked the land with no other rights except a share in the produce. Around cities such arrangements were increasing throughout this period as merchants bought up land and worked it to maximum profit using day laborers. This same working arrangement would have been practiced on many ecclesiastical estates, as the system left the landholder free to sell or sublease the property as he pleased, avoiding peasants' privileges, ancient or recent.

Among rural society also were agricultural servants who worked year round or were hired just for planting and harvesting. They lived in cottages, but did not own them, and found work on the farms of others for a little pay. They tended to be sedentary, living in the same cottages for generations.

An agricultural boom during the sixteenth century put more land under cultivation. Irrigation projects were initiated and swamps were drained, while previously forested land came under the plow. Many of these expansions were accomplished with urban capital and the new farmers living in the city were generally the leaseholders.

Livestock   Cattle trading was well underway by the sixteenth century. Animals raised in Denmark, Poland, Hungary and Ruthenia (today roughly Belarus and Ukraine) were in great demand for meat and leather. Among leading destinations for the cattle trade were Hamburg, Antwerp, Lübeck, Köln, Nürnberg, Frankfurt, and Venice. Herds ranging from about 30 to 300 animals were driven to market by the rough and ready drovers of the time. They lived mostly out of doors and carried their belongings in a saddle pack.

The lives of cattle drovers was hard and basic. Progress was slow along the special tracks they were obliged to follow; four miles a day was good with a rest every third day. The pace was deliberately slow, so the cattle would not lose much weight and their value diminish. One drover for every 20 or so head of cattle was typical along with a forager who arranged inns and pasture in advance. There were various custom posts, where the animals had to be registered and fees paid. The business was large, as thousands of cattle annually supplied the European market.

The industry was controlled by nobles from whom the merchants bought the animals and then hired the drovers. Peasants could only sell their animals in local markets. Cattle plagues in 1518 and 1559 eradicated entire herds and left many drovers unemployed.

Commercial sheep owners required room and fodder for their animals in the winter months and pasturage in summer. Sheep were typically kept in one area over the winter and then moved to another pasture for the summer. For these migrations, known as transhumance, the owners hired shepherds.

Spain and England were the two countries with the greatest numbers of sheep, and the transhumance often caused friction. Millions of sheep on the move strayed onto farms and village pastures creating an enormous amount of damage to crops. In Spain, the sheep owners formed an association, the Mesta, which received royal recognition that gave the shepherds the right to drive their animals across fields and through villages along designated corridors. The export of wool and meat from which the king gained revenues was too valuable to worry about farmers' complaints.

In England, too, the sheep were a mixed blessing. As European cloth centers grew in importance, sheep were kept to maintain the supply of wool. Landowners found that these animals were more lucrative than grain crops and used whatever means they could to fence in previously open land to contain the animals. Beginning several centuries earlier, the process, known as enclosure, was the source of much conflict between sheep owners and grain farmers. Forced from the land, many farm families moved to the cities to look for work. Often destitute, they begged for a living when jobs were scarce.

Fishing   Fish from both fresh and oceanic waters was an important element of diet and eaten everywhere in Europe. In Scotland, for example, foreign trade was based entirely on the fisherman, the shepherd (for wool), and the huntsman (for skins).[2] The North Sea and Baltic yielded huge catches of herring and cod for shipment all over the continent that was pickled, dried, or salted for the winter months.

The hardy fishermen and their families faced numerous dangers in their quest for a living. It was a long and risky journey from the coasts of Europe to the shores of Newfoundland, where the cod was abundant. Dense, disorienting fog, ice, and pirates were always a threat, and in the North Sea, the Baltic, and the Mediterranean, a sudden storm could send a ship to the bottom.

The industry was of great benefit to Catholics who were prohibited from eating meat on Fridays. Mediterranean seafood was usually sold in local markets or on the shore directly from the fishing boats and consumed within a day or two.

Gold and silver poured into Europe from Spanish discoveries in the New World. The bonanza of an entire mountain **Banking** of silver at Potosí in Bolivia in 1544 sent prices soaring in Europe. Along with an increase in silver production in the mines of central Europe and an increase of the gold trade with Africa, there was too much money around for the amount of available goods. With little access to money, the very poor suffered proportionately, and food riots were frequent. Money came in the form of coins of gold, silver or copper, often mixed with nickel or some other metal.

This century marks the period of credit expansion across Europe. Lending also increased, usually through merchants and rich peasants. The recipients of the loans might be destitute farmers whose crops had failed due to bad weather, others who wished to expand their holdings, a master craftsman who wanted to buy another premises, and other merchants who had lost a ship and its precious cargo at sea to storms or pirates or had been ruined by war.

A type of rural loan developed in which a farmer could pledge his land as collateral if he owned it. He could also put some of his anticipated crop against a loan. This was risky, of course, since a crop failure could ruin him. If a harvest failed, it might be possible to forestall the loan until the next harvest but with several bad years in row, he would be perpetually in debt. Widespread crop failures did occur in the late sixteenth century and again in the first half of the seventeenth that ruined both debtor and creditor. Such cases led to relocations of people and riots. Many were in debtors' prisons. By around 1600, interest charged on loans was approximately 10 percent. Large transactions could take place with major currencies such as the German mark, the French livre, or the British pound, but these were not in coins but markers used by merchants.

Another way of carrying on commerce was through bills of exchange that could be assigned to a third party in payment of debt. These bills became a kind of negotiable bond. Checks, or bank notes, a signed piece of paper authorizing a banker to withdraw money and pay it to the person whose name was on the paper, were also employed.

No money was required when two merchants held accounts at the same bank. One could simply go to the bank and order a transfer of money into the other's account. If they lived in different cities, they opened accounts at each other's banks and performed transactions through representatives in the relevant city.

Trade Fairs At large trade fairs, such as those at Frankfurt or Lyon, merchants came from all over Europe. They did not carry great amounts of coin. Instead bankers appeared at the fairs and kept track of the transactions on paper and could debit or credit the merchant's account accordingly.

At Medina del Campo in Spain, for example, all the streets and squares of the town were a marketplace. The primary purpose was to promote wool, textile sales, and books. It was regularly attended by some two thousand merchants and about fifteen bankers. At the great fair at Piacenza in northern Italy, millions of scudi changed hands on paper.

These seasonal clearing operations became permanent with the opening of exchanges known as the Bourse or Longa, an early form of stock market. They opened in London in 1517, Antwerp in 1531, and Amsterdam in 1611. The Amsterdam exchange that first opened as a bank was the only institution in the city allowed to pay or transfer bills of exchange more than 600 florins in value. All except small merchants had to have an account there. As the city grew, it eventually became the chief clearing house of Europe. The bank was backed by the city government and was the most reliable on the continent.

Guilds (Urban Industries) Almost everyone with a common interest or craft, formed themselves into a brotherhood or guild. They received their chartered right from the king or prince of the realm. Some guilds were organized as service trades and included doctors, teachers, notaries, and barber-surgeons. They performed a service rather than manufacturing a product. With demand relatively constant they maintained a steady clientele.

There were some trades that sold but, with some exceptions, did not produce such as innkeepers and grocers. Owning several such establishments provided potential for wealth, but balanced against costs, there was small chance of becoming rich. The really wealthy merchants made their fortunes in wholesaling.

Craftsmen formed associations based on their trades including textile workers, masons, carpenters, butchers, candle-makers, glassworkers, shoemakers, bakers, and so forth. The guilds maintained the secrets of traditionally transmitted technology, the mysteries of their crafts. The founders were generally free, independent master craftsmen.

It was important to recognize the honor of the craft and to insist on the dignity it brought its members. Thus, behavior of the members of guilds was strictly supervised as everything the individual did reflected on the group as a whole. Anyone who brought shame to the group was liable to be expelled.[3] One of the requirements was the legitimate birth of its members.[4] When the city of Augsburg suffered from overpopulation caused by migration from the country to the town, the guild members were instrumental in closing off trades to outsiders and restricting how many migrants could reside within the town.[5]

Guilds maintained funds to support infirm or elderly members, widows and orphans of guild members, funeral benefits, and a traveling allowance for those needing to look for work in other regions.

Long periods of apprenticeship made it difficult for people to establish shops of their own or, without the approval of their peers, to acquire materials or knowledge, or to sell in certain markets where the guild held monopolistic rights.

Guilds that engaged in fine crafts such as gold and silver jewelry or exquisite silk clothing and expensive materials and sold their products to wealthy clients were the most prestigious. The excellence of the work in metal, wood, or cloth and the exalted stature of the clients elevated the craftsman himself. Goldsmiths were universally of high status, but even they could end up destitute when a noble client failed to pay.

Not unlike today, status and connections were important. People who worked as confectioners carried more prestige than ordinary bakers although they might belong to the same guild. Carpenters were lower than joiners who made cabinets, chests, or ornate small boxes or performed detail work on window frames, ceilings, and decorative doors. Some had their own wood-working shops, others traveled to construction sites to perform a job. They often worked under contract to produce specific furniture pieces for the wealthy.

Shoemakers who produced fine leather or velvet shoes were more highly considered than those in the same guild who lacked these skills. Some members made new shoes but did not repair them. The cobblers who repaired them were not allowed to make them.

The shoemaker's shop was usually also his home, although some might maintain a stall at the local market to sell their products. Wealthy customers had their shoes made to order. The same kind of hierarchy would apply to hatters and other fine crafts.

Unskilled workers were not organized into guilds. Fishmongers, itinerant dealers, carters, or messenger boys had no such organizations to rely on in the event of illness or unemployment.

In Germany, jobs were posted by the master in a designated building sometimes owned by the guild or at an inn. Here, journeymen could find work. If a new man came to town looking for a job, he was obliged to report to this kind of employment office and could only take a job listed there. Masters were required to do all their hiring there.

For a young middle class boy, the road from apprenticeship to master craftsman would have been long and arduous. The time and strictness varied among guilds but in general, a boy or sometimes a girl in certain trades was placed with a master from about age seven to ten. An agreement was made whereby the child had to serve and obey the master and promise to remain in return for the instruction. In turn, the master agreed not to use the boy as a servant or be abusive toward him. The length of time for the apprenticeship varied from two to seven years. Disputes often arose over the amount of time given to serving the master and to learning the trade. Boys and girls were often apprenticed to a relative, where the situation might be more agreeable.

Once the agreement was finished, if the boy had learned the craft or trade well, he would receive a letter of introduction informing other masters of the craft that the young man was now a journeyman and eligible to be hired by a master and receive pay for his work. He sometimes traveled going from one master to another in order to learn different techniques and at the same time make business contacts.

No contract was involved in employment, but the job might last for many years. The ambitious journeyman dreamed of becoming a master and owning his own business. The contacts he made were of importance for prospective work. He also decided on his future home and found a wife to manage it. Few guilds accepted unmarried masters.

It was made relatively easy for sons of guildsmen and of masters to become members of the guilds themselves but more difficult for others by the raising of entry fees or by setting quotas then filling them with relatives. The piece of original work that was required to become a master could always be rejected as unworthy.

In the sixteenth and seventeenth centuries, journeymen were increasingly barred from mastership and were becoming simply permanent employees with no prospects of owning their own shops. Towns began to discover that guilds hindered economic progress and set about freeing crafts from guild control.

Wholesale merchants did not make things, and there were no journeymen. The family business was almost always passed on to members of the family who, once they had learned the business, were placed in an appropriate position.

Rural Industries Village or cottage industries that did not involve agriculture revolved around the blacksmith, the barber, the miller, the baker, cobblers, carpenters, and weavers. Villages often differed in their activities. In coastal areas, they might be devoted to fisheries, elsewhere to raising dairy cattle, to vineyards or orchards, still others to grain. Many peasants milled their own grain at home while others used the services of a mill, usually owned by the lord of the manor and for which they paid a fee.

In large towns the iron works might have several furnaces and forges and a number of workers, but in a village there was often just one man operating a bellows and a single forge. He might also farm to supplement his small earnings as a blacksmith. In addition, he could also be the one to see if a wound required cauterizing or a broken bone set. An alternative would be the barber who generally had experience in tending wounds.

Woodcutters, generally the poorest of workers, obtained a permit from the lord who owned the forest. Working as independent contractors, they cut down the trees and then sold them to lumbermen who carted them away to sawmills. The lord of the manor to whom the trees belonged took the lion's share of the profit. The work was hard and when the woodcutter aged and his strength failed, he had little or nothing to fall back on.

For poor peasants, in the countryside where rigid guild restrictions did not apply, weaving presented a chance to earn a little extra money. A sheep farmer sheared his animals and sold the wool to a merchant who then distributed it to peasants where it was spun into cloth in the home. The merchant collected the woven cloth and sold it to processors who finished and dyed it. From there, it was sold to various industries or persons such as tailors who turned it into clothes. This system of manufacture used credit at nearly every level. Textile manufacturers in the cities who farmed out this work to the villages paid less for the work than in the city. This was one way for entrepreneurs to bypass the guild system. Pay discrepancies between cottage and urban craftsmen were due to the fact that the country workers were semi-skilled, never having served as apprentices. The cottagers also maintained agricultural plots for food not available to town craftsmen, and working at home reduced overhead costs.[6] Often, the textile production was geared to the winter months when all farm hands were not required for planting and harvesting. Cottage industries also gave country women a chance to increase the family finances by working at the looms. Along with food production, textiles made up the largest industries, employing the most people and generating the most wealth.

Besides the mineral wealth flowing to Europe from the New World, central and eastern European mines underwent rapid **Mining** development during the time of the Reformation. New ones were opened, and established mines were going deeper underground.

The state owned the natural resources, and if ore was discovered on a family's property, the state claimed it. Usually the right to mine was purchased from the king or the prince of the realm, often in the form of an annual fee, by a wealthy entrepreneur who exploited the mine and sold the ore. The use of copper became more prevalent during the period for coins and for use in making cannons and cooking utensils. In the sixteenth century, copper was generally replaced by cheaper iron.

Lead used in roofing, armaments and piping, was mined on or near the surface of the ground and smelted close by to avoid expensive transportation costs. Smelters were situated in or nearby forests, where wood was readily available to turn into charcoal required to heat the furnaces to sufficient temperatures to extract the metal. The unhealthy work took its toll in lung diseases from the poisonous gases emitted in the process.

From the foothills of the Bohemian mountains, copper and tin deposits supplied the metal for the bells, statues, and doors of the great gothic cathedrals. Silver talers (coins) were minted here in 1519. The word "dollar," first applied by the United States to silver coins, derives from taler.[7]

One of the great German families controlling enormous capital, the Fuggers, financed copper smelters and used their resulting fortune to help support the Habsburg dynasty.[8]

In England, the most important mines were in Cornwall where vast quantities of tin and copper ore were found. When the miners of Cornwall went to the New World, they took with them their knowledge of deep, hard rock mining and helped develop some of the great mining areas of the United States.

Entire families worked the mines in England and Wales: women above ground, small children serving as messengers and doing odd jobs. At 12 years of age, boys could join their fathers underground.

To house their workers, mining companies constructed rows of cheaply built cottages and rented them to the miners. If a man had an accident, or otherwise was incapable of work, he lost his dwelling as well as his job.

Miners were born and died in these squalid company houses. Parents, children, and grandparents often crowded together. There was no overall mining guild, and isolated communities had few facilities for recreation.

Light in the mines came from candles placed on ledges along the wall of the shaft or attached to the miners' hats. They had to pay for their own candles and tools, the price taken out of their pay.

Dangerous rock falls, collapsing tunnels, gas explosions, and ladders of rotten wood often caused death and injury. Medical services were mostly nonexistent. An injured miner out of work had to rely on charity. Mining communities had their cripples sitting in the street begging, attesting to the price paid to extract metals for a pittance.

Coal was also widely mined and burned in England and Wales where air pollution became a fact of life. Despite the health problems associated with it, coal and its irritant consequences were considered a necessity.

There were usually three eight-hour shifts and a worker beginning at six in the morning arose about four if he had to walk several miles to the mine, negotiate hundreds of feet of vertical ladders, and then walk underground to the worksite. Eight hours of moil in cramped and frequently wet conditions left him exhausted. He returned home to wash off the coal dust, eat dinner, and get some sleep before the shift began anew.

HOLY ROMAN EMPIRE

By the end of the medieval period, much of Europe was under the jurisdiction of powerful monarchies such as Portugal, Spain, France, England, and Scandinavia.

The union of territories in central Europe ruled over by an emperor consisted of hundreds of smaller units under the immediate mandate of princes, dukes, barons, counts, margraves, knights (which might rule over only a village), and free cities. This large territory was linguistically and ethnically diverse and nearly impossible to administer effectively. It was feared by neighboring countries, such as France, for its territorial ambitions and was itself fearful of the westward expansion of the Ottoman Turkish Empire.

Seven noble electors selected each Holy Roman Emperor from the Austrian House of Habsburg whose lands were large and wealthy enough to enable the dynasty to impose its candidate on the other German states.

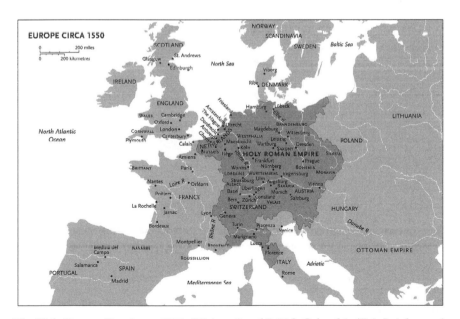

The Holy Roman Empire, c. 1560. (University of British Columbia/Eric Leinberger.)

The emperor, residing generally in Vienna, was often in conflict with the Church and subordinate rulers of the empire. Much of the land in the hands of the Church was beyond his grasp, and the political semi-independence of the nobility gave rise to disputes over taxation and territory.

Castles dotted the countryside and every few miles there was a different lord, a new jurisdiction where tolls had to be paid for goods crossing their lands. Many nobles were eager to expand their possessions and influence.

Free Cities   There were 80 free cities in the Holy Roman Empire that were not subject to the will of a landowner. These cities owed allegiance only to the emperor and not to an intermediate prince or lord. The free city was obliged to render hospitality to the emperor when he visited and to meet certain imperial taxes and military manpower.

Such an arrangement, for practical purposes, left the city politically autonomous and managed by the city magistrates. They had relatively large populations such as Augsburg, an important city of southern Germany, with a population of about 30,000.

At the apex of the municipal society stood the burgermeister and the so-called honorability that made up the city council composed of the rich, patrician families that monopolized the city government and administered its various sources of income at their pleasure. With their wealth and their aristocratic privileges, the patricians lorded it alike over townspeople and neighboring peasantry who were subject to the municipality. The town council assumed the chief rights over municipal lands, imposed duties, and sold guild privileges and rights of citizenship as a source of profit.

City inhabitants lived within the walls whose portals and ramparts were guarded at night. The streets of most such cities were crowded and bustling with activity during the day, and deserted after dark, the citizens tucked safely in their houses.

RURAL LIFE

The vast majority of people lived in villages of less than one hundred where came roving actors hoping to perform their plays, traveling salesmen peddling their latest concoctions of elixirs, migrants looking for work, quack doctors and dentists, and fairground performers and, on less auspicious occasions, beggars, roving bandits, or companies of soldiers who demanded to be quartered.

Brigands roved the countryside looking for opportunities—many of them mercenary soldiers who, between wars, had no pay. They gathered up whatever spoils they could find although locals often fought back with savage ferocity to protect the little they owned. Remote towns were easy targets for both brigands and soldiers, and often, if overwhelmed, the peasants had to plea for their lives and those of their families.

Pilgrimages were a source of relief from daily village life and some locals took on the role of guides, taking groups to nearby shrines and churches that had a special significance such as a purported holy relic.

Medieval and early modern villages consisted of a manor house, where the landholder, knight, or baron lived with a group of peasant houses nearby. The latter were usually one-bedroom huts made from wooden beams, mud, and straw. Windows in these murky dens were rare and a hole in the roof allowed smoke from the fire to escape. During winter months, warmth was generated by allowing the farm animals (goats, sheep, chickens, geese, and cattle) to sleep inside the house. Entire families slept on a straw or wool mat, allowing for almost no privacy. A small church served both as a place for worship and as the center of all events occurring within the village.

The lord maintained his authority in order to preserve the social structure while the priest served the villagers with religious instruction, giving advice and sometimes news. He was often the only one who could read. He could keep the peasants under control by telling them often that their role in life was God's mandate.

Those who possessed few goods and little land could easily fall into abject misery by the least accident. Illness or injury, the failure of a crop, death of a cow, fire or flood, or the death or bankruptcy of an employer could lead to dire consequences. An entire community could be subject to extreme poverty through sickness such as malaria, smallpox, or plague.

CHARITY

Most large cities in Europe at the time of the Reformation hosted charities, including orphanages for abandoned children and homes for the elderly as well as offering some relief for the destitute. In general, the Catholics were more accepting of beggars, whereas the Protestants, rejecting the premise that good works led to salvation, insisted the poor be put to work and become productive members of society wherever possible. In the event, however, much discrimination took place as to whether or not a person was truly in need of assistance.

In an attempt to verify this, both Catholic and Protestants strove to restrict benefits to members of their particular religious or secular communities whereby the poor had to provide proof of residence. Outsiders were automatically turned away.

In addition, those in charge followed strict rules in ascertaining the moral comportment of the mendicants, linking their behavior to Protestant and Catholic standards, respectively. As a result, many were denied much needed relief.

NOTES

1. See Elliot, 64. For population estimates and demographic trends, see also Watts, 20.

2. Warrack, 10.

3. Roper, 37.

4. Ibid., 38.

5. Ibid., 39.

6. Seccombe, 182.

7. Klein, 224.

8. For details see Elton (1963), 23–159 passim.

3

THE CATHOLIC CHURCH

Not unlike a powerful authoritarian state, the Church had its monarch (the pope), its princes (the prelates), knights (the priests), and all of Europe as subjects. Ecumenical councils acted as legislative bodies; canon law enforced its code of behavior. Ecclesiastical courts punished the wicked, and the Curia functioned as its fiscal body. The Church could declare war, negotiate treaties and collect taxes.

At the beginning of the sixteenth century, everybody believed in God, heaven, angels, saints, purgatory, the devil, and his agents. Nearly everyone was a member of the Roman Catholic Church that did not tolerate freedom of religion or deviations from its own doctrines. Those who digressed were punished by excommunication, by imprisonment, or, in more extreme cases, by death.

Priests could be regular clergy (monks) who lived in sheltered monasteries in a world of self-denial and abstinence or secular priests who lived in the community and performed the church services. The latter were concerned with the temporal world and with the people and their anxieties. The Catholic Church considered itself the only institution authorized to interpret the Bible; the translation of which from Latin into a vernacular language was forbidden. The true Christian respected the seven sacraments as well as religious oaths for monastic life, the infallibility of the Church, the authority of Church councils, Church tradition, and the legality of the ecclesiastical institutions created by Rome.[1]

For the vast majority of Christians, the Church would have been a source of solace and of refuge from the harsh realities of everyday life. Its doctrine, ceremony, and the promise of life ever after in a heavenly state of bliss would more than make up for suffering on earth if one obeyed the rules. Many Catholic priests did their best to soothe the conscience of sinners, aid the hungry and sick, and console the dying.

PURGATORY AND INDULGENCES

The Catholic Church believed that salvation was a process of purification and that the soul could be cleansed through confession and blessings, by engaging in a crusade or pilgrimage, by good works, prayers, saying the rosary, almsgiving, Communion, and attendance at Mass. Nevertheless, it was believed that few could escape purgatory, which further purified the soul from earthly sins.

It was also held that Christ and his disciples had accumulated a huge amount of merit while on earth that was deposited in heaven. There were plenty of these credits to go around, and one way of obtaining them was to purchase an indulgence that helped wash away sins and shorten time in purgatory. It was believed that the pope had the authority to draw upon this treasury that could even be used to help relatives and friends by making their stay in purgatory shorter and less painful.

One type of letter of indulgence, the "Peter Indulgence," was initiated by Pope Julius II in 1507 to financially promote the construction of Saint Peter's Basilica in Rome.

MONASTIC LIFE

Some monks and nuns partially sustained themselves by producing and selling goods such as cheese, wine, beer, liquor, fruit, and jellies or by donations. Rental or investment income and funds from other organizations within the Church also kept them far from hunger's door.

The life of prayer and communal living was one of rigorous schedules with prayers taking up much of their waking hours. Between prayers, some monks sat in the cloister working on projects of writing, copying, or decorating books. Others were assigned to physical labor of various kinds such as the cultivation of vegetables and other food. Monasteries offered a resting place for weary pilgrims or travelers and often with large libraries at their disposal, they were sources of information for scholars. Families sometimes gave up a son to the monastery in return for blessings. During times of pestilence, monks and nuns helped provide for the sick.

Monasteries varied in size. Some mandated isolation from the outside world; others interacted with the local village or town. As they gained wealth from their lands and from donations and stipends, they also sometimes became more lax. Viewed by many as institutions of easy living, their inhabitants were at times considered exploiters of the poor. Stories of what went on behind the walls between priests and nuns were abundant. It seemed to some that monasticism was an unnatural way of life with its inner secrets and was perhaps contrary to God's will.

Women were drawn into convents that offered protection; some of them also nourished their intellectual growth there—not available to them outside of the establishment. Convents, like monasteries, often housed libraries and contributed to the production of illuminated manuscripts.

Admittance to a religious order was regulated by Church law as well as by the rules adopted by the particular order. After a lengthy period of probation, a woman under temporary vows wishing to be admitted permanently was required to make a public profession of chastity, poverty, and obedience, not unlike their male counterparts in monasteries and confirm this by a solemn vow that was binding in Church law. One of its effects was that members were no longer free, and should they subsequently wish to leave the order, they would have to seek papal permission. To just walk away was severely punishable. There were many young women who were forced into the convent life by their families, for although some convents expected a fee for enrollment, the amount would have been much less than the payment of a dowry if the girl found a husband.

WEALTH OF THE CHURCH

Political power, material possessions and privileged position in public life were too often the primary ambitions of many of the higher ecclesiastics who were chiefly concerned with increasing their personal wealth by uniting under their jurisdiction several prebends or episcopal sees into the hands of one individual to allow for a larger income and greater power.

Church wealth in land and buildings, along with tithes, donations, inheritances, priceless artworks, and libraries, were often a source of contention between secular rulers and ecclesiastical officials. Further, these lands were exempt from taxation by secular governments unless with papal consent.

Every increase in Church lands, such as from wills to the Vatican from those who expected holy benefits, diminished state tax revenues on property. Secular rulers viewed swelling Church coffers as containing riches that rightfully should have accrued to them. Many of the nobility began voicing their objections to this flow of wealth from lands under their control to Rome. Decentralized Church authority gave bishops and abbots a good deal of individual power and lucrative positions in their jurisdictions, while the pope and the Curia gave direction and maintained unity in the details of Christian belief. Local nobles were only too aware that if their relatives became abbots and bishops, some of the wealth of the

Church would likely come their way. Such positions were often for sale to the highest bidder.

The Church was quick to collect its 10 percent of the produce of the peasants on Church lands, and while its teachings stressed charity, critics were not slow to recognize that the costs of charity were small in relation to the enormous income of the Church. Bishops lived in sumptuous luxury in palaces with servants, lavish entertainment, costly material goods, expensive dress, and tables of the finest food available.

There were men of the Church, however, who considered this ostentatious wealth and power obscene and far removed from the basic spiritual principles of Christ. They recognized the need for reform and adherence to fundamentals. But great care was called for not to antagonize Church authority and be accused of heresy.

CHURCH IN THE LIVES OF THE PEOPLE

The Church physically held the dominant place in the village, towering above the community on a hilltop if there was one. It also held the dominant place spiritually and often politically. It collected fees for baptism, marriage, burial, and other services. People's fear of the afterlife was its major asset that influenced how they thought about heaven and hell, emphasizing the torments of hell, the sufferings in purgatory, and the promise of paradise if people followed its tenets. Religion and superstition made up an important part of most aspects of Catholic daily life. Church and monastery bells continually reminded the inhabitants of towns and villages of the presence of God and the danger of committing sins.

In the past, investigation of heresy was a duty of the bishops, but Pope Gregory IX established the papal Inquisition whereby men and women who had once been members of the Catholic faith and had deviated from Church practices were tried and, if found guilty, handed over to secular authorities for execution. The hypocritical practice allowed the Church to remain unstained by the specific act of killing its victims.

CORRUPTION AND ABUSE

The years leading up to the Protestant Reformation were beset by moral corruption, greed, and abuse of position in the higher echelons of the Roman Catholic Church that included simony (investing one's wealth or using influence to purchase an ecclesiastical office), pluralism (as some influential bishops held several or more dioceses simultaneously), and absenteeism or the failure of some bishops to reside in the diocese they administered.[2]

Abuses arose in the way many ecclesiastical benefices were conferred often for the personal interests of the petitioner rather than the spiritual needs of the faithful. The lives of the higher ecclesiastics in Rome, in tune with the Humanist and Renaissance ideals, became more worldly than spiritual, leading to a love of luxury and profligacy. Ignorance and lack of training among the lower clergy left much to be desired.

Although the Church imposed clerical celibacy as a legal principle, in practice it was often ignored. Clergymen kept mistresses who were supported with Church funds, and male offspring of bishops or abbots (referred to as nephews) often found lucrative positions in the Church, universities, or the law. The female children (or nieces) might find themselves administering convents or marrying members of the nobility.

In 1492, Rodrigo Borgia became pope under the name of Alexander VI. His immoral way of life outraged many Christians. At his coronation he appointed his 18-year-old son, Caesare, to the Archbishopric of Valencia; however, Caesare neither went to Spain nor took religious orders. The pope's daughter, Lucrezia, married three times, had children with other lovers, and was the subject of much scandal. Tales of wild orgies at the Vatican were rampant, but anyone who denounced such abuses could be excommunicated or worse. Free preaching was prohibited, and all papers and books that were tainted with the ideas of previous reformers such as Wycliffe or Hus were burned.

A boy could become a bishop, a profitable position, if his father paid the price. Then there were dispensations or exemption from normal Church laws and practices available to those who could afford them.

The sale of sacred relics believed to have the power to heal and bring good fortune was another matter of contention. For some skeptics, this was pure superstition, of no value, and most often, a swindle. A splinter of the true cross, a tooth, or a piece of bone of a saint, some object said to have been once used by the Virgin Mary or by Christ Himself—all were peddled throughout Europe.

Among the uneducated, village priests were generally treated with respect. They gave counseling and advice in matters both in and outside a religious context and were usually available to assist with family problems.

But priests were not always in favor with their parishioners. In 1524, the parish of Saint Michael in Worms deposed its priest, Johann Leininger, who then made an official complaint. The matter was taken up by the town council, and church wardens and parishioners were asked to explain their actions. They had often complained, they said, of the scandalous life of the priest who lived in sin with a woman and had sired a child. In addition, the woman had taken on the position of sexton. Leininger was also accused of misusing church funds: an expensive green cloth had been bought to make Mass vestments, but the priest had used it to have a coat made for his son. He had also misspent 10 gulden belonging to the church and then given his parish registers to the dean of the cathedral, although they were under the control of the church wardens. Finally, he had refused to administer the sacraments to a gravely ill woman until he was first paid the Mass penny.[3]

While Spain, England, and France had usurped the right of the pope to appoint bishops and other high clergy in their realms, people of the Holy Roman Empire, especially the secular rulers, resented the pallium, the large tax payable to Rome for the investiture or change in the diocese of an archbishop, bishop, or abbot. The tax had to be raised by the inhabitants. In addition, the entire income of the first year after the investiture (*annates*) accrued to the papal treasury. This constituted a continuous drain on the local economy. Added to these onerous costs were the journeys to Rome, where prelates during their residence held court in a style of sumptuous magnificence, all paid for by the parishioners.

It was to the benefit of the Church to maintain an ignorant, illiterate, and unenlightened peasantry. Even people who could read Latin were not allowed to read the Bible. Possession of it was a criminal offense and could result in the execution of the accused. Sometimes translators and publishers were burned along with their work.[4]

The Catholic Church could use the scriptures selectively. The peasant population remained in perpetual fear of hell's fires, making it easier to extract their last pennies. Moreover, the sale of indulgences for remission of sins committed up to the time of purchase was now being practiced as never before with a view to meeting the increased expenditure of the Vatican. Even the monk, Martin Luther, asked why people should pay for a church so far away and one they would never see.

The unifying cultural foundation of Europe for well over a thousand years, the Roman Catholic Church, was complacent in its power and failed to recognize the coming maelstrom that would engulf the continent. Careful inquiry into the scriptures and a desire among some Catholic scholars to return to the earliest and basic principles of Christianity were ignored until it was too late.

NOTES

1. See Ferro, 52–53.
2. See Chadwick, 11 ff. for a conciliatory point of view.
3. Scribner, 123.
4. For more information on abuses, see Walker, 283–284.

4

WITCHES, MAGIC, AND SUPERSTITION

Since remote times, witches, village healers, and spell-makers in Europe had been both respected and feared because of their powers to bring forth good or evil, health or death. By the sixteenth century this had not changed. Much of western Europe engaged in massive witch hunts from about 1550 to about 1680 when an estimated 100,000 villagers were sentenced to death for sorcery, the vast majority either spinsters or widows.[1]

Those suspected represented a threat to Church authority, accused of being in league with the devil and casting spells. The penalty for witchcraft was death by strangulation, drowning, public burning, or decapitation.

It was widely believed that the condemned had an intimate knowledge of the use of herbs and other ingredients to concoct potions, which could both cure diseases or cause harm to recipients. Rituals, magic words, snakes, and lizards were often part of their ceremonies. They could prevent storms and make crops grow, and if malevolent, they could ruin a crop, family, or individual.

A common type of sorcery, sympathetic magic, involved a piece of clothing, jewelry, or a lock of hair that belonged to the person on whom an evil spell was to be cast. The victim who strongly believed he or she would sicken and die, sometimes did.

It was also thought that witches could fly, breaking away from earthly constraints to travel in the spiritual world, riding on demons accompanied by crows and ravens. They could also change their shape and become goats, cows, or other animals, making it difficult for witch hunters to find them.

AGENTS OF THE DEVIL

A prominent charge was that witches participated in activities known as the Witches' Sabbat. According to the Church, such festivals were secret and involved obscene rites with the devil. Alleged witches often confessed under prolonged torture that they had been to Sabbats where they pledged service to Satan and admitted that Sabbat ceremonies began with new initiates having sex with the devil or his demons. Initiation ceremonies might also include sacrificing an animal or child. The torturers were eager to hear such stories, and the victim, preferring death to gruesome prolonged agony (that would continue until the desired outcome), was ready to confess to anything.

Christians believed that Satan was able to counter some of God's designs and saw this as an apocalyptic struggle between good and evil in which no one was certain whether events happened because of divine or evil influence. It was impossible to determine how much of human

A depiction of a witches' sabbath, by Frans Francken the Younger, 1607. This early seventeenth-century painting shows some of the alleged practices of witches, including flying on brooms, murder, spells, and bubbling cauldrons. (Kunsthistorisches Museum, Wien oder KHM, Wien.)

conduct was based on individual freedom, how much determined by God, angels, stars, fortune, or luck, and how much was regulated by profane intervention. The question that always arose in learned circles was how these forces could be influenced in such a way that one could avoid misfortune while fulfilling God's laws and gain eternal life.

In 1568, Jean Weir, a physician, spoke of the existence of 72 princes of the underworld, and over seven million infernal spirits formed into 111 legions each with 6,666 fiends.[2] Others proclaimed more than one billion demons organized into legions, cohorts, and companies, each containing over six million individuals.

It was believed there were demons confined to the air responsible for storms and lightning and others to the ground living in forests. Still others were in the sea (female devils), but all had one purpose—to torment man. These kinds of stories were believed not only by the average person but also by the elite and by educated priests. People were frightened by the different forms, human and animal or even vapor and invisibility, which devils could take to conceal their presence. Theologians of the time attached great importance to the incube (male demon) and succube (female demon) who could invade and possess the human body. In such cases, they would call for the victim to undergo exorcism.

PROTECTION FROM EVIL

Evil was everywhere and had to be countered by any and all means authorized by the Church. Talismen such as trinkets or candles, blessed by a priest, would ward off evil spirits. On the day of the Feast of the Purification of the Virgin, candles of all sizes were brought to the church to be blessed. Large ones were brought by heads of households, slim, tapered ones by women and girls, and penny candles by boys. They were piled up in baskets before the altar and after being blessed, were taken home and used in family devotions. The large house candle symbolizing Christ was lit by the death-bed or carried along behind the bier in funeral processions. It was also lit during bad weather to ward off crop-damaging hail, storms, or malevolent spirits. The tapered candles of the women were lit during childbirth and placed by the hands and feet of the mother to discourage the presence of malignant spirits. Penny candles were lit on All-Souls Day and Advent for family devotions.[3]

Holy water, blessed by a priest, had similar properties to charms and candles as protection against evil forces that caused hail, lightning, thunder, and severe storms. The Augsburg ritual book relates that whoever was touched or sprinkled by the water would be free from all uncleanness and all attacks of evil spirits. Further, all places where it was sprinkled would be preserved free from harm, and no pestilent spirits would reside there.[4] Holy water could heal sickness, shield domestic animals from wolves, and protect plants and seedlings over which it was distributed. It had beneficial power over homes, food, herbs, grain and threshing floors, and much more.

In Paris there were some fifty religious buildings in the *Ile de la Cité* alone, many of which had been built to commemorate a saint.[5] Saints played a large role as everyone looked first to them to cure illnesses, insure a good harvest or safe childbirth, as well as stave off evil spells and malevolent spirits.

Each saint was assigned certain responsibilities, and everyone knew which one to appeal to for which ailments, which pilgrimages to undertake to benefit their well being, and who would take care of them and watch over them as they traveled. A great number of saints' relics, some in the form of powder or potions, were carried. Servants often kept a piece of bread in their pocket, blessed by a priest, to protect them, prevent them from contracting rabies, and to kill rats. Many people believed that the end of the world was imminent, but meanwhile, God was keeping His eye on them. His pleasure was manifested when the harvest was good; His ire when it was bad.

CROWS, RAVENS, AND CATS

Crows and ravens were both despised and revered. It was forbidden in England to kill either of them. It was possible to incur a large fine for harming ravens for if they did not consume carrion, the putrified flesh would poison the air.

It has been asserted that the English did not harm ravens because they believed that the legendary King Arthur had been transformed into one, and his return was awaited by the people. This belief, in fact, continued in Wales and Cornwall until almost the end of the nineteenth century.

In 1662, a Scottish woman, Isobel Gowdie, when confessing to witchcraft, said that crows were a favorite form for witches to take when traveling at night. The Brothers Grimm, in their collection of German legends, reported that a man and woman from Lüttich were executed in 1610 for traveling about in the form of wolves while their son accompanied them as a raven.[6]

Cats, especially black ones, have always been a target of superstition and cruelty and associated with witchcraft and magic. To come across one at night signified the devil or a witch was nearby. It was believed that witches transformed themselves into cats in order to cast spells. They assembled at night and howled, copulated, and fought under the direction of a huge tomcat thought to be the devil himself. For protection against a cat's evil powers, one had to maim it such as breaking its legs. A maimed feline could not attend the Sabbat or cast spells.

Every year, cats were killed by the thousands in France into the seventeenth century.

Beliefs related to cats varied from place to place. In Brittany, if a cat crossed the path of a fisherman, his catch was doomed. In Anjou, the bread would not rise if a cat entered a bakery.

These animals also figured into folk medicine. To suck the blood from a freshly amputated tomcat's tail would help cure bodily wounds incurred by a fall. For pneumonia, it was beneficial to drink the blood from a cat's ear mixed with wine.

Cats were victims in other ways. In London during the Reformation, a Protestant crowd shaved a cat to resemble a priest after which they dressed it in priestly vestments, and then hanged it on the gallows at Cheapside.[7]

MINERS AND GHOSTS

Like almost everyone else, miners' lives were replete with superstition and magical stories. They were afraid of spirits who lived in the dark shafts, and tales were abundant of unattached hands carrying candles, strange voices in the dark warning of cave-ins, and ghostly black dogs indicating disaster was imminent. Underground, in the flickering candle light, shadowy apparitions could easily play on the imagination of people raised on such beliefs.

THE PEASANTS OF LORRAINE

Workers on isolated farms out in the countryside were particularly prone to terrors of the night in the form of supernatural beings as well as from ordinary brigands.

In Lorraine, in eastern France, an area lying astride important crossroads between France and Germany, the people suffered, perhaps more than most from invading armies, battles, pillage, devastation, and robber bands of unemployed soldiers. Afflicted by poverty and starvation, they were also terrorized by their belief in sorcery and evil demons. In addition, they lived in fear of the Catholic Inquisition whose severe judges were determined at any cost to root out the causes of evil perpetrated by the devil. Anyone could be tortured if denounced as a participant in satanic rites.

A magistrate in the town of Nancy, charged with clearing evil-doers out of the region, boasted to the Cardinal of Lorraine that he had sent 800 sorcerers to the stake to be burned. Arrogantly, he claimed that his justice was so effective that 16 people had killed themselves rather than face him.[8]

In 1602 a judge, M. Boguet, commissioned to destroy nests of devils said to be in the Jura mountains, repudiated the use of torture to which he believed the true disciples of the devil would be immune. He studied carefully the rites of the Sabbat and came to the conclusion that in the Jura, the devil himself appeared as an enormous black sheep, a candle between his horns, to preside over the orgies. The sorcerers approached one by one and lit their candle that burst into long bluish flames. They knelt down and kissed Satan's *derrière*. Then came the time of public confession when the sorcerers told the prince of the underworld of their exploits since their last meeting together. Those who caused the most wicked abominations such as having people and their livestock die, the most illnesses, or the most fruit spoiled were the ones most favored by Satan.

Boguet was greatly struck by the frenetic dances that sometimes caused women to abort as well as tales that the old men were the most agile. The judge spared the accused from torture and took care to soften the inevitable death penalty by recommending that they be strangled before the flames engulfed them. This judge's book on sorcery (*Discours des Sorciers*) was studied by many and became a manual for members of parliament. He decimated the population of the Jura, and if his own death had not intervened, he may have exterminated the entire region.[9]

NOTES

1. Watts, 201.
2. Erlanger, 31.
3. Scribner, 6.
4. Op. cit., 10.
5. Erlanger, 20.
6. Sax, 77–78.
7. Darnton, 91–92 ff.
8. Erlanger, 59.
9. Loc. cit. See also, Watts, 203.

5

SPREAD OF THE
REFORMATION

Religious reformers made rapid strides in the imperial lands of the Holy Roman Empire, where the territorial secular rulers were often inclined toward the new religious point of view as were some members of the Catholic clergy. Reformist leaders used all means available to condemn and ridicule the Catholic Church and inform a mostly illiterate society of their beliefs. Besides the printing presses, woodcuts, engravings, songs, satire, drama, and the pulpit were all means to instruct the masses.

GERMANY

How the religious lives and practices of the people were disrupted by the anxiety, passion, and upheavals of the time is well illustrated in the case of Germany.

Local congregations, anxious to hear the new orthodoxy, pressured their village and town councilors to hire a preacher sympathetic to the Reformation. Unsympathetic city officials found themselves confronted by an angry populace.

When no church was available to itinerant evangelists, as was often the case, they preached in the market place, the churchyard, or wherever there was a willing audience. Church services were now changing; in some cases, the preacher allowed questions from the congregation during

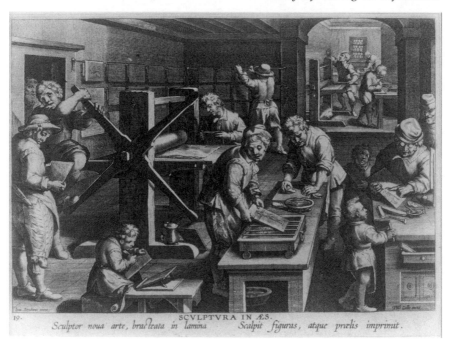

SCVLPTVRA IN ÆS.
Sculptor noua arte, bracteata in lamina   Sculpit figuras, atque prælis imprimit.

Interior view of a workshop with men and boys engaged in various activities in etching, engraving, and printing. Print by Philippe Galle, c. 1600. (Library of Congress.)

the sermon. Elsewhere, clerical garb was not worn. In one case the preacher wore a long red coat, fashionable shoes, and a Scottish red beret.

In some instances, congregations became unruly; in Regensburg, a Catholic preacher was heckled during the sermon. In 1524, in Ulm, a priest who began his sermon with a prayer to the Virgin Mary, was driven out of the church with vociferous abuse.

Where reforms were accepted by the populace, a once-passive congregation sometimes turned into an unrestrained shouting match. Disputes with priests reached the point where town councils forbade public contradiction of preachers, and city officials everywhere reimposed discipline by prohibiting anyone from speaking during the Mass.

Even in private homes, evangelical sermons were given, and peoples' lives were filled with debating religious issues—the most popular place being at inns but also at spinning bees, Church ales, on the job site, as well as in the village square where pamphlets were distributed and read out loud to any gathering. The dinner table, too, always provided a setting for conversation on religious topics.

Songs and poems scornful of the orthodox clergy were widely circulated. Some towns prohibited such activity that could lead to public disorder. There were cases where crowds of Lutherans would invade a Catholic church and by singing loudly, attempt to drown out the church music.

Tempers flared in Magdeburg in 1524 when a weaver who sang Lutheran hymns was imprisoned. Two hundred citizens marched on city hall to demand his release. A number of German cities passed censorship laws threatening authors and publishers with fines and imprisonment, forcing their activities underground.

Hans Häberlin, a lay preacher from the village of Wiggensbach, was detained in 1526 for unauthorized preaching. At the time of his arrest he was speaking to a crowd of about eight hundred peasants gathered in a field. In spite of setbacks and opposition, the Reformation spread throughout the Holy Roman Empire finding fertile ground in many regions.[1]

THE PROTESTANT MOVEMENT IN SWITZERLAND

The religious movement in Switzerland started under Ulrich Zwingli, a priest. The Swiss confederation of the time was made up of 13 nearly autonomous states (or cantons) along with some affiliated states. In Germany and Switzerland, there was at first agreement on reformist issues, but the relative independence of the cantons brought on conflicts during the Reformation when the various regions supported different aspects of doctrine. Some followers of Zwingli, for example, believing the Reformation too conservative, moved independently toward more radical ideas.

The movement first spread to the major German speaking cities such as Zürich, Basel, and Bern, but large numbers of people lived in villages or hamlets tucked away in the high mountain valleys. These places were snowbound in winter and the locals had to be self-reliant. Some were reached only by paths leading ever upward hewn out of the sides of mountains with precipitous drops to river gorges far below. Vertiginous bridges of stone and wood crossed over deep abysses 1,000-feet below. The hamlet might consist of a dozen log houses in a clearing surrounded by dark pine forests where bears still lurked in the sixteenth century and could be a danger. Snowcapped mountains loomed all around. Compared to the lowland cities with their pollution, thieves, noise, periodic plague, and civil regulations, people of the hamlets lived a serene life in the fresh air with room to expand. They raised chickens, geese, sheep, goats, and cows; grew vegetables in the short summer; and pretty much lived by their own resources. Milk, often made into a soup and cheese were the primary staples. There was no shortage of wood for fires and warmth and in winter close to the fire on a straw mattress was the best place to sleep. Most of the mountain peasants were poor, but some with more livestock and a little money would send their children for some schooling in the valley towns.

Young children occupied themselves with homemade toys in the form of puppets, toy soldiers and horses, dolls, throwing rocks at a target, racing and pole-vaulting, When boys were a little older, perhaps as young as eight, they became shepherds and took the livestock up higher into the mountains to the summer pastures. This too was a dangerous life. Shepherds sometimes became lost when enveloped by dense clouds and fog. Sometimes, bears after the livestock menaced the guardian, falling rocks and avalanches were always a threat, a sudden unexpected snow storm could bury the shepherd, and food and water could run out days away from the hamlet. Sleeping on straw mattresses teeming with lice and fleas was uncomfortable enough, but if the lice carried typhus, the shepherd's life was in danger. Usually barefooted and with little more than a tunic, the boys from impoverished families had little choice but to follow in the path of their fathers. There were, of course, some young men who preferred not to tend sheep and goats in the highlands and left the villages and hamlets for opportunities in the cities and took their chances on survival. When work was nowhere to be found, they resorted to stealing chickens and geese, onions or carrots in the fields, and begging in the streets.

Mountain people were not entirely isolated and would sell their wool and cheese in the larger villages when weather permitted the journey into the valleys below, and there they could barter for flour, wine, and luxuries such as pepper or spices imported from clearing houses in Amsterdam and brought to the cities and towns of Switzerland by mule carts.

News of the reform movement gradually reached the villages and hamlets by traders, visiting friends, or relatives. There was generally some visitor who could read and brought Protestant pamphlets to the outlying communities.

Zürich Embraces the New Faith
As the sixteenth century advanced, Zürich contained about 10,000 inhabitants. The city's economy focused on the surrounding hinterland that provided commercial agricultural produce. Power was held by an urban oligarchy of leading families. The surrounding villages and farmers were obliged to sell their products at fixed prices in the city and purchase their requirements from the city shops. Censorship allowed no criticism of the administration. The little industry and trade was reserved for the privileged few who operated in the sphere of public or ecclesiastical authority. In the twisting narrow streets, the merchants and artisans had no say in the functioning of the city and were banned if they complained. Zürich was both spiritually and economically corrupt. A few priests lectured ineffectively about the abuses of indulgences and corruption of morals, but little changed.

Already well known for his dynamic preaching, Ulrich Zwingli was appointed people's priest at Zürich where he gave his first sermon on January 1, 1519. During his university days in more liberal Basel, he had become familiar with the doctrines of humanism and was sensitive to ecclesiastical abuses.

At the end of January 1519, when Bernhardin Sanson appeared at the gates of the city peddling indulgences, parishioners turned to Zwingli for advice. He let it be known that indulgences were sold on false pretences, and as a result, the Council of Zürich denied Sanson entry into the city. Hoping to reduce the effects of the reforms called for by Luther, authorities in Rome disclaimed supporting Sanson, and he was recalled.

After 1520, Zwingli's theological opinions became more radical. He attacked moral corruption, accused monks of laziness and high living, rejected veneration of saints, cast doubts on the notion of hell fire and the efficacy of excommunication. Attacks on the assertion that tithing was God-given contravened the economic interests of the Church, and some canons came to oppose him. Zwingli professed not to be an innovator; his teachings were based only on scripture. How much he was influenced by Erasmus and Luther is unclear.

Zwingli was chosen to fill a vacancy among the canons of the cathedral in spring 1521, retaining his post as the people's priest. He was now a citizen of Zürich.

In March 1522, on the first fasting Sunday of Lent, he ignored the rules while friends distributed smoked sausages, an action he defended in both a sermon and a publication.[2] Noting that there was no general rule on diet in the Bible, Zwingli reasoned that no sin had been committed, and hence no punishment should proceed from the Church. The city council requested that the issue be clarified. The bishop responded, reiterating the traditional position on fasting.

Soon after, in July 1522, Zwingli and other humanists petitioned the bishop in an attempt to rescind the requirement of clerical celibacy. The bishop insisted that the ecclesiastical order should be maintained, but Zwingli was not dismissed. When he rejected the right of the Church to judge on ecclesiastical matters because of its own corruption, other Swiss clergymen began to join his cause.

With no clarification on the issues, tension continued to grow between Zürich and the bishop, and among Zürich's confederation partners in the Swiss Diet. On December 22, 1522, the Diet proposed that its members put a stop to the new teachings, but the Zürich city council had other ideas. On January 3, 1523, it invited the city's clergy along with those from outlying regions, as well as a representative from the bishop, to a meeting to hear the views of the various factions, after which the council would decide who would be permitted to continue proclaiming their beliefs.

Attracting some 600 participants, the Zürich disputation met. It came as a severe blow to the Catholic Church when the council decided not only to let Zwingli continue his preaching, but to allow any preacher to teach as long as it was in accordance with scripture. The secular members of society were setting the rules that had been the prerogative of the Church.

In September 1523, Zwingli's colleague and pastor of Saint Peter's Church, Leo Jud, adhering to a literal reading of the second commandant "Thou shalt not take unto thee any graven images" asked for the removal of icons from churches including statues of saints. Demonstrations followed, whereupon the city council held a second disputation to discuss not only icons but the very essence of the Mass. Catholics felt that the Eucharist was a true sacrifice, but Zwingli declared that it was only a commemorative action. Men were in attendance who also wanted the process of reform to move at a more rapid pace and who, among other things, wanted to replace infant baptism with adult baptism—a time when people understood what they were doing. They were led by Conrad Grebel, one of the founders of the Anabaptist movement. The arguments, pro and con, resulted in the question of who actually held the authority to decide on these issues—the city council or the Church.

Eventually, a compromise was reached that allowed pastors to leave images in their churches if they wished as long as they instructed the congregation about the consequences of worshipping idols. The hope was that people would eventually want them removed. The council later decided on the removal of images within Zürich, whereas rural communities were granted the right to remove them based on majority vote of their congregations.

When Zwingli's major adversaries left the city, resistance from those hostile to reform, collapsed. An attempt by the Bishop of Constanz to defend the Mass and the veneration of images resulted in a rupture of ties between the city and the Church. Pastors, no longer required to celebrate Mass, began to modify their services as each saw fit.

Zwingli translated the ceremony of Communion into German, and on Maundy Thursday, April 13, 1525, he celebrated Communion in its new form. Instead of silver cups, wooden ones were used to show humility, and at the sermon there was no music or singing. Zwingli advocated limiting the celebration of Communion to just four times a year. He also asked for the abolition of monasteries to turn them into hospitals for the poor. His advice was followed. Remaining nuns and monks were pensioned off. Church properties were taken over by the council, and new welfare programs were instituted. The most extreme branch of the Reformation in Switzerland led by Conrad Grebel rejected the role of civil government in Church affairs and demanded that a congregation of the faithful be established for this purpose. Grebel encouraged the emerging Anabaptist movement.

On August 15, 1524, against Grebel's wishes, the council insisted that all newborn infants be baptized, and nonconformists were forced to pay a fine. This was later changed to banishment. For rebaptism of anyone, the death penalty was imposed. Felix Manz defied the mandate and was arrested and drowned in the Limmat River that runs through Zürich. The Anabaptists departed the city for a more congenial place.

Success of the Reformation in Zürich and elsewhere became a political as well as a religious issue between the **Religious** cantons since the economy of some regions depended to a **Civil War** large extent on mercenary soldiers and the pay they brought home. The Swiss people were proud of their mercenary solder pike men who had turned the tide of many battles. Mercenary soldiering was also an outlet for the young men of impoverished hamlets and towns who brought home their pay that helped improve the lives of their poor fami lies and members of the communities. Their abolishment was a major tenet of the Swiss Reformation that led to friction among the cantons.

The League of the Five Cantons was formed in 1524, to combat the spread of the reformed faith. Tensions ran high. A Protestant pastor was burned at the stake in Catholic Schwyz in 1529. In retaliation, Zürich declared war. Open war was avoided and a peace agreement was drawn up.

At a religious conference in 1529, Luther and his friend and colleage, Philipp Melanchthon, opposed any union with Zwingli. This led to a schism in the reform movement caused by Luther's insistence on the real presence of Christ as opposed to Zwingli's teaching on the symbolic presence of Christ at the Eucharist.

Two years later, war broke out, and the Catholic cantons defeated the forces of Zürich. The 48-year-old Zwingli was killed. The cantons agreed to a peace treaty allowing cities that had already converted to remain Protestant. Cantons remained free to choose their religion. The peace prescribed the *cuius regio, eius religio*[3] principle that would also be later adopted in the peace of Augsburg in 1555. Catholic cantons made up a majority in the Federal Diet of the Swiss Confederacy.

The city and the canton of Zürich adhered to the ideas of Zwingli, along with other parts of German- speaking **Geneva and** Switzerland. In the west, French-speaking Switzerland, **Calvinism** on the other hand, developed its own particular brand of the Reformation, organized in Geneva by John Calvin, a Frenchman who originally pursued a theological education and then law. He later converted to Protestantism (exactly when is unclear), but his doctrine distinguished itself from Lutheranism and Zwinglianism by strict moral precepts. Unlike the citizens of Zürich, Bern, Basel, and other Swiss cities that became Protestant in the 1520s, the people of Geneva did not have close cultural ties with the reformed churches in Germany and German-speaking Switzerland. The canton of Bern, determined to see

Protestantism spread throughout Switzerland, sent reformers to Geneva in 1533. After considerable conflict, Geneva officially became Protestant in 1535.

A successful lawyer, Calvin was invited to Geneva by Guillaume Farel to establish the new Reformed Church where he altered the nature of Protestantism, modeling the social organization of that city completely on biblical principles and designing a catechism to impose his strict moral code, derived from a literal reading of Christian scriptures, on all the members of the Church as well as the citizens.

His reforms did not go over well, however, as the people of Geneva realized that they had thrown out one dogmatic church only to see it replaced by another. Calvin's reforms simply imposed more oppressive orthodoxy on the city. As a result, Calvin and the Protestant reformers were banished from Geneva early in 1538. He moved to Strassburg where he spent his time writing commentaries on the Bible and finishing his prodigious work on Protestant doctrine, *The Institutes of the Christian Church*.

The city of Geneva, meanwhile, became unruly, and the city fathers invited Calvin to return. He was convinced that the entire human race was wicked and sinful, and people could not save themselves just by their own efforts but depended on the grace of God who, omniscient, already knew who would be saved and who would not. Those destined for salvation were the elect or chosen ones.

Some of Calvin's followers, Theodore Beza, for example, asserted that since God did not intend everyone to be saved, then Christ died only for the elect, for those predestined to go to paradise. This view of double predestination implied that the rest of mankind would go to hell. Calvin's vision of an ideal Christian society would be founded on the elect.

Miguel Servetus, a Spanish theologian and humanist, stopping off in Geneva on his way to Italy, was arrested there. His views on baptism and the trinity differed from Calvin's, and he was burned at the stake. Heresy was not tolerated.

Nonbelievers were ruthlessly pursued, and any form of entertainment such as gambling, dancing, singing, drinking, theater, festivals, displays, and poetry readings were all forbidden. Musical instruments and pictures were removed from churches. Absence from church without a good excuse was punishable.

By the mid-1550s, Geneva had become a Protestant focal point. Those expelled from their own countries including France, England, Scotland, and the Netherlands, found shelter there, and soon nearly a half of the population comprised foreign Protestants. Adopting radical Calvinist principles, many who had arrived as reformed moderates left as devoted Calvinists.

Anything that was clearly evident in scripture had to be followed diligently and with dedication. Beliefs, church organization, political organization, and society itself were to be based on the Bible. Following citations in the New Testament, Calvin divided Church organization into four levels: there should be five pastors to preach, a larger body of teachers to instruct the population in the Calvinist doctrine, 12 elders imitating the 12 apostles and chosen by the council to supervise every aspect of city life, and finally, deacons to care for the sick, the elderly, the widowed, and the poor.

For the citizens of Geneva, like it or not, Calvin's council wielded the power. Theaters and drinking establishments were closed, and only inns were allowed some moderate drinking accompanied by sermons. Swearing was forbidden as was card playing, and church services required attendance three or four times a week. All residents were obligatory members of the Church. Private houses were inspected from time to time to be sure they adhered to the moral standards set out by Calvin. Not unlike the Spanish Inquisition, members of society were encouraged to report their neighbors for violations of moral precepts. Women's hairstyles and clothing had to meet certain standards of modesty. Lace, jewelry, and brightly colored clothes were looked upon as ungodly. Children had to be named after biblical figures. Penalties for infractions of the code were severe, and capital punishment by burning was not uncommon, especially for heresy involving witchcraft or Catholicism.

Even though the views of Luther, Zwingli, and Calvin had similar theological points of view, it did not take long before their followers turned to conflict. Luther forced a rift with the Catholic Church by deviating from established dogma. Zwingli rejected the literal view of the Eucharist, which eventually ruptured relations with Luther. Calvinism, going further, broke with Zwingli and Luther. Luther also fell out with Erasmus.[4]

While Geneva at that time may seem bizarre to many people today, it should be remembered that the God-fearing people of the sixteenth century rejoiced in the restrictions placed upon their so-called saintly city. They believed humility, unpretentiousness, and piety were the will of God. All assumed they would be one of the elect.

TROUBLE IN STRASSBURG

Elsewhere in the Holy Roman Empire, the free city of Strassburg was undergoing religious problems. The Imperial City, a crossroad of European commercial routes was comparatively wealthy. Many people, poor and rich, passed through its gates. The city had a thriving book trade, and evangelical works, such as those of Martin Luther, were in demand.

Strassburg contained over twenty thousand inhabitants in the early sixteenth century not including thousands of peasants who lived beyond the walls but under the jurisdiction of city institutions. Industry was practically unknown except for cheap woolen goods. The people were by and large anticlerical, stimulated by humanist scholars and dislike of the bishop who owned much of the surrounding land and controlled the monasteries and clergy. Violent protests against city officials, composed of the upper crust families, and against the Church were not uncommon. From 1519, anti-Church pamphlets were common in Alsace.

Lives of Peasants and Village Clergy Conflicts periodically arose between poor peasants and village priests, sometimes just as poor. Clergymen often made loans to peasant farmers, but if the farm failed, the peasant defaulted leaving the priest even poorer than he was before. Many clergy depended on the income from these loans.

A number of parishes had long before been incorporated into ecclesiastical institutions such as chapters or monasteries, and peasant income also supported wealthy cannons and Church administrators. Around Strassburg as in other places, clerics often held more than one benefice, and the peasant complained that there were too few priests, and the quality of their service was abysmal.

The city elite and the bishop of the Cathedral controlled the outlying lands and collected the tithes and rents. Bad harvest and inflation had left many destitute, but stirred by Luther's numerous tracts on the gospel and on individual freedom that inundated Alsace, they demanded justice. The city council met some of the claims of the gardeners (the largest guild in the city) by putting a few restrictions on the Catholic clergy and passing reform bills. It was not enough, and the peasants' demands grew.

The gardeners were the most downtrodden, low paid and unhappy. In 1523, a large group of them withheld payment of tithes, rents, and dues to their landlords. The next year, 400, mostly gardeners, attacked convents and monasteries they felt were corrupt, smashing statues.

Gardeners and artisans including tailors, furriers, barrel makers, potters, shoemakers, tanners, butchers, vintners, and other commoners joined together, discussed their problems, and often petitioned city councils for improvement in their working conditions and lives. Sometimes their leaders were imprisoned or banned from the city for several years. The city council was slow to act on their demands.

Peasants protested against the Strassburg Cathedral chapter on whose land they worked and attacked a convent in 1525. Another 2,000 rebels, consisting of many Strassburg gardeners, plundered the abbey of Aldorf. Pillage continued for three days until the duke of Lorraine and his army ended the upheaval with much peasant and artisan bloodshed.

Reform leaders preached in the countryside and peasants listened and sometimes revolted when they heard that Jesus favored the poor and not the rich.

For many, the pace of reform was too slow. The city council composed of nobility and guild representatives, an oligarchy like that of Zürich and most other cities of Europe, made cautious concessions ascertaining their own positions of power were not endangered. By 1524, radical reformists were demanding more rapid socio-economic and religious change.

Matthew Zell, the first major reformer influential on the city council, welcomed and supported Martin Bucer, a native of Alsace, on his arrival in the city. That the common people were eager to hear the voices expounding the New Gospel was evident from the great crowds that came to hear Zell, expelled from the church, preaching from a wooden pulpit made by the carpenters' guild. His congregations numbered more than 3,000 members.[5]

Bucer, like so many other reformers, had first trained for the priesthood. By the end of 1523, the city council published a mandate allowing evangelical preaching in the city. Bucer became a star. He would become leader of the Reformed Churches in Switzerland and South Germany after the death of Zwingli repudiating the idea that the rite of Mass was a true sacrifice.

Meanwhile the city council vacillated over the religious issues confronting the populace, while the number of citizens supporting the Reformation continued to rise, and hostility for the Catholic clergy grew. Conrad Treger, the prior of the Augustinians, attacked the reformed preachers and labeled all the burghers of Strassburg heretics. Angry mobs broke into monasteries destroying religious icons. Many opponents of the Reformation, including Treger, were arrested. The council belatedly took action requesting an official statement from the evangelical ministers. Bucer summarized the teachings of the Reformation in 12 articles that included justification by faith alone, rejection of the Mass, monastic vows, saint veneration, purgatory, the traditional liturgy, and the authority of the pope. He emphasized obedience to the government. Treger, released from prison, left Strassburg ending open opposition to the Reformation. Bucer spent much of his time attempting to repair the differences between Luther and Zwingli in their divisive views of the Eucharist.

THE NETHERLANDS

The Protestant reform engulfed the Spanish-held Netherlands of the Holy Roman Empire. The Netherlands consisted of French speakers in the south (Flanders and Brabant), Dutch speakers in the center (Holland), and Frisian in the north (Friesland).Towns such as Amsterdam, the Hague, Rotterdam, Dordrecht, and Antwerp were wealthy centers under the leadership of merchant families. Dutch burghers were educated, energetic, and independent minded people.

Reformation in the Netherlands was initiated by popular movements and reinforced by the arrival of Protestant refugees from Germany and France and later from England under Mary Tudor. Charles V, the Holy

Roman Emperor, issued strict orders against the printing and preaching of the works of Luther, but records of the period name numerous people suspected of heretical opinions.[6]

The earliest presence of the Reformation was in the form of Lutheranism, and two monks who had read Luther's works were burned at the stake in Brussels in 1523. Followers of Luther, however, active in the 1520s did not develop into a popular movement and remained small and intellectual. The first expression of the new religion came from Anabaptists in the 1530s who followed the leadership of Menno Simons from Friesland, ordained in the Catholic priesthood. Influenced by Luther's works, he left the Church to become an evangelical preacher and allied himself with the Dutch Anabaptists. Teaching that neither baptism nor Communion conferred grace upon an individual and that Grace was bestowed only through faith in Jesus Christ, he attracted large audiences. Although not the founder of the sect, his influence was such that many Dutch Anabaptists adopted his name, and became known as Mennonites.[7]

Meanwhile, Dutch publishers, risking their lives in major cities, clandestinely took on the dangerous but lucrative work of publishing heretical works for a growing market.[8]

In the 1540s, Calvinism took root in the French-speaking south, imported by missionaries from Geneva, and grew rapidly. Charles V proclaimed two brutal edicts in 1550 whereby mere suspicion of heresy was enough to burn the suspect at the stake.

When his son, Felipe II, a Spaniard and Catholic through and through, took over his share of the Habsburg Empire, which included Spain and the Netherlands in 1556, he was even less tolerant and installed the Inquisition while curbing the traditional rights of the nobility and townsmen.

Felipe's methods to bring the Netherlands to heel increased the unpopularity of Spain and the Catholic Church, equated as the same oppressors. In 1566, a radical mob of Protestants looted and destroyed hundreds of churches, and anti-Catholic riots spread across the country.

Felipe II unleashed Spanish troops on the Netherlands under the command of the bloodthirsty duke of Alba whose barbaric actions resulted in open revolt. Between 1567 and 1573, thousands of Protestant leaders were executed. The war of independence waged by the Dutch against Spain began in 1568.

William I, prince of Orange, led the revolt and eventually took control of most northern towns. In 1579 the Union of Utrecht, an alliance of all northern and some southern provinces, was formed. Those that joined the union would become the Netherlands; those that did not would become Belgium. In 1581, the Union of Utrecht proclaimed independence from Spain. The new nation suffered a series of reverses in the ensuing war. Alba's firm grip impelled the southern regions back to Catholicism causing a flood of refugees to the north where Protestantism flourished and where the sea beggars with attacks on Spanish shipping and troops in the north helped secure quasi independence.

Meanwhile, the Dutch were turning to Calvinism as refugees from Flanders and the Brabant poured in. The seven northern provinces that eluded the Spanish grasp came to be recognized by England as independent Protestant states.

With a spirit of toleration in the Dutch Netherlands, the region came to be recognized as a safe haven for persecuted people of all kinds of religious shades and attitudes.

In 1573, William I proclaimed himself a Calvinist. In 1584, Balthasar Gérard, a supporter of Felipe, felt that William of Orange had betrayed the Spanish king and the Catholic religion. Felipe had declared William an outlaw and pledged a reward of 25,000 crowns for his assassination. Gérard decided to collect it. William was shot down on the stairway of his own house after a meeting with Gérard, but his son Maurice continued the warfare until his death in 1625. Finally in 1648, the Eighty Years' War of attrition ended, and the Netherlands received unconditional independence at the Treaty of Westphalia. Belgium remained under foreign rule until 1831.

NORTHERN EUROPE

While the Protestant Reformation was felt across all of Europe, the movement was strongest in the north. After some years of turmoil in the sixteenth century, all of Scandinavia ultimately became Protestant, as the kings of Denmark (who also ruled Norway and Iceland) and Sweden (who also ruled Finland) adopted the principles of the Reformation.

To a large degree, the reform movement introduced in Denmark was through the work of Hans Tausen, a disenchanted monk and a student of Luther. There is little doubt that the Danes were ready for a change. Imprisoned by his order, people came to his cell in droves to listen to him preach, and when he won over the prior of the monastery to his views and was released, there were few churches of significant size to hold the crowds. He addressed the people in the market place from a church tower.

When the Franciscans refused to allow him to preach in their more ample church, a mob broke in by force. A compromise was arranged whereby friars were to preach in the morning and Tausen in the afternoon. The bishop, unhappy with these proceedings, sent armed men to the church to arrest Tausen. The parishioners, who had carried their weapons with them, drove off the bishop's men.

In October 1526, King Frederick I took Hans Tausen under his protection, appointed him his chaplain, and charged him to continue to preach the gospel to the citizens of Viborg who were made responsible for his safety.

On the death of his benefactor, Frederick I, Bishop Ronnow of Copenhagen wanted him banished. The people took up arms against the bishop and would have killed him but for Tausen's intervention. The bishop rescinded his accusation, allowing Tausen to preach. Christian III, son of the dead king, an open reformist, won an ensuing civil war and the crown in 1537.

In Sweden and Finland, the Reformation was spearheaded by the Swedish King, Gustav Vasa, in 1523. When the pope remonstrated over Gustav's interference in Swedish church affairs, the official connection between Sweden and the papacy was severed. The crown confiscated Church property, and from then on the clergy were subject to civil law, and all ecclesiastical appointments required royal approval. Official sanction was given to Lutheranism that was to be taught in the schools and preached in the churches.

SOUTHERN EUROPE

Spain, Portugal, and Italy remained predominantly Catholic. In a country such as Spain, a united state under a strong Catholic monarch, and a powerful Inquisition supported by the people, such religious transformation could not have arisen. As soon as a spark glimmered, it was quickly extinguished.

Subjected to the will of the Inquisition, the few Protestants in Spain were forced to live precariously, for even having visited a Protestant country was enough to put one under suspicion of apostasy. Even foreigners had to go before the inquisitors for the slightest infringement of the rules such as failing to remove one's hat when the bishop's carriage passed by. There had been a few defections in Spain, but the Inquisition maintained tight control over all religious activity, and heretics were summarily burned at the stake. With inquisitorial police everywhere and neighbors ready to denounce one another for any suspicious behavior, Protestantism remained confined to a few very secret worshippers.

Portugal, under Spanish domination for much of the period (1580–1640), followed policies similar to those of Spain. The country remained untouched by the Reformation.

The Reformation had very little impact on Italy as a whole. The only Protestant communities were those of the Waldensians, who lived in isolated mountain valleys. These groups had existed before the Reformation but then, due to common beliefs, they integrated into the Reformed Church.

Because Luther's works were published in German, Church censorship in Italy successfully kept his works from the literate public as well as the general populace by banning preaching and reform ideas. There were no city or state officials asking for reformed preachers as was the case in German-speaking areas.

Church officials regarded any kind of reform as a threat to their position, and high offices were controlled by powerful families. There were a few isolated incidents in which followers of Luther or Zwingli tried to make inroads in Italy, but even the mention of their names could be dangerous. At one point in 1531, Lutheran ideas were discussed at the University of Padua, but papal authorities wasted no time suppressing this activity.

EASTERN EUROPE

Protestant reformers cut deeply into the fabric of the Catholic states of Poland under tolerant rulers. The teachings of the reform movement found adherents throughout the country.

The most fervent Protestants were to be found in the cities of Danzig, Thorn, and Elbing, which were still mostly German. The majority of Poland's nobility had converted to Protestantism, and the policy of tolerance attracted many of the refugees from other lands. A new Protestant-dominated nation was about to be born.

Then came the miscarriage. In 1550, the king, Sigismund Augustus, announced he would remain Catholic and that heretics would be expelled from the country. This did not happen as many of the nobility were Protestant, and the common people were not affected by the religious split. Following monarchs were thoroughly Catholic, and a divided Protestantism, while not vigorously persecuted, just faded away.[9]

WESTERN EUROPE

Assembled at Meaux by Guillaume Brigonnet was a group of French evangelical humanists. There, Jacques Lefèvre produced **France** his French translations of the scriptures. Lefèvre did not attack the papacy or seek a break with the Church, but the town gradually acquired many Protestant residents. Similar small circles appeared in other towns such as Amiens and Metz in Lyons and Grenoble. There was little coordination among the far-flung groups that were inspired by Erasmus, Lefèvre, Luther, Zwingli, Bucer, and even the Anabaptists. Growth and expansion was inhibited by opposition from the Sorbonne and the Parliament of Paris. King François I supported Lutheran princes in the Holy Roman Empire in his struggle against Charles V but had no axe to grind with the pope as did Henry VIII of England.

The citizens of France did not have the spiritual or political need to embrace the new faith. The peasantry, especially, stuck to their saints and pious practices. There was no rush into heresy, and the powerful French bishops kept their dioceses under control.

In 1534, with the affair of the placards, the king clamped down, then for a time relaxed the oppression, but at the end of his reign, some 3,000

Waldensians were massacred in Provence along with many Protestant artisans at Meaux.[10] Calvinism, however, was on the rise, but Catholics were still in firm control.

England   Dissenters were not unknown in England and provided a small nucleus for a Protestant foothold. The Lutheran movement was reinforced by the trade with Antwerp whereby numerous heretical books and pamphlets invaded the country. After about 1520, such ideas were discussed by students at Cambridge under the auspices of the Augustinian friar, Robert Barnes, a disciple of Luther (martyred in 1540). Ties with the Vatican were severed in the reign of Henry VIII, and the Anglican Church emerged. Thomas Cranmer and Thomas Cromwell inclined toward Protestantism; the latter worked toward forming alliances with other Protestant states such as Saxony. They both were sympathetic to the dissemination throughout England of the scriptures translated by Tyndale and Coverdale.

WOMEN IN THE ADVANCE OF THE REFORMATION

In countries outside the Holy Roman Empire women also played a significant role in the spread of reformed ideas. Elizabeth Dirks, for example, from a good family was sent to a convent in East Friesland where she began to question whether life in a convent was truly a Christian way to live and became interested in Anabaptism. She decided to flee, but she was apprehended a little later in still Catholic Holland. Hustled off to prison, she was asked for names of her family members and students whom she had taught. She refused to reveal anyone in the Anabaptist movement. When asked by the examiners if she believed one was saved through baptism, her response was that she did not. She also stated that only Christ, and not priests, could forgive sins. Severely tortured, she still refused to answer their questions. On March 27, 1549, Elizabeth was forced into a sack and drowned. The criminal court records of her ordeal were published in 1660.[11]

Catholic women in the hands of Protestants fared little better. Women in England who harbored Catholic priests were persecuted in the reign of Elizabeth I. Such was the fate of Anne Line, a convert to Catholicism, who was hanged as one of the 40 Catholic martyrs of England and Wales in 1601 for that crime. Margaret Clitheroe was accused of the same crime but refused to plead either guilty or not guilty (in such cases, the trial could not proceed, and torture was applied). A board was placed over her body and weights added to it, resulting in her being crushed to death.

Margaret Ward was hanged for helping a Catholic priest escape from a London jail. She was arrested and clapped in irons, flogged, and hung up by the wrists. This treatment continued for so long that afterwards she was severely crippled before her execution.

The (Catholic) Act for the Advancement of True Religion was passed in 1543, prohibiting women from reading the Bible in public, but this did not deter Anne Askew. Arrested and stretched on the rack, she endured this treatment for months but revealed nothing of her acquaintances. Too badly crippled to walk, she was carried to the stake and burned as a heretic in 1546 in London at the age of 25. Protestantism was not to be recognized officially in England until the reign of Edward VI.

NOTES

1. For the above sources, see Scribner, 51–57, 65.
2. Published on April 16, under the title Von Erkiesen und Freiheit der Speisen (Regarding the Choice and Freedom of Foods).
3. "He who leads, selects the religion."
4. Luther, 390.
5. Elton, G. R. ed. (1965), 107–108.
6. Duke, 15.
7. See Hillerbrand (2007), 123–125 for more detail.
8. Duke, 29.
9. Hillerbrand, Op. cit., Chapter 11.
10. Dickens (1966), 99.
11. Hillerbrand (1964), 242–245.

6

HOLY ROMAN EMPIRE

OBSERVATIONS OF A SIXTEENTH-CENTURY TOURIST

Fynes Moryson, son of a well-off English gentleman, left England in 1591, sailing to Stade near the river Elbe where his travels began through the Holy Roman Empire. In his accounts, he commended the Germans for their integrity but found them inclined to be somewhat dull.

He admired the German women for their propriety—covering themselves from head to foot if in the street. People who were not married did not kiss publicly; and if they were married, they only did so discreetly. Even to touch a woman's hand in greeting or departure was strictly against etiquette.

Honesty was a characteristic of the inland Germans who would not cheat a client nor sell an item for more than its value. Buyers paid the asking price without bargaining.

At feasts they had no intimate interaction and discourse or playful activities. Instead, there were long orations, one following upon the other, interspersed with short toasts.

In short, Fynes found the Germans large in body, short in wit, modest in speech, just in their dealings, strict in dress, and heavy drinkers.

Germans were excellent in what Moryson called the manual arts because of their diligence in their chosen professions. They were content to do a good job in one industry unlike in other countries where, besides their professions, men tried to gain a superficial knowledge of many things for discourse and ostentation. The Germans produced the printing press, excellent clocks, and water-driven mills for use in mines and for sawing wood. Mills, on

Artisans and City Life

riverboats, could be moved from town to town when needed. With these inventions, they made labor easier and saved on costs. Children's cradles were supported by wheels as were beds designed for the ill, too weak to walk. For ease of labor, plows also had wheels.[1]

The various artisanal trades had their yearly feasts that were not as rigid as most events. People paraded through the streets in the morning and once having dined, moved on to a public house to spend the afternoon either dancing or sitting at the tables, singing, talking, and drinking. When the festivities were finished, they marched back to their homes as they had come.

Unlike open English shops, the artisans in Germany worked behind closed chambers with stoves or ovens supplying heat in the winter months. Apprentices also worked here for six years under less harsh conditions than in England, according to Moryson. They had more holidays and more leisure time, with Mondays off work. If a client entered a shop to buy a pair of shoes or boots, no one offered assistance, but all continued working. The buyer selected his footwear himself and tried it on. If it was satisfactory, he paid the price asked along with a mandatory tip (*drink-geld*), drinking money for the workers. A small tip was scornfully refused.

He noted in addition that many educated Germans he met spoke Latin and had some skill in mathematics and music. Women carried chalk in their purses to help them quickly add up figures.

People begging for alms sang in the streets, and poor students during holidays went from house to house, generally receiving hand-outs from the wealthier homes.

Each city and fair sized town had trumpeters who lived in the steeples of churches along with their families. Stoves were provided as were chambers to live in. Daily at noon, they sounded trumpets on the highest part of the steeple. When anyone approached the town along the road, by horse, carriage or even walking, flags were hung out on the steeple to inform the citizens of the new arrivals and especially the innkeeper who could prepare for clients. In addition, patrols walked the streets at night to keep an eye out for mischief or fire. As they walked, they shouted out periodically to the effect:

> Loving sirs let me say to you
> The clock eleven has now struck
> Look to your fire and your light (candles)
> That no mischance befall this night[2]

Many cities also maintained (at public cost) musicians who played at the inn each day at noon when the councilors went for dinner, as well as at public feasts. At festivals, the louder the music, the better the Germans liked it. It seems they were fond of singing birds and both in the better houses and those of the artisans, birds could be seen enclosed by a wire behind the window or flying about freely. In Leipzig, Moryson observed nightingales in the better homes that made sweet sounds for those passing.

For reading matter, literate Germans had little interest in foreign authors but preferred their own in science, philosophy, and divinity.

As men often got into arguments and fights, even when drunk, they did not kill each other, for the penalty was imme- **Dueling** diate execution. When two gentlemen went into a field to duel, there were no referees or moderators, but they did battle with the flat of their swords, being careful not to thrust or stab. When the first blood was drawn, the fight was over, and they usually shook hands. The loser bought the drinks for all who witnessed the event.

Most people of any means had a stove in the house to heat water for the bath they took on Saturdays. The women could **Bathing** often be found sitting in doorways drying their hair in the sun. The cities also had public baths for use on those days, used by both men and women who only covered their private parts, if anything, and they were often attended by maids and servants who washed and dried them. The various hot springs or mineral waters were popular, and men often brought mistresses rather than their wives to bathe with them. Although it was forbidden, apothecaries sold sex-stimulating drugs to trusted patrons.

Moryson found many unfamiliar customs in Germany, one of which involved the cherished storks. The cities **Other Cus-** and even private homeowners often built nests of wood, **toms and** saving the birds much effort; and it was considered good **Amusements** luck to have them nest nearby.

At the time of public fairs and the ringing of bells, thieves and condemned fugitives could freely enjoy the festivities, but they had to be gone by the second ringing of the bell.[3] Moryson claims to have seen a woman (who had already had a finger cut off for a crime), beheaded for failing to leave on time.

Drinking and dancing in public houses at feasts or in private homes was the highlight of entertainment for the Germans. In addition, they had shooting contests with crossbow and harquebus, sleigh-riding through the streets when snow covered the ground, and hunting and hawking, although the latter was generally off limits to all but the princes. At the time, there were still bears, wild oxen, wolves, wild boar, and rabbits in Germany. The princes all had herds of red deer and harts freely roaming their forests that were a curse to the peasants as the animals ate their crops and trampled their fields. During harvest time, the country people stayed up all night to try and scare away the animals (especially the red deer) from their wheat fields and vineyards by whistling and making loud noises, but the animals learned that they could not be harmed and seldom moved away. To kill a landowner's deer, boar, or a wild goat could lead to either execution or having one's eyes put out. Wolves, it seems, were fair game for all.

Moryson observed at first that in spite of religious differences, the German Protestants were surprisingly tolerant of each other; but he was not aware of the animosity that lurked beneath the surface of public life. Eventually, however, he arrived at the conclusion that Calvinists and Lutherans hated each other with a passion.

NÜRNBERG

Nürnberg, in the state of Bavaria, was indicative of urban living in many German towns. The merchants of the city were frugal in business and lifestyle, and some were very rich. Like other townsmen, they took care of their civic duties such as standing guard on the walls at night and received no special treatment in the taxes they owed or if they broke the law.

The city stood in a good location for trading purposes. In 1450, a census revealed about 30,000 inhabitants, and another, in 1622, showed a population increase to some 40,000–50,000, of which more than half were artisans. Nürnberg became a focus of the German Renaissance during the fifteenth and sixteenth centuries, and was also an early center of humanism, science, and printing. In 1534, it was the first of the imperial cities to embrace Protestantism.

The free imperial cities tried to control the number of people low on the economic scale by setting a fee for citizenship. Nürnberg set this at 100 gulden, which was high and more than many other free cities charged. Also required was a minimal amount of property. A dye master wishing to establish a shop in town with rights of citizenship, for example, needed 350 gulden: 200 gulden in property, 100 to become a citizen, and 50 for a craft license.[4] It was not the same for all crafts. A linen worker needed only 50 gulden in property. Such cities were also home to a large class of noncitizens such as piece workers in cloth industries, day laborers, and assistants to artisans and merchants—many of whom were transient and lived a day-to-day existence.

Everyone had their rank within society, and all were expected to behave accordingly. In the cities, people lived on certain streets depending on their work or profession, and their mode of dress would be appropriate to their class. The manner of clothing was set out in sumptuary laws, as was the way in which houses could be decorated.

Among the artists who were born or lived there, the painter and print-maker Albrecht Dürer was the most prominent and well esteemed by his contemporaries. Others, such as sculptors, painters, and woodcarvers, adorned the city with their works, which brought together the Italian Renaissance and the German Gothic traditions. Scholars went to Nürnberg to lecture, and a printing press was established there. The first pocket watches, known as Nürnberg eggs, were made there around 1500. An interest in culture on the part of the prosperous artisan class found expression in the contests of the master singers, among whom the shoemaker-poet Hans Sachs was the most well known.

Foreigners such as William Smith of London who resided in the city from the 1570s to the 1590s lauded its virtues and presented some aspects of life in letters back to England. He mentioned the liveliness of the city and remarked on the clothes, the government, festivals, and morals.

Smith recorded that the city was well painted, and gutters and spouts for rain water were of copper, gilded, and fashioned like flying dragons. The buildings were high and stately but only up to four storeys. They commonly had three or four garrets, one above the other,—in which the wealthy stored their grain. Few houses were made completely of timber; lower storeys were generally of stone.[5]

After Augsburg and Köln, Nürnberg was one of the most populous cities of Germany, but as in most major towns, there was a wide disparity of wealth. Smith was impressed with the good order and cleanliness and that many lanes were paved. The city was well provided with public hot water baths and wells that served most of the houses. He also stated that no dunghills existed along the streets but were found only in odd corners, and that people did not urinate in the streets. Refuse could not be thrown out of the house until after ten o'clock at night under penalties of fines or imprisonment.

Each family was allowed to keep one pig that had to be housed outside the city when it became six months old.[6]

Since not all cities had such stringent laws as Nürnberg, some merchants found it behooved them to relocate to other places such as Augsburg where mercantile supervision was less onerous, and laws were not enforced so scrupulously.

In crowded environments, disease was always at hand to strike down the vulnerable. Between 1560 and 1585, major epidemics racked the city. First came plague, then smallpox, then plague again and dysentery, followed by measles and, once more, smallpox. The latter took 5,000 lives in the year 1585. Most victims were children. The city suffered a population decline that took years to recover.[7]

There were many towers. Smith figured about 200, each with lodging for watchmen. The streets were patrolled every night by a man who blew a horn at the foot of each tower to make certain the watchman was not sleeping. If the blast of the horn was not acknowledged, then the watchman had to be asleep, and subject to eight days in prison on bread and water.

Criminals or suspected criminals received little in the way of justice. They were generally allowed to say something on their own behalf, and this would be followed by close questioning from the magistrate. If the accused did

Crime and Punishment

SCOPVS LEGIS EST, AVT VT EV QVE PVNIT EMENDET, AVT POENA
EIVS CAETEROS MELIORES REDDET AVT SVBLATIS MALIS CAETERI SECVRIORES VIVA T.

Pieter Brueghel's *Justicia.* Justice stands blindfolded as people around her are
being tortured. Engraving, c. 1559. (Library of Congress.)

not plead guilty, they were escorted to the torture chamber where in due
course they would confess to anything.

Convicted thieves were beheaded if they were citizens of the city or
hanged if they were not. Hanging was considered by far the worst punishment since the agony was prolonged.

A conviction of arson brought the perpetrator to the stake to be burned
alive. Anyone who swore a false oath had two joints of their forefingers
amputated, and blasphemers had their tongues cut out. For lesser crimes,
punishment included whippings and banishment from the town.[8]

Trials lacked witnesses and lawyers for the defense, and judgments
were already in place before a hearing. The law required evidence of guilt,
and a confession was extracted by any means available.[9] For serious
crime, execution followed immediately.

The Church generally had no sympathy for the accused. Pain and suffering were unimportant. Individual clerics who were charged with care
of their souls explained the beliefs of the Church in the hope that their
faith would be renewed and they would die with a prayer on their lips.[10]

City Regula-
tions
Smith, an innkeeper himself, speaks of the hospitality of
the city council. A person arriving in town with two or
more horses presented his name to the magistrates who

immediately sent him pots of wine and bid him welcome. If the guest was a nobleman, he received one wagon laden with wine, another with oats and a third with foodstuffs. He also found the citizens honest and as good as their word. If a purse was dropped in the street with money or other valuables in it, for example, its owner was more than likely to have it returned. Smith lamented that such was not the case in London.

The city council in Nürnberg, as in other cities, regulated everything. Nothing was kept secret. The authorities took note of the amounts spent on weddings, clothes, christenings, feasts, parties, gifts, and funerals. Draconian details of these and other events were laid out in manuals to be adhered to by the public. It was forbidden to be secretly betrothed, and if a man wished to serenade his lady, the payment to the musicians was restricted to bread, cheese, fruit, and a cup of wine, which could be passed around only once. For a newly married couple, only one party and seven guests were allowed. For all sorts of entertainment or ceremonies, there were manuals to be followed, and any breach of regulations was subject to fines. In addition, a list of guests had to be sent to the office that dealt with weddings and funerals. Dancing after a wedding could only continue until ten o'clock. These are but a few of the many burdensome restrictions placed upon the citizens.[11]

AUGSBURG

The free city of Augsburg, with a population of about 30,000, ranked on a par with Nürnberg and Strassburg. The life of the city was trade, but monasteries, convents, and parish churches were in abundance. There was a cathedral, containing relics of saints, towering above the buildings and its extensive land holding surrounded the city beyond the walls. Its power rivaled that of the city council. Lodgings for numerous clergy were tucked away in its shadows, and here, business was good for prostitutes. Market day was particularly active and noisy with throngs of servant girls bargaining with stall keepers.

Nearby thieves and swindlers sat dismally in the stocks having lost all semblance of dignity. When their time was up, they were banished from the city. The great houses and gardens of the rich merchants contrasted with the cramped quarters of the workshops and one-room hovels of the craftsmen.

Martin Luther visited Augsburg in 1518, and from then on his supporters grew in numbers as did problems for the city council. By 1524–1925, the council, made up of aristocrats, wealthy merchants, and guild masters, was under threat. Radical evangelical preachers and followers carried out direct action that included throwing salt into holy water, tearing up missals, and other annoying deeds. The council ejected one of the instigators, an evangelical monk, from the city, causing a riot. Many of those who gathered to protest the expulsion were poor weavers, laborers, and some guildsmen. The council feared more social unrest from the people who united behind Luther and took the bold step of secretly executing two weavers.[12] Unsure of its citizens, the council then stationed armed mercenaries in the city. In Augsburg as elsewhere, the Reformation took on a social and economic dimension as the poor resented the wealthy upper class that ran city hall.

By the late 1520s, the evangelist preachers and the political elite began to form alliances, while radical Lutherans started to associate with the Anabaptist movement, persecuted by both Lutherans and Catholics. Throughout the 1530s, propaganda leaflets flooded the city mostly directed at monks and Catholic priests who were condemned for every imaginable, and especially sexual, sin.

In 1537, Hans Welser (a disciple of Zwingli) and Mang Seitz, were elected mayors of the city. The Reformation was now firmly established. Tensions continued, however, between rich and poor, guildsmen and aristocrats.

CHANGES IN MANNERS

Some of the old medieval customs became offensive to the new religious orientation. In Saxony, a newly married couple bathed together and emerged from the water wet and naked to distribute refreshments to a crowd of friends.[13] Consummation of the marriage was closely observed by half a dozen or more people to ascertain that the couple had performed this function properly, and there could be no dispute about the legality of the marriage. Such practices began to change about 1550 with the spread of the Reformation as a more prudish attitude toward nakedness and sex set in. Similarly, defecating and urinating in public places became taboo.

Village weddings that were once accompanied by drums, bugles, and crowds of noisy people having a good time as they escorted newlyweds home were beginning to be toned down by city ordinances to just a few members of the family. The old, obscene, riotously enjoyable merriment of the past had no place in solemn Christian ceremony.

PATRICIANS AND BURGHERS

Wealthy families sat on the councils of most towns and had a firm grasp on all administrative offices, made all decisions, using and distributing finances as they saw fit. Guild and other taxes were exacted, but as guilds grew and urban populations rose, the town patricians found themselves confronted with increasing opposition. The burgeoning

Albrecht Dürer, *Peasant Couple Dancing*. Engraving, 1514. (Library of Congress.)

burgher class incorporating well-to-do middle class citizens felt their increasing wealth justified a claim to some rights of control over town administration and began demanding seats on the town assembly.

They felt the clergy had failed to uphold its religious duties. The opulence and laziness of Church officials aroused much ill will, and the burghers demanded an end to the clergy's privilege of freedom from taxation as well as a reduction in their number.

URBAN WORKERS

Most urban workers were unskilled labor and hence not organized into guilds. Some were petty retailers such as fishmongers, rag and bone men, carters, unskilled construction workers, and the like.

Service trades were always a possible occupation for a young urban man and included many professions from doctor, teacher, barber, and notary to bathhouse keeper. These groups also formed guilds, but there was no masterpiece to produce. In some places, examinations were required, however. Special service trades might offer opportunities in some areas that were not found in others; for example, some cities had licensed tour guides.

A trade depression, changes in fashion, or an invention rendering traditional work methods obsolete could bring destitution to city workers and to specialized communities such as the silk weavers.

PEASANT WEDDINGS AND RELIGIOUS HOLIDAYS

Outside of the cities, life took on a different aspect when the dreary, monotonous routine life in the villages was interrupted for religious

Peasant Wedding. Pieter Bruegel the Elder, 1568. This painting depicts a peasant wedding scene. The feast is held in a barn. The bride is seated in the center under the canopy. Flatcakes are being brought in on a door that is off its hinges. (Kunsthistorisches Museum, Wien oder KHM, Wien.)

holidays or at marriages when the entire village would turn out to partake in the festivities.

While the pipers played, they danced in the streets or nearby fields. More wealthy peasants treated the festivities with great generosity, spending a good portion of their income to entertain the locals. On these occasions, coarse manners and heavy drinking were normal. While the peasant consumed about a gallon of beer or wine per day, at weddings he went well beyond this.[14]

The marriage event was not unlike a church holiday that was celebrated in a robust and irreverent manner with prodigious drinking that often alarmed the clergy. By the sixteenth century, some 20 saints' days were observed each year involving religious festivities. Romping around the village dressed in an array of costumes often made up of household utensils such as pots and pans, beer barrel armor, tub hats, egg shell necklaces, ladles, and other implements and accompanied by flutes, horns, and barking dogs, the din was deafening, giving much delight, especially to the children. The threat of danger was ever present, however, and men always carried knives or swords.

TIME AND WEATHER

The day for most rural dwellers within the Holy Roman Empire, and indeed in most of Europe, was regulated by natural sunlight and by the rhythm of the seasons. Artificial light from lamps was expensive, so oil for lamps was carefully rationed. Men and women in both city and village worked long days in summer and less in winter. By the sixteenth century, most cities and small towns had a municipal clock that chimed the hours. These were welcomed by the Church so that religious offices could be carried out at approximately the correct time.

In divided communities of both Protestants and Catholics, thorny problems arose over who would control the bell tower and ring it at the appropriate time. Mass-produced calendars had been available since the invention of printing, and these listed feast days, fairs, and phases of the moon and were extremely popular at all social levels. But much confusion arose over the changeover from the Roman Julian calendar, which was not so accurate, to the Gregorian calendar that was more precise. According to the Romans, the solar year had 365 and one-quarter days, and to counter this, a day was added every four years to correspond to the seasons. These calculations, however, were slightly off in the measurement of the solar year because a day was lost every century. By the end of the sixteenth century, the calendar was 11 days off with these computations, and on the day of the switch to the more precise Gregorian calendar, October 4 became October 15. Most Catholic countries adopted the pope's new timetable immediately. Protestant countries were furious at what they saw as the arrogance of the Vatican in its attempt to further its influence even more and refused to adjust to it for the next century. Much confusion ensued; a traveler leaving a Catholic city on January 1, on a two-day journey, might arrive in a Protestant city on December 21 of the previous year. Another reason Protestants objected to the new calendar was because it showed Catholic religious days not appreciated in Protestant households.

A major factor in the lives of the peasants in the Holy Roman Empire and all over Europe was the weather. Famines of catastrophic proportions were always just around the corner. Harvest was an anxious time. A severe hail storm, intense frost, or heavy rain and flooding could reduce the yield to a fraction of what was required to maintain a family. Sometimes deep snow came early, and harvest and transportation of the crop were hampered. During the growing season, wheat, barley, vines, and other crops were always in danger of a disastrous turn in the weather.

Drought, too, could be a major cause of crop failure as rivers, streams, and wells dried up. Over a prolonged period of time, a chronic shortage of water left the farmer helpless and desperate. It was often the weather that left families starving, eating roots and boiled bark, and, unable to pay their taxes, losing their homes. From property holder to landless laborer was often an anomaly of the weather. In bad times, droves of miserable humanity would shuffle to the church for a handout of a piece of bread or to a larger city to seek work or beg on the streets.

Women and men working together in the fields at harvest time. *Roxburghe Ballads.* Charles Hindley, ed. (1874) vol. ii, 182. (Rare Books and Special Collections, University of British Columbia Library.)

TAXES AND THE LAW

The nobility and the clergy paid no taxes. The bulk of the burden, therefore, fell as usual on the peasants. Princes often attempted to force freer peasants into a state of near slavery through tax increases and the introduction of Roman Civil law, more conducive to their desire for power since it reduced all lands to private ownership and eliminated the feudal concept of land as a trust between lord and peasant with the concomitant rights and obligations. In adhering to the remnants of the Roman law code, they not only heightened their wealth and position within the empire (through the confiscation of property and revenues) but also their dominion over their subjects.

Peasants could do little more than passively resist. Even then, the prince now had absolute control and could punish them in any manner he wished. Blinding or chopping off of fingers were common enough practices for disobedience. Until Thomas Münzer and other religious radicals like him rejected the legitimizing factors of ancient law and sought Godly law as a means to rouse the people, uprisings remained isolated, unsupported, and easily quelled.

Some ecclesiastics exploited their subjects as ruthlessly as the regional princes. The Catholic Church used the authority of religion to extort money from the people. In addition to the sale of indulgences, they fabricated miracles, set up prayer houses, and directly taxed the population.

WOMEN

Within the Holy Roman Empire, as elsewhere, women had no political voice, were not permitted to vote, and were not to serve on governing bodies. Exceptions might be widows from noble families who controlled land while their sons were still under age.

The average life span was 30 years for men and 24 for women, and anyone who reached 40 was considered old. Women bore an average of six or seven children, many of whom did not survive. Of those who did, 45 percent would die before the age of 12. About 10 percent of the men would never marry, and around 12 percent of the women found themselves shut up in convents, often unwillingly. Apart from marriage or religious orders, there were few places in respectable society for a single woman.

NOTES

1. Moryson (1967), 299.
2. Ibid., 350.
3. Loc. cit.
4. Ozment (1986), 19.

5. For Smith's description see Hampe, 6–7.
6. Ibid., 7.
7. Ozment (1986), 22.
8. Loc. cit.
9. Hampe, 18.
10. Ibid., 4.
11. Ibid., 10–15.
12. Roper p. 9–14.
13. Watts, 83.
14. Simon, 27.

7

ENGLAND AND SCOTLAND

TUDOR ENGLAND

The upper and middle classes in England became better off under the Tudors, the royal house that ruled England throughout the sixteenth century. This was an age of England's growing naval strength, exploration, and increasing commerce, and after about 1525, population numbers began to increase, while production rose more slowly. Nobles and the upper middle classes invested money in land and the economy and generally grew wealthier as gold and silver entered the country from trade and piracy. A price revolution that first hit Spain as riches flowed in from the New World now caught up with England as costs increased fivefold during the century.

Wage laborers, farm hands, and other members of the lower echelons, however, became worse off as wage increases failed to keep up with the rising cost of living, and real earnings declined. In today's parlance, inflation was rampant, and people on fixed incomes or set wages suffered. Even an impecunious nobleman, whose livelihood depended on fixed rents, might find himself hard-pressed and have to sell off some property. By the end of the century, in poor, remote parts of the country, many people living on starvation wages died from hunger.

A small percentage of people lived in cities such as London where tradesmen tended to live in the same quarter For example, butchers and slaughterhouses occupied the same street called the Shambles. **Towns**

Sewers or drains were few, dirty water and garbage such as decaying vegetables and offal was cast into the streets. Rats thrived as did disease such as smallpox, measles, typhus, scarlet fever, chickenpox, and diphtheria. Outbreaks of the plague occurred every few decades killing 10 to 20 percent of the inhabitants of any town. Numbers recovered, however, as there were always poor country people who moved into the cities looking for work.

While everyone was officially required to clean the area in front of his dwelling at least once weekly, cities were generally dirty, crowded, and foul-smelling. In London, there were not many public toilets, but what they had were situated beside streams. In the majority of towns, there were none, so everyone used any spot that was convenient.

Water came from wells, transported by water carriers who brought in the heavy containers on their backs. In some towns, pipes or channels had been put in place to bring it in from the countryside.

Streets, at night dark and dangerous, were narrow, and upper floors of buildings jutted out, sometimes practically touching those on the opposite side. Apart from the possibility of being robbed, people had to face a variety of hazards as they made their way along dark unpaved lanes such as deep holes in the road, low hanging balconies, or a horseman in a hurry. If someone were trampled by a horse, the rider would seldom even look back. In London, a boy could be hired to light the way with a lamp, but most people avoided going out after dark.

Tudor Homes   By the sixteenth century, houses no longer had to be defensive. The very wealthy usually had large mansions in the countryside, employing as many as 150 servants. These homes were built with many chimneys and fireplaces that were needed to keep the huge rooms reasonably warm and to prepare the food.

People of more moderate means had solid half-timbered houses comprising a wooden frame with wickerwork and plaster as fill. Sometimes they were filled with bricks. Although roofs were usually thatched in the countryside, in London tiles were used due to the ever-present danger of fire.

Furniture remained basic but for the well to do, oak would be used in the main since it was expected to last many generations. Chairs were used more than previously, but they were costly and even in affluent homes, children and servants commonly sat on stools. Windows of glass, held together by strips of lead, were also expensive, and anyone who moved to another residence, would take the windows with them.

The very poor used bands of linen saturated in linseed oil for windows. Chimneys were totally unaffordable for these people whose houses usually had a hole in the roof for the smoke from the fire to escape. Most peasants lived in small huts with floors of hard earth, using benches, stools, a table, and perhaps a wooden chest as furniture. Their mattresses were packed with straw or thistledown spread over ropes across a wooden frame.

In contrast, the walls of mansions were paneled with oak in an effort to avoid drafts, as were four-poster beds hung with curtains. Wallpaper was sometimes applied and tapestries hung to retain the heat. Carpets, another luxury item, were usually hung on the walls rather than placed on the floor that would often be covered with reeds or straw together with aromatic herbs, normally replaced once a month.

The rich lit their homes with beeswax candles, while other people utilized malodorous candles made from animal grease. The very poor used rushes dipped in fat before lighting. Clocks were in evidence in some of the more opulent houses, although the rich carried pocket watches or pocket sundials.

Gardens of the wealthy often had a maze for pleasure and games, hedges of sundry shapes, and fountains decked out with flowers. Poor people might have a small space beside their houses, used to grow vegetables and herbs.

In 1596, a flushing lavatory with a cistern was invented by Sir John Harrington, but the idea was slow to catch on, and most people continued to use chamber pots or cesspits.

The farmhouse in Tudor times was usually constructed of wood and plaster with a thatched roof; although by the   **Farmhouses**
end of the sixteenth century, better-off farmers were building houses of stone or brick with tiled roofs. The main living room served also as the kitchen and had an open fireplace with a brick oven beside it. There would be a long table at which the farmer, his wife, and the servants

The Family Meal. *Roxburghe Ballads*. Charles Hindley, ed. (1874) vol. i, 116. (Rare Books and Special Collections, University of British Columbia Library.)

took their meals together. Sometimes the children would stand while the adults were seated. Little other furniture was there except a few benches and a dresser on which were placed the plates and drinking vessels. Just outside the kitchen door would be a brew house and dairy. A well and a wood stack would be close by. The barn, stables and tool sheds stood in the farmyard. Laborers lived in cottages scattered around the house, and sometimes these consisted of little more than walls, a roof, and a stone hearth. The smoke exited through unglazed windows and the door. Pigs and chickens wandered in and out. Each cottage would have a small plot to grow vegetables.

In August and September, grain was harvested, and threshing began in the barn with flails, usually short clubs attached by rope to long staves that separated to beat the stalks. The grain was cleaned and winnowed in the breeze on a flat pan-like basket to carry off the chaff. (A goose wing could be used as a fan to create a breeze.) Next came plowing the land that had been left fallow or that was covered in stubble from the previous harvest. This was also the time to collect acorns for the pigs, beechnuts, and honey from the beehives and for gathering in the fruit. November was the time to slaughter some of the animals, both for salted meat to carry the family through the winter months, and since there was not enough hay to feed them all.

After Christmas plowing began again, newborn animals were anticipated, and the crop was sown. Pruning, mending hedges and fences, carting manure to the fields, and many other chores kept everyone busy. By March, the barley was sown and children would be sent into the fields with slings to scare off birds that gathered for the easy pickings.

The housewife tended the herb garden, oversaw the sowing of flax and hemp, and worked the dairy making butter and cheese using milk from both cows and ewes. In June, sheep shearing was underway, in July, hay for the animals was collected, and August was devoted to the harvesting of grain. At this time, the farmer hired reapers who were paid sixpence a day (plus meals or a shilling a day without). When the work was finished, the poor were allowed into the fields to carry away anything they could find that had been left over from the harvest.[1]

Social Classes   Vast amounts of land were owned by the nobility in this highly structured society. Below them were the gentry and the wealthy merchants, also landowners who like the nobility, were usually educated and unwilling to perform undignified manual labor. Further down the scale were the yeomen who owned their land and were sometimes well off financially, but who had no issues about working together with the farmhands. At this level, too, were the craftsmen who made the items necessary for everyday living such as shoes, tools, and clothes. Generally, both yeomen and craftsmen were literate.

Tenant farmers, on the next rung of the social ladder, leased their land from the well-to-do owners and struggled to make a living and feed their families.

At the bottom were the wage laborers, generally illiterate, who walked a fine line between work and mendicancy. They made up over 50 percent of the population, living at subsistence level with little food, shelter, or enough clothes to keep warm. A rising population meant a shortage of work, leading to many unemployed.

It was possible to move up a social notch or two: an ambitious wage earner with intelligence who was willing to persevere, could become a yeoman if he had enough money to purchase a coat of arms and call himself a gentleman.

About a third of the population lived in poverty, but Tudor law, while tolerating cripples, was harsh on able-bodied beggars deemed vagabonds, unable to find work at home, and who left their parishes in order to find it elsewhere.

The Poor and the Destitute

There had been laws against such transients for a hundred years, but in 1530, the old and infirm poor were issued with licenses to beg. A jobless man roaming the streets without a license could be taken to the nearest market place, tied to a cart, and whipped before being ordered to return to his parish. In 1536, another law was passed subjecting vagabonds to a whipping for the first offense and part of their right ear to be sliced off for a second, with a view to easy identification. A third offence led to the gallows. This was again modified in 1547, to condemn anybody found loitering for three days to work for anyone who would hire him for whatever wages offered. If no one took him on for a wage, then he had to work for food and drink alone. If he refused, then he could be sent before the local magistrate and ordered to become that benefactor's slave for two years. If he tried to escape, he would be made a slave for life and branded. This law was abolished in 1550, when flogging was again made the penalty for nomadism.

A severe vagrancy law was once again imposed in 1572, whereby for a first offense, the beggar was whipped and branded on the right ear. In the case of a second offense, he would be executed by hanging. The punishment in both cases could be commuted if someone employed him. However, for a third offense, he would be hanged regardless.

In 1576, new laws were passed concerning the old and disabled that ordered parishes to put them to work in their own homes by supplying them with materials such as flax, hemp, and wool. Those who resisted were sent off to a correction center where life was often brutal.

Four years later, parliament passed the poor law whereby every parish was commanded to put up a workhouse for these people. There, they were forced to work to their fullest ability. The original purpose of the workhouse was to remove such people from the urban scene. Inmates could be let out to work if it were available, but they were confined when it was not. The death penalty for vagrancy was finally abolished in 1597.

The Anglican Church

In England, the Reformation followed a different course than elsewhere in Europe. The changes within the English Church proceeded at a slower pace as reformers oscillated between the wish to continue the Catholic traditions and the desire to take up the new Protestantism. The result was compromise.

England had already undergone anticlerical movements in the fourteenth century that had given rise to the Lollards and John Wycliffe who had translated the Bible. However, anyone found with a Bible in English was considered a heretic and burned at the stake.

The Reformation in England took on a different character as it was initiated by Henry VIII's desire to divorce his queen, Katherine of Aragon in order to marry Anne Boleyn, which the pope would not permit. As a result, in 1534, Henry cut off his ties with the Holy See making himself Supreme Head of the Church of England by the Act of Supremacy. Between 1535 and 1540, the policy of the dissolution of the monasteries led to attacks on Church land and property, which were taken over by the crown and the nobility.

Henry died in 1547 and was succeeded by his son, Edward VI, who was nine years old at his coronation (and only sixteen at his death). Under his rule, the reform of the Church of England was established officially.

Mary, daughter of Katherine and Henry, a fierce Catholic, reigned next, from 1553–1558 and immediately began the restoration of the Catholic faith. She promoted the return of property such as furniture taken from the Church during the dissolution of the monasteries, but permitted the nobles to retain the lands they had acquired. During Mary's sovereignty, some 300 Protestants, including about 56 women, were burned in the Marian persecutions, their holdings given over to the state; but instead of being discouraged by the number of martyrs, the Protestants became more avid than ever in their hatred of their monarch who by then was known as "Bloody Mary."

Elizabeth followed Mary on the throne, and an uneasy compromise was reached which veered between extreme Calvinism on the one hand and Catholicism on the other; but it remained relatively successful until the seventeenth century. England became Protestant in doctrine but retained much of the Catholic ritual. For example, the Church had officiating bishops, but at its head was the state.

Elizabeth's response to the religious divisions resulted in 1559 in two acts of the English parliament: another Act of Supremacy reaffirmed the Church of England's independence from Rome with Elizabeth at its head, and the Act of Uniformity set out the rules now governing the English Church including the use of the Book of Common Prayer, published in 1549, that was not popular. Conservatives disliked the changes, and Protestants believed it contained too much Roman Catholic usage.[2] Everyone subject to the queen was required to attend divine services on Sundays and holy days under penalty imposed by the Protestant bishops and justices. Injunctions called for the removal from churches of Catholic shrines, tables, candlesticks, and all other decorations with the exception of the crucifix. In 1570 the pope excommunicated Elizabeth and absolved all Catholics from their allegiance to her.

During her reign, the detection and arrest of Catholic priests in England was hampered by upper class women who often sheltered them. Craftsmen constructed what were called priest holes in the mansions of the country estates for hiding priests and the paraphernalia required for Mass. The chambers were well disguised in the walls, and often a thorough search of the premises did not reveal them. Life for the hunted priest was a nightmare. He often suffered after days of confinement in the cramped hole with little or nothing to eat or drink while

Allegorical group of eighty men and one woman, Elizabeth I, who were prominent in the Protestant Reformation. Engraving by Fredrich E. Eichens. (Library of Congress.)

he listened to his pursuers knocking on walls and ripping away boards. Sometimes he had to sleep in a sitting position with no room to stand. Many were caught and taken off to prison along with the owners of the house in which they were sheltered. If visitors were staying there, the priest might have to spend weeks or months in the same clothes, vermin swarming on the straw-covered floor, and the open bucket for excrement emitting a nauseating stench.[3]

Puritans The early Puritan movement of Calvinist inclination sought reform in the Church of England so that it would resemble more closely the Protestant churches of Europe, especially Geneva. They enlarged the Geneva Bible and demanded change, wanting to purge all vestiges of the Catholic faith from the island. They also felt that the Church of England was incapable of true reform. Too many pastors were scarcely literate and not worthy of their office. About all they could do was to read passages from the Book of Common Prayer, but they failed to inspire people with dynamic orations. Puritans were also unhappy with the fact that bishops were chosen by the crown and not by the body of worshipers.

Convinced that ornaments and ritual, including music and genuflection in the churches, was idolatrous, Puritans opposed the wearing of the surplice as too reminiscent of Catholic priests. In addition, they wanted to do away with ecclesiastical courts and refused the Book of Common Prayer. They also objected to the imposition of its liturgy by force of law. Queen Elizabeth considered them subversive.

Preparations for the Sabbath began the night before when all food had to be cooked and clothes made ready. That evening they retired after supper for family devotions after which they would read the Bible for some time before going to bed. No labor at all was tolerated on the day itself, which began at sundown the night before.

A normal Puritan service began with a prayer, then reading of the scripture, a sermon, another prayer along with the Lord's Prayer, the creed, a psalm, and finally, the benediction. Reading of the scriptures continued at home after the service. This simple act of worship was extended throughout the whole of the Sabbath, which was not considered to be a day for idleness or sport.

Puritans were rigorously opposed to the state interfering with Church affairs and refused to do military service. They were often referred to as dissenters or nonconformists. Their movement eventually led to the formation of various reformed denominations.

They had a reputation for extreme piety, believing they were chosen by God for a special purpose, and their lives should be lived in a God-fearing manner. They were accused of believing sex was a sin, being opposed to any kind of enjoyment including sports and recreation, and of wearing drab clothes to demonstrate holiness.

During the seventeenth century, legal action was instigated against the Puritans because they refused to follow the Act of Uniformity that demanded preachers read from the official prayer book during services, wear Anglican vestments, and support the Anglican ceremonies. At this time, the Church of England also demanded that young men hoping to become teachers and working toward a degree from the universities of Oxford or Cambridge, be compelled to sign the Act before they could earn such a degree. The Puritans were forcefully persecuted and could expect anything from being imprisoned indefinitely to being burned alive. They wanted to purify the Church of England. They did not seek full separation from it but rather a reformation of it directing the Church back to the Bible.

They constantly strove for the holiness they imagined could be found in saintly living, and religious education was heavily emphasized and played a fundamental part in their lives. Preachers focused on reading the Bible, expounding on the meaning of the texts, discussing key points of doctrine as well as applying it to their lives.

Usually a small, plain building, the Puritan church would be for many months of the year a place where people suffered in unbearable cold. Sometimes women carried small foot stoves of hot coals to warm their feet during the lengthy services. The men sat on one side, women on the other, all in assigned seats. Children separated from their parents were expected to remain still and in absolute silence. Music was not considered appropriate; instead, the Puritans listened intently to dire warnings of sin and punishment if they did not follow the strict orders of the denomination.

Those Puritans, who found the persecution orchestrated by both Catholics and Protestants intolerable, left England. Some went to the Netherlands and various other parts of Europe, and some settled in the New World.

The pendulum in England swung back and forth between the Church and reformers, and uprisings and martyrs were **Martyrs**[4] inevitable. William Tyndale, for example, a nonconformist student seeing the writing on the wall escaped from England. He was betrayed and captured in Antwerp and clapped into prison for heresy. From his cell, he wrote the following letter (originally in Latin) to the governor in 1535:

> I believe, right worshipful, that you are not ignorant of what has been determined concerning me [by the Council of Brabant]; therefore I entreat your Lordship, and that by the Lord Jesus, that if I am to remain here [in Vilvoorde] during the winter, you will request the Procurer to be kind enough to send me from my goods, which he has in his possession, a warmer cap, for I suffer extremely from cold in the head, being afflicted with a perpetual catarrh, which is considerably increased in the cell.
>
> A warmer coat also, for that which I have is very thin; also a piece of cloth to patch my leggings: my overcoat has been worn out; my shirts are also worn out. He has a woolen shirt of mine, if he will be kind enough to send

it. I have also with him leggings of thicker cloth for the putting on above; he also has warmer caps for wearing at night. I wish also his permission to have a candle in the evening, for it is wearisome to sit alone in the dark.

But above all, I entreat and beseech your clemency to be urgent with the Procurer that he may kindly permit me to have my Hebrew Bible, Hebrew Grammar, and Hebrew Dictionary, that I may spend my time with that study. And in return, may you obtain your dearest wish, provided always it be consistent with the salvation of your soul. But if any other resolutions have been come to concerning me, before the conclusion of the winter, I shall be patient, abiding the will of God to the glory of the grace of my Lord Jesus Christ, whose spirit, I pray, may ever direct your heart. Amen.

W. Tindalus[5]

After being confined in prison for a year, he was burned.

Lawbreakers and Prisons Tudor towns were dangerous at night, and every man carried a sword or dagger. Some travelers carried a 12-foot or 13-foot pike on their shoulders when on the road; others a brace of pistols on their saddles.[6]

In London, as elsewhere, there were not only professional robbers but also discharged, penniless soldiers and laborers with wages so low they could not buy a new shirt. In spite of savage punishments, criminals operated wherever victims could be found. Here, too, innkeepers were often in cahoots with thieves for a share of the booty when a likely man of means appeared at the door.

Criminals in the hundreds were caught and executed every year, but most escaped justice. If the offense exceeded the theft in value of over two shillings, the penalty was hanging, being taken down alive, and quartered.

People in prison for lesser offenses or debt, depended on the good nature of the jailer or the charity of friends and the public. In some places in England, they were secured for the night, fettered and chained together in groups of five or more. Stocks in the market place were also used to confine rowdy drunkards and even those who had spoken disrespectfully against public officials. Some had their ears nailed to the pillory (afterwards cut off). English justice was also severe for women. Those who abused their neighbors, even verbally, were publicly whipped or tied to a stool and dunked in a pond. More persistent offenders were banished after being paraded through the town in a cart.

Constables were harassed by the people at large, especially by students who were permitted a degree of toleration. Apprentices, too, were generally ready for a fight and brought their clubs into the streets. On one occasion, the police were no match for them, and the army had to be called in.[7]

SCOTLAND

At the beginning of the sixteenth century, the northern country of Scotland seemed wild and primitive to the rest of Europe. The Stuart kings were dominated by the nobles who warred with one another and, along with the Church, exacted heavy taxes from the people, many of whom had lives fraught with extreme poverty.

Scotland's foreign relations focused on ancient hostility with England and on a long-standing alliance with France. Economically and politically the country was in bad condition—even the soil was poor and difficult to cultivate. There was no industry, and the few cities were small. The country people were extremely poor and superstitious, and the Church was content to keep them that way.

Although Scotland was independent, it was far from united. The northern Gaelic-speaking clans had little to do with the government in Edinburgh. Based on family ties, allegiance was primarily to the clan and its chief and not to any central authority. The king was irrelevant. Only in the central lowlands did the king's government rule, but there, too, power was mostly in the hands of a few nobles.

Protestant influence began to make headway in Scotland, entering the country via merchants from northern German towns. The first evidence of this is a law passed by the Scottish Parliament in 1525, banning Lutheranism. The spread of the Reformation in Scotland was accompanied by barbarous acts of cruelty and treachery, but it generally found a sympathetic audience throughout society.

The powerful Archbishop James Beaton of St. Andrews and his nephew, Cardinal David Beaton, were staunch supporters of Rome. Archbishop Beaton despised Protestant beliefs and went to great lengths to prevent them from spreading.

In Scotland, Patrick Hamilton, a student of Luther, began to preach the new doctrine and soon found a following. Invited to a conference at St. Andrews by Archbishop Beaton, he was arrested for propagating heretical views. Beaton had made sure that the king, James V, was indisposed, lest he intervene on behalf of Patrick, a relative. Patrick was tried as a heretic by the archbishop and burned at the stake in 1527.

The death of Hamilton, a member of the royal family, demonstrated that the Catholic Church recognized no social boundaries when it came to preserving its supremacy. However, instead of creating fear of repression, Hamilton's death attracted people more than ever to Lutheran doctrines.

Meanwhile, Scottish nobles had drawn up a common bond calling themselves "Lords of the Congregation of Jesus Christ."[8] They asked John Knox to assist their cause, and he returned to Scotland in May 1559. He instituted reforms giving the common people a voice in Church affairs for the first time. The populace was so receptive to his preaching against idolatry, they destroyed Catholic churches and their idols, burned and pillaged monasteries, and assaulted priests. Riots followed Knox's preaching from town to town, and war ensued to end French presence in

Scotland. The Lords of the Congregation were aided by troops from England under Queen Elizabeth. The battles ended with the Treaty of Edinburgh, which gave Scotland freedom from interference in its affairs by either England or France. The Reformation Parliament of 1560 repudiated the pope's authority, forbade celebration of the Mass, and approved a Protestant Confession of Faith drawn up by Knox.

After the split with Rome, it was uncertain for a century or so whether the Church in Scotland would be Episcopal or Presbyterian. Charles I, King of Scotland and England, preferred the Episcopal form, while the Scottish people insisted on the Presbyterian. They prevailed, and Presbyterianism was permanently established in Scotland by constitutional act in 1689.

The Scottish Catholic Church[9] Almost half the wealth in sixteenth-century Scotland lay in Church coffers. A merchant of the first rank in his day, Andrew Halyburton was also Scottish Consul at Middleburg (Netherlands), where he transacted business mostly on behalf of Scotsmen buying and selling and charging a percentage for his services. According to Halyburton's ledger, items exported from Scotland were meager, consisting mainly of wool, hides, and fish, reflecting not the produce of a skilled society but, rather, that of the simple sheep herder, hunter, and fisherman.

Imports into Scotland included some dye, gunpowder, equipment for building, and materials for Church decoration; but the foremost items were luxury materials followed by wines, spices, and specialty foodstuffs such as olives, dates, and figs. In Halyburton's ledger, the first account is that of the Archbishop of St. Andrews, followed by bishops and nobles, all of whom were involved in importing items of great luxury. It appeared that cardinals and bishops lived as well or better than kings.

There was no such thing as banking in Scotland at the time, and those with money to spare generally invested it in precious metals, jewels, and expensive furnishings. This was especially true of the Church, for even the nobility had little in the way of precious metal; pewter was more their style. The farmer, who slept on the ground in a mud hut lined with straw with a dirty blanket around him and a log for a pillow, had every reason to question the sincerity and fitness of the men of God and their Church.

Monks tended to live in idleness and comfort, paying little heed to their religious duties, and most of the preaching in Scotland was done by friars who often had little education. The convents were in the same state, housing generally illiterate, undisciplined sisters. Parish churches were neglected and without sufficient funds to pay qualified priests. Further, the moral standards of the secular clergy suffered as attested by the large number of children they sired.

As in other parts of Europe, the poverty of parish priests stood in sharp contrast to the wealth of those more important members of the Church hierarchy, whose lucrative positions were often maintained within the family. Many noble families drew good incomes from the control of Church offices.

Fynes Moryson, the English traveler, described some of the dinners he attended while in Scotland and the accouterments he encountered. He observed that dishes were almost always of pewter, the wealthy sometimes owning **Dining in a Castle** as many as 40 dozen plates of varying sizes, whereas in lesser households they would have three to four dozen. Drinking cups and the jugs and basins for washing the hands were silver or pewter.,

Guests invited to a castle for a meal would enter the great hall on the first floor via a winding, stone staircase and be greeted by two servants, one holding a metal bowl and the other holding a pitcher of water to pour over the hands. The most important were then seated at a long, narrow table, slightly raised, and serving as a line of social distinction. The long wooden boards of oak or fir that were used as the table sat on a pair of trestles and were removed and placed against the wall when not in use. A fire would be burning in a large, open fireplace, a tapestry hung from the wall, and a rug lay in front of the fire. Rushes or grass covered the floor.

The lord of the castle would sit in the middle of the table in a high-backed chair, a canopy suspended above him. Others sat on benches with loose cushions, while less influential guests sat at side tables. All had their backs to the wall, so food could be served from the middle of the room.

With the exception of the servants, everyone would have their heads covered, the women using kerchiefs in the form of two horns draped from a mound of real or false hair. Such coverings prevented fleas, lice, or scabs falling into the food.

The tablecloth, generally green, was made of imported material; candles were lit to increase the light from the overhead chandelier. The silver saltshaker, a most important table piece that was put in a prominent place in the middle of the table, could be of great size and intricate design. Plates were usually pewter, although wooden ones were also used in some houses. Spoons were pewter or silver; forks were not used since people ate with their fingers: two fingers and the thumb were the rule for eating from the common dish and for also lifting a cup. Basins, towels, and table napkins were provided for washing the fingers. If needed, guests tended to use their own knives that they carried on them. Cultivated people were taught not to be greedy, not to stare at others who were eating, and not to roll their eyes at the table. They should drink in moderation, diluting their wine with water. At the end of the great hall, musicians entertained from a gallery as people ate.

The hall itself was sparsely furnished with perhaps a side table for pitchers and plates, a chest for towels and napkins, and a comfortable chair for the lord. Furniture was strictly functional and not used for decoration. The great barren halls of Scotland contrasted sharply with those in France, England, Italy and elsewhere.

Bedrooms were also scantily furnished in Scotland as they were in England at this time, usually containing a bed, table and a chair along with a few tapestries on the walls. Bedrooms for guests had just the beds and perhaps a stool and chest for clothes. Nothing else was considered necessary. Every castle or mansion had a bake house, a brew house, and a kitchen with only the bare necessities.

The Manse of Stobo

The solid mansion of Stobo in Glasgow provides a good example of the disproportionate wealth of some Church members as compared to the rest of the populace. It belonged to a priest, Adam Colquhoun, rector of the university, who drew his income from a sparsely populated district at the same time as the benefice of Stobo brought with it enormous earnings, enough to ascertain that Adam Colquhoun's relatives (churchmen also owned property in the area) lived well. It was one of many houses in the district of Stobo where the clergy that served the cathedral found residence. The manse was a far cry from the castle described previously, and while it may not be representative of the homes of all Catholic clergy, it does give a glimpse of the more opulent and ostentatious life they led. It is also an example of why the common people and many nobles despised the haughty and self-aggrandizing churchmen.

A tower-like building with stone walls three foot thick, it was entered via a winding staircase onto which the doors of several apartments opened directly. Fireplaces were in the hall as well as in the priest's room, but all rooms were dark since the windows were very small, and the walls were dense. The back of the building faced south and had galleries overlooking an orchard and garden, and all the furnishings were of the highest quality.

The hall had panels of tapestry on the walls showing scenes of plants and animals, huntsmen, or scriptural stories, a large fireplace and a cupboard standing against the wall with shelves arranged so that the contents, including some forty dishes of silver, were displayed. Here, too, was a fine buffet covered by luxurious Flemish quilted material. Other furnishings were of carved wood and included a variety of chairs and footstools.

The bedroom contained a bed, the frame of which was of carved wood, decorated with gold. Pillows filled with down and the sheets, pillow cases, and coverings were the best money could buy. In the daytime, the bed was covered with rich velvet lined with cotton. Panel tapestries lined the walls for beauty and for warmth, and curtains could be drawn around the bed to keep the occupant free from drafts.

This chamber was furnished lavishly. A chandelier hung from the ceiling, and besides the bed, there was an oak bench, a carved wooden chest for keeping valuables, various storage boxes and a locked, leather trunk.

Within the chest, he kept a rosary, a gold cross, a chain, various rings of gold, and other items of value. On top of the chest stood a silver water vessel, a sponge, some combs, and a brush.

At the same time as the common people suffered under the demands of the Church, they were forced to witness priests flaunting their wealth on the streets of the cities such as Glasgow, indulging their personal vanity with sumptuous clothing and jewelry.

The priest of Stobo's everyday costume seems to have consisted of a velvet doublet lined with scarlet, a scarlet vest worn over a white shirt, and black hose with silk garters and gold tassels. His damask gown, lined with marten sable, was fastened with a gold button. His shoes were of velvet, his gloves of cloth interwoven with gold and silver. A silver toothpick was kept in the bag at his waist. There was no sign of frugality or asceticism displayed by this son of the Church!

Other rooms in his house included one containing an altar hung with velvet (the most expensive of cloths) with fringes of gold, on top of which were the sacred vessels for celebration of the Eucharist. Next to this room was the oratory where the sumptuous vestments were kept, and a carved desk with religious and secular books that were expensively bound and decorated with gold and silver.

The kitchen had two functional tables for preparing the food and various pots, pans, and items needed to provide feasts. No stools or chairs were provided for those who worked there. His barn was well stocked with wheat, oats, hay, peas, and hoards of salted meat and fish, butter, and cheese. In addition, there was a stable with riding equipment and even armor, although members of the clergy were not supposed to bear arms. Here, too, was all equipage needed for practicing archery, and a silk leash and collar studded with silver for his dog or dogs. He kept a parrot for company, a crane, a tame deer, and characteristic of his time, a mistress.[10]

A merchant typically lived above the shop where he worked his trade. A low curtain would form a partition behind which he could keep chests containing necessary items. A house such as this gives an idea of the transition **Merchants' Houses** in progress in the sixteenth century toward more modern concepts of privacy for the family (as opposed to life in a castle filled with nobles and their large retinues). A prosperous merchant was able to introduce new ideas, art, and fashion into his life through trade with other countries.

There was often an entrance to the upstairs living quarters from the outside. The main room would probably be decorated with a few wall hangings and contain a long table covered by a piece of tapestry. A couple of small windows, glazed or shuttered, generally faced the street.

At the table would be the merchant's seat and a bench for his wife and children. Alongside the table was generally a serving counter upon which were placed dishes of tin or silver. Of course, some merchants were wealthier than others, and this would be reflected in the decor. A salt-shaker was an integral component of every table, and its design and decoration (gold, silver, or glass) would indicate the owner's prosperity. Also in this room might be an oak aumrie (cupboard) containing various precious belongings such as a rosary, rings and jewelry.

Next to the hall would be a bedroom, sometimes equipped with a curtained bed, a place for clothing to be laid, a box for clothes or linens, and a traveling trunk. On the wall might be hung a brush, a comb, and a towel. A basin for water, a mirror, and a spinning wheel might also be present. Two rooms were fairly standard for a merchant's house. A merchant could own a horse, a plow and a cart, and other tools for him to work a piece of land leased on the outskirts of town.

At this time chairs began to be used that were convertible into a small table used for chess or cards. They were usually light-weight and could be moved in front of the fire or to the window so that women doing needlework could look outside as they sewed. As other furniture came into use from the continent, people started to enjoy it not only because it was useful, but also for its beauty. Carpets, rugs, and books duly took their place in homes.

The merchants represented a rising class just before and during the Reformation, who enjoyed more prestige and material benefits than previously.

Mirrors are not mentioned in Scotland until 1578, and clocks, although found on churches and city halls, were not used in private houses until businessmen, who needed to keep appointments, began to use them. The alarm clock is recorded in Scotland as early as 1564, but many still used the hourglass.

Innovative items that were introduced into the well-to-do households from France about this time included fans, shoehorns, painted buttons, and cups. Tobacco also became popular in spite of King James' negative views on smoking.

In 1556, the town council of Edinburgh decreed that there should be an English version of the Bible in every substantial household.

Dinner on the Farm Eating a meal for a farmer and his family contrasted greatly to dining at the castle or in the house of a wealthy merchant. At noon the wife set up the trestles in the middle of an earthen floor, placing boards on top to serve as the dinner table. In better class farms, a linen cloth was spread over the part where the farmer and his family sat. At the other end of the table sat the hired workers. When no cloth was available, a chalk line or the position of the salt dish separated the upper and lower halves. Before eating, people uncovered their heads and grace was said after which the males replaced their hats and kept them on. Although the farmer washed his hands before eating, the workers seldom did.

The house itself was usually wood-framed and constructed of stone, clay, or turf with small windows covered over in bad weather with skins or shutters. The thatched roof had a hole in the center for smoke to escape from the hearth below. Sometimes animal skins covered the doorway. In poor houses and cottages, kitchens and living quarters were the same room.[11]

For some years, the new Church of Scotland developed along the lines of the Elizabethan Church in England. Bishop-rics continued to exist, and the Book of Common Prayer was followed. Difficulties arose when the widowed Mary returned to Scotland to take up her position as queen and did not recognize the new church. Although she found it expedient to make peace with the Protestants, she was a staunch Catholic through and through and hoped to restore the Church of Rome in Scotland. To this end, she was prepared to use force if it became available, but for such force she was dependent on France or Spain, neither of which was willing to help.

The New Church

The deposition of Mary Stuart in 1566 marks a turning point in religious history. Her son James VI, still a baby, succeeded her, so the government fell into the hands of nobles who made certain that James was brought up as a good Protestant.

For the majority of the common people, life remained difficult. They suffered from an increase in population in the sixteenth century that caused shortages of grain leading to famines, and contagious diseases such as measles and smallpox were rampant. Prices rose faster than wages, vagrancy laws in the latter half of the century clamped down on wandering beggars looking for work, and poor relief was given only to those in their home parish. Laws were passed against adultery, fornication, drunkenness, breaking the Sabbath, and witchcraft.

Small country communities still centered around a castle, a manor house, or a church. Communications between towns remained poor.

NOTES

1. Salzman, 39ff.
2. Walker, 364.
3. Bainton (1973), 247.
4. Hillerbrand (2007), 104.
5. Jacob Isidor Mombert. "Tyndale's Letter from Prison" Bible Research. http://www.bible-researcher.com/tyndale3.html (accessed March 19, 2010).
6. Salzman, 59–60.
7. Ibid., 63–65.
8. See Cowan, 116–118, for details.
9. Warrack Lecture II, 32 ff., for much of this section.
10. Loc. cit.
11. Sanderson.

8

FRANCE

Like much of Europe, urban France was responsive to new ideas on religion that entered the country from Germany and the Netherlands. In 1519, the German printer Johann Froben sent 600 copies of Luther's works there, and from then on France provided a market for further controversial publications. As early as 1523 statues of the Virgin Mary were desecrated in Paris and at Meaux. But these were small matters in light of what was to come.

The bulk of the population of France lived in the countryside either in small towns, hamlets, or on isolated farms. About nine out of ten inhabitants of the country depended directly on agriculture that provided not only food but also the raw products such as hemp, flax, and wool for urban textile industries. The main staple was bread, and much of the land was sown with wheat, barley, rye, and oats depending on the region and type of soil. Land not under cultivation or forest and scrubland might provide the peasants with mushrooms, game, timber, and edible roots.

Plots around the houses for gardening might be planted with vegetables such as melons and pumpkins, vines and cucumbers. Peasant life was one of constant labor, planting harvesting, tending the crops, caring for the sheep and pigs, repairing tools and taking produce to market. Most lived a hand-to-mouth existence, and any abnormal condition such as persistent bad weather or ravages by war spelled famine and death.

The king's claims to govern the Church derived from the Concordat of Bologna in 1516 that confirmed François I's right to make appointments to benefices, but allowed the pope to collect a year's revenue from each post and to veto unqualified candidates, a veto he seldom used.

The king acquired enormous powers to dispose of the Church's wealth, and he could (and did) use the offices of prelates to provide positions for his relatives or faithful followers. This often meant that lords of the church were worldly people, lacking in theology and spirituality. No restraints prevented one person holding many simultaneous titles. Numerous bishops lived well on their revenues and never visited their sees, preferring to remain in their palaces or at court. These arrangements amalgamated Church and state, while the University of Paris (the Sorbonne) acted as arbitrator and watched over the Church-state complex deciding on matters of heresy or nonconformity to Catholic principles.

THE AFFAIR OF THE PLACARDS

François I reigned during the formative years of the Reformation in France maintaining an attitude of tolerance, not being especially interested in religious matters. This changed with the Affair of the Placards when anti-Catholic posters appeared in public places in Paris, in major provincial cities, and even insolently on the door of the king's bedchamber at Amboise on the night of October 17, 1534. The message was a direct attack on the Catholic Church, supporting Zwingli's position on the Mass that denied the physical existence of Christ in the sacraments.

The incensed king and much of the citizenry of Paris and elsewhere now viewed the Protestant movement with deep hostility. For Protestants, inroads into the minds of the French people were off to a bad start. The insult was too much to overlook, and suspected Protestants were rounded up, imprisoned, some were burned as heretics. During the reign of Henri II who came to the throne in 1547, persecution of Protestants intensified and many, among them John Calvin, fled the country.

Religious Intolerance   In 1551, the Edict of Chateaubriand dealt with matters of heresy. All public careers were off limits to Protestants and petitions for mercy were disallowed. Bible reading and discussions or arguments on religious matters were banned. The life of a Protestant was dangerous, covert, and apprehensive. Who could be trusted? Informers received a share of the goods of condemned persons. Teachers were watched, and the printing of books was regulated. Reading matter from Protestant countries could not be imported, and none could be printed in the country that had not been approved by the theological faculty of the Sorbonne. French clandestine printing presses had to be well concealed from spies.

In 1557, the Edict of Compiègne ordered judges in civil courts to order the death penalty in cases of heresy. Filthy, dark, dank, rat-infested, prison cells where Protestants awaited trial, were filled well beyond normal capacity. The Protestant prisoner could only look forward to a confession of his sins and expose all those whom he knew to be heretics at his trial and have a quick execution, or he could be stretched on the rack for his silence until his joints were separated, and then be carried off to the stake.

Struck by a lethal blow to the head during a tournament in 1559, Henri II died leaving four sons by his marriage to Catherine de Medici, among them the future kings François II, Charles IX, and Henri III. François II died within a year, and the throne passed to ten-year-old Charles IX with his mother as regent.

The crown's tolerance or intolerance on religious matters had a great affect on peoples' lives and could lead to unexpected consequences. Catherine's ambition was to calm religious tensions between Catholics and Protestants and to see the continuance of the royal Valois line by preserving the throne for her sons.

Catherine granted the Protestants right of public worship in 1562, making a formidable enemy of the powerful aristocratic Catholic Guise family of which some members were great landowners, bishops, and cardinals. The Guises hated Protestants (called Huguenots) and had a lot to lose if Huguenots called the tune.[1] The House of Guise constituted the most powerful Catholic family in the country, which was over 90 percent Catholic.

When 30 Protestants, worshipping on a farm at Vassy, were murdered by retainers of the second duke of Guise[2], Catherine ousted the dangerous Guise family headed by the second duke and his brother, the Archbishop of Reims and Cardinal of Lorraine, from the royal court. By removing the Guises, whose agenda for taking over the country was already suspect, she made a dangerous adversary. They could muster support from the French populace (by promising to defend the nation's faith) and from Catholic Spain, Bavaria, and the papal states.

Catherine strove for compromise. She was only too aware that if one of the two enemies defeated the other, it would spell the end of her dreams for her sons.

At the beginning of the sixteenth century, the French economy was in a prosperous state. The majority of peo **The Common** ple including the peasants were better off than before. **People** The population grew, and the lower classes ate better and were more mobile in seeking work in other regions where labor was in demand. Towns and cities also increased in population sometimes more than doubling the number of inhabitants. However, by the middle of the century, inflation far outstripped wages, and peasants began losing their land as it was grabbed up by the upper classes. Vagrancy increased, and towns were hard pressed to care for the poor. By the end of the century, peasants ate poorly, tensions among the classes rose, and revolts were common. The gap between the middle and lower classes grew wider as the former grew more prosperous.

Famine was the primary threat to both country and city dwellers. A few bad seasons in a row could be devastating. In good and bad years, the grain was no sooner harvested and ground than the agent of the local bishop arrived to claim the Church's share. To stake his claim according to the terms of the lease, the lord of the manor soon followed. The farmer then had to sell at market part of his crop to pay the king's taxes and set aside the seed for the following year's planting. There was generally little left to sustain the peasant's family especially if his plot was not large. In bad times he might have to sell any animals he possessed to pay the rent. As a last resort he borrowed the money against future crops on his land to pay the debts. When he fell behind in his payments due to another cold winter and wet summer, some or all of his land was taken from him by the moneylender in foreclosure.

Given such a chain of events, the peasant farmer might try to feed his family by making bread from tree bark or grass, but eventually, starving, he would take his family off to the city where he lived on hand-outs from begging or any odd-jobs he could get.

When the harvest failed, as happened numerous times in the sixteenth century, and hunger stalked the towns as well as the countryside, prices soared as those with money hoarded grain to sell it at the highest price. Even the town craftsmen, laborers, and merchants were reduced to a subsistence level of living.

France by history and geography was highly varied, and conditions in one region did not necessarily apply to other regions. In some places farmers could supplement family income by putting the household to work spinning and weaving for a little pay from textile manufacturers, but in remote areas this was not always possible.

CONSPIRACY OF AMBOISE 1560

The Guise family strongly opposed the more tolerant policy of Catherine toward Protestants, keeping young Charles IX under their thumb. To thwart the power of Guise over king and country, the Protestants plotted to kidnap Charles IX from the clutches of their enemies by arresting the Guise brothers. They were betrayed and failed. Catherine forsook her policy of toleration and compromise and now took up a hard-line Catholic position issuing an edict taking away freedom of worship from the Huguenots and ordering their ministers out of the country.[3] The Guises exercised merciless vengeance killing large numbers of Huguenots and casting the bodies into the Loire River. The stage was set for civil war. Leaflets, tracts, and sermons from the pulpit promoted the concept that any religious views outside of the Catholic Church constituted heresy. The struggle against Huguenots took on the form of a Holy War. In an attempt to avoid this, Catherine renewed her policy of moderation. This did not please the very Catholic city of Paris or the Guise. The people of the city listened intently to the ardent and vehement sermons of their priests against the Huguenots and the crown that tolerated them. Parisians were of two kinds: those who put religion before law and were ready to kill for it and those of more moderate disposition, merchants, and traders, who disliked Huguenots but preferred to live and let live in peace under the law.

In the grimy narrow allies of the back streets of Paris, the destitute and despaired found a *cause célèbre* in the words of their priests. The Huguenots in Paris remained in the shadows and held secret services in private houses.

Catherine's daughter, Marguerite of Valois, married the Huguenot, Henri III of Navarre, on August 18, 1572. The wedding took place in Paris. A large contingent of the Huguenot nobility came to Paris for the wedding. This presented the opportunity to eliminate the Huguenot leadership.

MASSACRE OF SAINT BARTHOLOMEW'S DAY

Just before dawn on August 24, 1572, the slaughter commenced. Crowds ran through the streets, knives and cleavers in hand, breaking into houses and dragging out hapless Huguenots in a killing frenzy. The Seine River, where the bodies were dumped, ran red with blood

Navarre's attendants inside the Louvre palace were butchered although Henri himself was not hurt.

The slaughter continued the following day and spread to the provinces. the relentless blood bath reached Rouen, Lyon, Bourges, Orléans, and Bordeaux, continuing to the beginning of October. Current estimates put the number at about 3,000 killed in Paris alone. Felipe II of Spain welcomed the news of the carnage as did the Pope Gregory XIII. Protestant countries were appalled at the atrocities, and to explain the mass murder, Charles IX claimed the Huguenots had been plotting against the crown.

Rather than extirpating the Huguenots, the massacre intensified the bitter hatred between them and Catholics. They abandoned Calvin's principle of obedience, adopting the view that rebellion was legitimate under such circumstances. Catherine was now seen as an intolerant Catholic extremist.

The massacre was a catalyst for further religious warfare in France that would continue off and on throughout the sixteenth century. It generated a new mindset among the Huguenots. Previously obedient to the laws of the land and to officials, as Calvin had demanded they now brushed aside such considerations and called for the elimination of the monarchy and the king of France who had been party to the massacre. Not only were Huguenots fighting Catholics and the Church for freedom of religion, but they were also fighting the monarchy for political freedom.

In the 1590s, bad years for the common people, the weather had been cold and wet for three years, and there were three bad harvests in a row. Religious warfare destroyed transportation networks and food sources. Bread was scarce, and prices of food, fuel, and housing rose, while wages saw little increase. Taxes were high to pay for the wars and large national debt. The effects of war were so severe in northern France that two-thirds of the population of Picardy were widows and orphans.

Charles IX passed away on May 30, 1574, not yet 24 years old. The crown went to Henri III. Upon the death of the heir-presumptive to the throne, youngest son of Catherine, the duke of Anjou made the Protestant Henri of Navarre heir in 1584. Failing to convince Henri to renounce Protestantism for the sake of the people, Henri III banned the reformed religion and ordered all Protestants to renounce their faith on pain of exile. Further battles ensued between Huguenots and the powerful Guise Catholic League.[4]

EDICT OF NANTES

When Henri IV came to the throne after the murder of Henri III, he had second thoughts and realized that peace in the land would depend on a Catholic king. In 1593, he renounced his Protestant views. Nevertheless, on April 13, 1598, in Brittany, he promulgated the Edict of Nantes that granted the Protestants full civil rights, which resulted in the end of the civil wars. A court was set up, the *Chambre de l'Édit*, where both Protestants and Catholics could deal with problems and disagreements. It upheld their right to believe as they chose, Protestant ministers were to be paid by the state, and public worship was now legal in most of the kingdom although not in Paris, which was too volatile and where trouble would most certainly ensue.

The Huguenots retained control over the cities or strongholds they possessed as of August 1597. The edict also restored Catholicism in areas where it had existed previously and prohibited any extension of Protestantism in France. Nevertheless it was fiercely resented by the pope as well as by the French Catholic clergy. But, once there was no threat of a Protestant king, the Catholic League faded away. The edict brought a measure of peace, but France was still divided into Protestant and Catholic enclaves. The common people, however, could resume a normal life without threat of war and devastation to their property, but distrust lingered on. Protestants settled down to agriculture, trade, and manufacturing, becoming the most prosperous people of France. They engaged in maritime commerce and brought prosperity to themselves and the country. The burgeoning silk industry and the manufacturing of fine linen in the seventeenth century owes their origins to Protestant entrepreneurs.[5]

Abraham Bosse. Engraving, 1633. Louis XIII sits on his throne surrounded by courtiers. Eight men kneel in front of him receiving honors. Through the window fortifications can be seen with cannons, bell tents, and soldiers in formation. (Library of Congress.)

PEASANTS AND WAR

During the period of attempted reform of the Church in France and the subsequent civil wars, the country people frequently saw their houses razed, crops ruined, animals slaughtered, and anything of value carted away by armies or marauding soldiers. Poverty-stricken families made their way to towns in search of food, but often found themselves locked out at the gates.

During the many civil wars that racked France between 1562 and 1598, peasant life could be sheer misery. From time to time they were forced to quarter soldiers (without recompense) when an army—Catholic or Protestant—was on campaign. Through the sweat of peasants the privileged were fed and their grand style of living promoted, whereas in return, the peasants were mocked as artful, vulgar, and as dull-witted as their animals.

Those farmers who were well off with oxen or horses of their own as plow animals were reduced to a pitiful state of poverty during the interminable wars over religion. Soldiers confiscated the animals to pull their wagons and cannon and often simply ate them. Fields went unplowed, no crops were planted, no seedlings were produced for the next year's planting, and the people, living on roots and water, starved.

Even under conditions not ravished by war, life was hard for those who worked the land. In much of the country, means of transportation were destroyed, and food, especially bread, was scarce. Troops pillaged granaries and trodden-down grain fields. At the same time the cost of living rose, while wages remained low and taxes high.

In northern France, family farms were generally too small to support more than three people: the farmer, his wife, and a child. The heir had to wait until the father's death before marriage.[6] Inheritance was difficult for parents living on a small plot of land with several children. To divide the land equally among them would render each plot too small to make a living. To bequeath it to only one such as the oldest child, would leave the others landless.

Misery and debt mounted as the wars continued. Soldiers left along their marches a trail of murder, rape, pillage, and smoking ruins of farmhouses and barns. Many farmers were forced to leave the wasteland of their farms and join the multitude of vagrants roaming the countryside and were often forced into one army or another.

MIDDLE CLASS

While the peasants were undergoing difficult times, the middle class was increasing its wealth. For example, in Calais, on the north Atlantic coast, there was an active maritime trade with other French ports, as well as with the English, and the Dutch.The quality of life improved. Town dwellers now had time to spend on leisure in gambling dens and taverns.

In England, Italy, Germany, and many other countries, commerce was an honorable profession, but not in France or Spain where work was beneath the dignity of the nobility. Most of the pious, prudent, parsimonious, and obsequious middle class merchants lived in their quarter of the city and seldom ventured out of it except on an occasional visit to the fresh air of the countryside. Most of them spent their waking hours sheltered from the elements by an arcade tending their sidewalk stalls, selling their fruits and vegetables, meat or wares, and sometimes shouting out bargains to attract customers. When evening descended and the light faded, they checked receipts, counted the money, swept out the shop and retired to their quarters. Religious or civic ceremonies offered some diversions to this routine.

HOUSES

In Paris, houses were constructed of large, unpolished stones covered with plaster. They had as many as six storeys, the roofs covered with tiles. Other cities employed timber, clay, and plaster to build their houses, which were not as high. Almost every house had a wine cellar in which cider, wine, and other beverages were stored. Some of the windows were glazed, and many had shutters that were closed at night. Streets were mostly just wide enough for two carts to pass. Houses in the villages were usually made of timber and clay with thatch, but those belonging to the wealthy were similar to the residences in towns. Palaces of the nobility were made of stone, and those of the king had carved stone and sometimes marble pillars.[7]

SERVANTS

Every household with enough money had servants, and the more they had, the more prestige the owner enjoyed. After 1565, it became illegal to employ a domestic without a certificate and proper papers. Those who had worked before had to produce a letter from their previous employer giving the reasons why they had left.[8] Servants were paid a wage or compensated in some other way for their work. In the latter case, the employee was forced to depend entirely upon the munificence of the employer. Generosity was fairly rare, however, and the compensation was sometimes as little as five livres or 100 sous a year for a man and perhaps 60 for a women. Compared to An unskilled urban worker who made about six sou per day or enough for two moderate loaves of bread, five livres did not go very far. The servant, of course, generally had clothes and meals supplied.[9]

A wealthy family dressed servants in uniforms, but conditions were often abysmal. Sometimes they were forced to sleep in dark hovels and often on the ground with only a blanket. Anyone who stole from the master was subject to hanging.

LIGHT AND WARMTH

Oil lamps or candles were used for light. For most people, the candles were made of suet, emitting an odious smell. More expensive wax candles were only used by the wealthy. There was no lighting in the streets at night, so people carried a torch or lantern and a weapon of some kind. Although sulfur matches were known at the time, they were seldom used.

It was generally not common to heat more than one room, so in winter, the bourgeois family tended to concentrate in the kitchen where food was cooked and where there was always some warmth available from the large fireplace and chimney that radiated heat. The whole family sat on stone benches around the fire, which also provided some light during the long evenings.

French people had long envied the Germans who had great wood-burning stoves. Since the time of François I, some royal houses in France had them; but in general, it was only toward the end of the sixteenth century that such stoves became more easily accessible to lower class society.

Churches were always freezing, and this was sometimes offset by braziers carried for prayers or for the service. A metal ball filled with hot embers proved a blessing for the numb fingers of the priest. Warming pans, some could be very large and made of silver, were used by well-off families before retiring to an icy cold bed.

Bells were used to signify the time to light fires for heat and light. Those of Notre Dame in Paris rang at seven o'clock, the ones at Saint-Germaine at eight, and the bells of the Sorbonne at nine. An ordinance of 1596 fixed the curfew at seven after the feast of Saint-Rémi up to Easter and at eight after Easter.

Fire-fighting equipment was, at best, rudimentary, although reservoirs installed on the roofs of buildings saved rain water, and an attached pump was used against the frequent fires.

Everyone seemed to be afraid of lightning, and many people carried a piece of coral or eagle feathers for protection. Masts of ships were protected on the upper end by sealskins, as it was widely believed that lightning never struck eagles, seals, crocodiles, turtles, or fig and laurel trees.

WATER AND CLEANLINESS

Some places in Paris, such as hotels, schools, colleges, and certain convents and monasteries had private water channels granted by royal patent after 1598. In addition, there were some houses with their own private wells, but their water was sometimes contaminated and dangerous to drink. Those who could afford it employed water carriers or recruited their valets to bring buckets of water from the public fountains fed by aqueducts around the city. Lower classes collected their own water from the Seine River, the recipient of runoff from the streets and sewers in Paris, but no doubt, they were immune to the germs and used to its foul smell.

On average, the bourgeois house used about 15 buckets of water daily that sometimes had to be carried up steep stairs to the third or fourth floor of a building. Once it reached the apartment, it was poured into recipients.

Water was a precious commodity and not to be wasted. Its primary use was in the kitchen for cooking and sometimes drinking, but it was not for personal hygiene. Taking a bath was out of the question short of being struck down with some terrible disease that required one. Many dwellings did not have even a washing bowl; a bathroom towel was unknown. Normally, people cleaned themselves by rubbing, scraping, and scratching their skin, or through perspiration—hence, public steam rooms were popular. They were not favored by either Catholic or Protestant clergy who denounced the steam parlors as places of debauchery and sin.

Few people washed except once in a while, their hands and, less often, their feet. They never washed their heads. Jean Duchesne, one of the queen's doctors, recommended cleaning the head, the ears, and scrubbing one's teeth. After eating, he suggested washing out the mouth with pure wine and washing the hands in cold water. Even better for the hands was to mix the water with wine or sage leaves that had been soaked overnight. In winter it was recommended to use warm water to wash the hands. The water could be warmed by rinsing it in the mouth. To clean the teeth one could also employ lentisque from the pistachio tree, rosemary, or some other aromatic wood. Most important, however, was to thank God after each meal.

The population customarily suffered from lice, fleas, bedbugs, and other vermin, and gentlemen suffered these parasites under their gold-braided jackets as much as the beggars under their rags. It was always difficult to refrain from scratching one's head, chest or other places when in polite company. When people complained to doctors about their parasites, they were told that to drive away fleas, they should attach several heads of kippered herring to a wire and put them under their straw mattresses.

People were warned not to spit or blow their nose at meals without turning one's head aside, away from the table. One must not attempt to catch fleas while dining, and when eating in company, everyone should refrain from scratching the head.[10]

ECCONOMIC CHANGES

At the beginning of the sixteenth century, as wealth began to be generated outside of property, the bourgeois soon came to equal and even surpass many nobles and high clerics in the accumulation of money.

Commoners were less seeking to demonstrate wealth by gaudy refinements and showy purchases enjoyed by the nobility but preferred to amass movable wealth. War was not on their agenda, the profession of war was left to the nobility, and they shunned ostentatious activities preferring to increase their monetary holdings. Frugal, modest, and avaricious, money brought them power, and they gradually took over the municipal administrations in the name of the king and then gained control of provincial assemblies and tribunals. The bourgeois took part in public parades and ceremonies. During the religious and civil wars from 1562 to 1598, the middle class reached new heights of prosperity.

Rich speculators and financiers found positions as ministers of the king and married the daughters of upper class families, or they purchased noble rank from the monarchy. Less successful merchants could only watch with envy.

Among the poor, the lowest classes, wages did not keep pace with inflation. The debasement of coins by the crown and the hoarding of wheat by merchants waiting for higher prices hurt the laborers both rural and urban. To make matters worse, French migrants flowed into Spain where wages were higher and sent home silver imported from the New World causing inflationary spirals. The peasantry faced increasing taxes by royal agents and those of the Huguenots, while many lost their land to money lenders and the elite. Thousands of landless people roamed the countryside destitute and miserable, harassed by ever-threatening laws against vagabondage.[11] Once the civil wars were over in 1598, and peace returned to the realm, the peasantry, revitalized, began to flourish again.

OUTWITTING THIEVES

France was a dangerous place. In 1595, the Englishman, Fynes Moryson, walked throughout the country and described his experiences. At one point along the way, he ran into some demobilized soldiers on their way home from a war. Moryson had hidden his gold inside his inner doublet, but the soldiers took this along with his shirt, sword, and cloak, leaving him practically naked. He was not completely destitute, however, since he had shortly before sold his horse for sixteen French crowns, which money he had put in a box, covering them over with a putrid-smelling ointment for scabs. A further six crowns he had wrapped in a cloth, which he tied up with thread sticking some needles into it. As they were stripping him of his clothes, the thieves took the box, but when they smelled the contents, they threw it on the ground. At the same time, seeing no use for the thread, they trampled it underfoot. As they rode away, a relieved Moryson retrieved his money, grateful at least to be spared having to beg in a foreign country.[12]

NOTES

1. The label Huguenot was first applied in France to those conspirators involved in the Amboise plot.

2. Ferro, 138.

3. Garrisson, 352–363.

4. The Catholic League was formed by Henri, third duke of Guise, in 1584. It was an extremist group, bent on the eradication of French Huguenots.

5. In October 1685, Louis XIV, renounced the Edict and declared Protestantism illegal. Some 400,000 Protestants left the country, depriving France of numerous skilled artisans, agriculturalists, and men of commerce. Other countries benefited from the mass migration, encouraging the refuges to settle in their lands. New Rochelle was founded by them in the state of New York.

6. Watts, 40.

7. Moryson, iii, 495–496.

8. Erlanger, 196.

9. For money and costs in sixteenth-century France, see "Money," http://www.lepg.org/money.htm (accessed March 19, 2010).

10. Warrack, 14.

11. Baumgartner, 266–268.

12. Moryson, (1967), xiii.

9

NETHERLANDS

On his retirement in 1556, Charles V split the empire, whereby his brother became Holy Roman Emperor as Ferdinand I, and his son inherited Spain, the Netherlands, Spanish territories in Italy, and the Americas, as Felipe II. Netherlanders soon began to despise their new religiously fanatic sovereign who taxed the commerce and appointed his own officials in secular and ecclesiastical posts. Felipe said he would die a hundred deaths rather than rule over heretics.[1] But heretics there were and in growing numbers. People had been arrested for failing to attend Easter Communion,[2] and bloody persecutions took place in Flanders.

SPANISH PERSECUTION

There were many grievances against Spanish rule under Felipe II, whose half sister, Margaret, Duchess of Parma, acted as regent from 1559–1567.

The duchess' chief advisor, Cardinal Granville, alienated the nobles in the early 1560s when he reorganized the bishoprics, Felipe II's nominees, to give the prelates more power on councils of state and introduced the Inquisition to bring an end to Protestantism. The nobility and city councils of the Netherlands considered this in direct violation of their rights.[3]

Margaret attempted to enforce the heresy laws in 1565 such as the placard laws introduced earlier that prohibited reading heretical literature on pain of death.

But the masses openly decried the injustices of Spanish and Church rule, opposing the tithe, high prices, taxes, the imposition of the

Etcher and engraver in studio with patrons. Engraving by Abraham Bosse, 1643. (Library of Congress.)

Inquisition in the Netherlands, and other arbitrary acts. They hated the self-serving Catholic clergy, who never lacked a good meal. Pamphlets began circulating, mocking and satirizing the clergy and the Church. The disparity in wealth was clear: a laborer earned about 75 guilders a year, while the Prior of the Batavian Monastery received 7,500 guilders annually. Churches and monasteries administered huge financial sums, and many of them owned at least half of all peasant farms. Exempt from taxation, the Church demanded a tenth of the grain, cattle, and fruit produced from the fields and orchards.

The steady influx of Calvinist disciples into the Netherlands around the middle of the century led to Protestant congregations springing up throughout the country.[4]

VIOLENT ACTION AND REACTION

On August 10, 1566, in a field near the town of Steenvorde in Flanders, a crowd gathered to listen to the words of a Protestant preacher. Fired up by his ringing condemnations of injustice and led by a former monk, the mob gathered up axes, ladders, ropes, and hammers and marched off shouting and singing hymns to the nearest monastery. The monks fled for their lives, and the building was reduced to rubble. Within a week, 400 churches, monasteries, and convents were attacked. Icons statues, pews, and choir stalls were hacked to bits: pictures were ripped from walls, altars smashed, windows broken, curtains shredded, columns battered down, and even the holy crosses were destroyed. In the big cities, church services stopped. Terrified priests and nuns dared not appear before the avenging crowds and hid as best they could.

The rioters rang the bells constantly, and when tired from their days' work, they carried home whatever they pleased from the holy sites. A swath of destruction lay across the land. Beautiful objects, paintings, and precious, richly decorated manuscripts were not spared. In the frenzy, private homes were not immune, and people buried their sacred treasures in back yards to preserve them.

As the Lutheran doctrine spread and people began to think of themselves as free men with no allegiance but to God, they refused to doff their hats and kneel in streets when a religious procession passed by. The long burning fuse of discontent had reached the powder keg.

As church services were disrupted and icons destroyed everywhere, Felipe II, residing in Spain, ordered his general, the duke of Alba, to transfer his army from Italy to the Netherlands to quell the uprising by any means. He was given a free hand and arrived in Brussels August 22, 1567, at the head of an army of 10,000

Alba's brutal tactics against rebels and reformers caused about 100,000 people to flee the country for Germany and England. Alba and his Council of Blood tortured and murdered anyone accused of treason against Spain or heresy against the Church. He plundered towns to pay his army and raised taxes to 10 percent on all sales, further inciting a furious public. The Inquisition dealt with heretics sending them to death and confiscating their property. The nobility were not immune. The atrocious suppression secured the south for Alba but only served to reinforce the will to fight in the more northern provinces.

The 80 Years' War for Dutch independence began in 1568 as a Protestant Dutch uprising to throw off the rule of Spain and its Catholic Inquisition.

SEA BEGGARS

In the 1550s and 1560s, violent gangs of hungry people began wandering the country robbing and plundering. Often monasteries and clerical travelers were their targets. By the latter half of the 1560s, they were known as the sea beggars. They attacked Spanish soldiers whenever the opportunity presented itself, and at sea they proved to be more successful than on land. They sank Spanish vessels and also those of other nations.

On July 10, 1568, they attacked and defeated a Spanish fleet. The feared sea beggars hated anything to do with popery and Spanish rule.

Mixing with the local population, they quickly sparked rebellions against the so-called Iron Duke (Alba) in town after town and spread the resistance southward.[5]

SPANISH FURY

Alba was dismissed from his command in spring of 1576; the king of Spain had exhausted his finances, and without supplies (except those stolen from the Dutch people), and their pay long in arrears, the Spanish soldiers mutinied. In a frenzied rage, the soldiers ransacked Antwerp, Europe's leading commercial city and brutally slaughtered some 8,000 citizens over a period of three days. Huge numbers of people fled, and

Surprise Attack on Maestreicht. Woodcut, Hans Burgkmair, 1775. (Library of Congress.)

anyone who remained and had nothing with which to placate the furious soldiers was executed on the spot. Houses of wealthy merchants were stripped and burned, their owners grateful if they managed to escape with their lives.

News of the incident, known as the Spanish Fury, incited the populace to fever pitch in their hatred of Spaniards. The determination of the Dutch to resist occupation was demonstrated at Maestreicht (Maastricht) in a siege that lasted four months. Two thousand soldiers held out against 20,000 Spanish troops. When the Spaniards broke through the walls, they slaughtered about 10,000 inhabitants.

During these struggles with Spain, life and property were far from secure as Spanish troops pillaged, the **Rebellion in** Inquisition sought victims, and high taxes imposed on **the North** the people were used to pay their oppressors. Periodic rebellions broke out in many places. A national leader was needed, and one arose in the person of William I of Orange.

Appointed governor of Holland by Felipe II in 1559, William joined both the Calvinist faith and the revolt against Spain. His leadership inspired the Dutch with a new lease on optimism and determination to throw out the foreigners who governed their country.

Seven northern provinces rebelled and declared themselves independent in 1579, becoming the Protestant United Provinces of the Netherlands (Holland). The southern provinces (Belgium and Luxemburg) remained with the Catholic Church, dominated by Spain. Meanwhile, throughout the long struggle for religious and political independence, the common people of the Netherlands attempted to live a normal life.

CHILDREN'S EDUCATION

After attending the local communal school, children went to Latin schools that had changed their emphasis from a religious to a secular one as the Reformation advanced. Education was primarily a privilege of the moneyed classes, and young men between ages seven and twelve were sent off to boarding schools in the larger cities. A good education was important for the individual but also, in the Dutch view, provided a benefit to society. Those boys not suited for training in the Latin schools took up apprenticeships to become bakers or craftsmen.

DIET

Rye bread was a staple of the diet, its price and quality regulated by city officials. The well-to-do ate white bread that cost more. Regulations prohibited bakers from making pastry, pies, cakes, and cookies; this was the exclusive job of other guilds. Although life was reasonably prosperous for some, for those people whose houses and lands were ravaged by Spanish troops and brigands, any kind of bread would do.

In the country a kind of soup was made of many different kinds of vegetables, chopped and cooked with stale bread and broth (potatoes were not known at this time).[6] Such a mush would be simmered over a fire in a large pan known as a cow kettle. Meat, usually pork, was sometimes added to this. Only the wealthy ate fowl and game (unless they were poached) because these foods were too expensive for most people.

At Christmas, a special cake would be made consisting of pears or quince, almonds, curds, and raisins mashed together with sugar and cinnamon. To this mixture, butter and several egg yolks would be added.

WINTERTIDE[7]

In the Netherlands as in other parts of northern Europe, life from day to day proved hardest in times when a severe winter settled over the land, and temperatures plunged below freezing and remained there for weeks or months. To keep the fire going was a real effort; as wood became scarce, the countryside was scoured for anything that would burn, and those that had wood to sell charged a price that was far too high for many. Hundreds of poor people perished in the countryside and in their homes from hunger or freezing. Fodder for farm animals was scarce during such times, and they died in the thousands. Wolves roamed freely in the village streets looking for food. Ships locked in the ice in the harbors brought trade to a standstill as supplies of local and imported grain dwindled, and prices skyrocketed. Since dealers in grain sometimes refused to sell if they were expecting prices to go up, citizens rioted in the streets, and bakers and grain depots were stormed and decimated.

The poor farmer, who managed to survive the winter with his chickens, eggs, cow and sheep, and his home-grown dried vegetables, was often robbed and cleaned out and, on occasion, even killed by vagabonds, gypsies, roaming soldiers, deserters, lepers, and tramps, anyone who was homeless and on the move. Before going on to the next place, they sometimes set fire to the farmhouse and warmed themselves.

HOUSES AND FURNITURE

There were no street numbers, so houses needed to be identified in other ways. A red boot hanging above the door, a pair of gilded tongs, or the house "on the right of the one with the picture of a horse," and so on made finding the dwelling in question easier. Inns and taverns had their distinctive signs hanging outside, often carved in wood.

Houses had both stone and wooden façades in the cities, many with thatched roofs. In poor houses, an open fire in the middle of the room had a large kettle suspended over it, used for simmering oatmeal, vegetables, or fruit.

People who worked at home, such as tailors, shoemakers, or cabinet-makers, used the front part of the house as a workshop or showroom. Such rooms were unheated and cold most months of the year, so the owner warmed his hands by retiring on occasion to the inner room where stood a fireplace. There, he sat on a stool or a bench. In some cases, the back of the bench would be reversible so that he could face the fire or sit with his back to it. On the bench might be a sheepskin, a cushion, and even a foot-stool for more comfort. But people in general were used to uncomfortable furniture, and for most a plain board with four legs was generally what they utilized. Padded and comfortable armchairs were unknown, and the floor would do if nothing else were available. Worshipers even brought their own folding chairs or stools to church.

In lower class homes, most utility items were homemade, such as a barrel chair with the upper half of one side cut away, half filled with cushions, and giving back support. Another item of furniture might be just a log split in half with two wooden legs at each end.

The fireplace was the main source of heat in the inner room of the dwelling where wood and mostly peat were burned. Within the fireplace were the andirons, and blocks of peat (from the marshes) and wood were put on top of them, so the chimney would draw well. The women often stood in front of the fire with their skirts gathered up, so the warmth could go up to their bodies. Suspended from a crossbar in the chimney of the fireplace was an adjustable hook to hang pots containing food at different levels above the fire. A spit for roasting chicken or duck over the fire would be found in most homes along with other utensils such as a metal or wooden porridge spoon for stirring and serving. Other implements for cooking included a very long-handled frying pan (so one could stand back from the hot flames and fry an egg), tongs of various shapes and sizes, metal tripods, and bellows.

A clay fire bell covered the fire overnight so that there might still be hot embers in the morning, which could be used to restart the fire. If not, then a flint was struck against metal to create a spark in a tinder box filled with singed cotton that was nourished along by blowing on it.

In the interior room of a middle class house was the feather bed, about waist-high off the floor, covered by a blanket and surrounded by curtains with a canopy above. Some shelves would be along a wall near the fire for dishes, along with a cabinet for storage, a few wooden stools, a bench or two with cushions, and a folding table against a wall when not in use. Several pictures and a cross bow might decorate the walls. A chandelier with three or four candles hung from the ceiling; it was used only on

Sundays and holidays such as Christmas. Windows were usually small and opaque, the diamond-shaped glass enclosed in lead frames.

In the back of the dwelling would be the kitchen that in modest houses would have another fireplace for cooking, more shelves for plates, pots, pans, and jugs, a washbasin on top of a cabinet and a kettle of water hanging above the basin. Water had to be carried into the house from the nearest well or public fountain in the village. There might be a small alcove bed in the kitchen for a child. In summer the kitchen fire was used for cooking, but in winter the interior room fire was used for this purpose. To maintain two fires at the same time was expensive, so the kitchen was left ice cold in winter. Outside the kitchen door, most houses had a cistern to catch and contain rainwater.

FIRE HAZARDS

A fire that destroyed a single farmhouse was not the end of the world since with neighborly assistance, the family could soon construct another dwelling. In the cities, fire could be, and often was, a disaster. To reduce the risk, houses were often built from a frame structure and the walls filled in with paneling consisting of twigs and branches woven together and covered over with a plaster made of loam, mud, and cow dung.

City ordinances regulated building. Tar and pitch were prohibited materials on the façade, and beds could not be built within four feet of the hearth. Fires were extremely dangerous; they could destroy a village or town in short order. Inspectors came around regularly to check the work and, depending on the city, could be very strict looking for the smallest deviation from the building codes.

Extinguishing a fire once it had taken hold was nigh impossible. People of all ages would arrive when the fire alarm was sounded, forming lines along which buckets of water were passed to be thrown on the blaze. Others would try to stop it spreading by tying wet cloths to the end of a stick to put out sparks that landed in the thatch of a nearby house. In a strong wind, such measures were almost useless.

The essential ingredient, water, had to be always available to put out fires, and in winter when the rivers, streams, and canals were frozen over, it was necessary to make sure there were openings in the ice from which to draw it. In many communities, leather sacks of water were kept in the houses for emergencies. In case of a fire, every household had to supply an able-bodied person to bring pails for carrying water. It was also mandatory to hang a lantern in front of every house in order to light up the dark streets if the fire alarm sounded at night. Houses with thatched roofs also had to have ladders standing by. When ordered by the city, everyone was required to have a two-handled tub of water outside the front entrance, and inspectors came around to take inventory and ensure compliance.

Gradually, in the course of the sixteenth century, more and more houses were built of stone, and thatch gave over to tiled or slate roofs. Outlets for smoke made of wood were replaced by brick chimneys.

HYGIENE

The back yards of houses were usually places to store unused articles in sheds along with housing pigs, chickens, and a cow or horse. There also would be hung the laundry, which would be done four or five times a year. Pots hung from the gutter of the roof for nesting birds, generally starlings, and when the young birds were nearly ready to leave the nest, they were gathered up and eaten.

Streets were a dumping ground for just about everything: kitchen leftovers, broken pottery, or china were thrown outside, and horses, cattle, chickens, and pigs left their droppings as they wandered through the smelly mess. If there was a canal or stream at the doorway, refuse was thrown into that. Outhouses were constructed over the water, and sometimes there would be a little landing next to it where pots and pans were washed.

Towns were infested with rats that ate the grain, cheese, fruit, or whatever else was available. They also gnawed the woodwork in the houses. Although they were not identified as carriers of disease, people tried ingenious ways to be rid of them. One device was a narrow, about seven-foot-long, wooden box with an opening at each end and compartments inside filled with nesting material. Once the compartments were full of rats, the ends were sealed and the animals drowned. Another was a plate balanced on two sticks of wood extending out from the kitchen counter. When the rat walked onto the plate to retrieve the bait placed on it, the plate tipped up and the rat fell into a bucket of water placed underneath. There were many such devices, but the rats bred faster than they could be eliminated. The streets, mostly unpaved, were a moving mass of rodents at night that would begrudgingly make way for the night watchman.

Water was a precious commodity not because it was scarce, but it had to be carried, usually by hand, from the source to the **Bathing** house. It was used sparingly for washing the body, but when it was absolutely necessary, a large wooden tub was available for the purpose. It was a time-consuming operation pouring pots and pitchers of hot water into the tub and then sitting there for a while, sprinkling some of it over one's head in an attempt to wash the hair. It was apparently more fun, although more costly, to go to the public bathing house at the local inn where men and women climbed into the same tubs, pots of beer in hand, to enjoy the bath and the company, much to the disapprobation of the Church.

THE INFIRM

Mentally deficient people and those suffering from diseases were found in abundance on the streets of Holland including many who were too sick to work and others such as lepers, who were obliged to shake the lepers' wooden clapper as they approached to beg, to alert the prospective alms-giver of their condition. As the Reformation gained momentum, however, life became more difficult for those in need. Having heard from the reformers that salvation depended on God's grace and not on good deeds, the latter became less popular as people liked the idea that it was not necessary to give alms in order to go to heaven.

There were people about who begged that appeared handicapped but were in fact fit and sound. They would complain of having suffered in the wars, women pretended to faint in the streets, and some would lie down in front of the doors of residences, groaning and crying out. Some women carried tiny babies saying they had just given birth and needed rest and food. Others pretended insanity or faked an attack in the market place, and when the audience gathered around, the pickpockets went to work.

THE PLAGUE

The bubonic plague appeared about every five years as a regular part of daily life; nobody knew where it came from. About all they could do was pray to God that it would not descend upon them. Many people scraped bits of sandstone off the local churches, placed them in a bag that they wore around the neck as a kind of holy talisman against the disease, which was blamed on many things such as eating apples and plums, mosquitoes, the dirty water of the canals, foreigners, or the Jews who were often rounded up and exiled. Everyone had an opinion as people died by the thousands.

The Catholic Church's view, however, generally prevailed. The priests maintained the plague came because of the sins of man and was a sign of the wrath of God. Hygiene was generally very poor, however. People wore the same shirt for weeks on end both day and night, a haven for fleas. No one made the connection between plague, rats, and fleas. Rats carried fleas that, in turn, carried the disease. Nearly everyone had fleas in their clothes and in their beds. Pitch was burned in barrels in the streets in attempts to purify the air.[8]

Calling for the surgeon was generally futile because few would come, considering it too dangerous. Those doctors who braved the plague

Pieter Brueghel the Elder, 1562. Triumph of Death. A dying man plays the lute as Death fiddles. Skeletons ring bells from a dead tree, emaciated figures (representing death) drive a horse and wagon filled with skulls. A crow sits on the horse looking down on the dying and the dead. (Museo Nacional del Prado, Madrid.)

received extra pay for perilous duty. They would perform the usual bloodletting, check the urine, and cover the boils with a poultice or with a dried toad. Usually a priest would be in attendance not only to give a blessing, but also to record the will and testament of the dying person in case there was something to be given to the Church.

Coffins were at a premium in a plague-ridden area. When an epidemic struck, corpses filled the streets waiting for burial. Those who had had money were buried within the Church, creating an almost unbearable stench, masked by huge amounts of incense. The less well off were buried in the church yard. To prevent pigs from digging up the bodies, iron grates were laid down. If the churchyard was filled up, the bodies were taken outside of the city and dumped into mass graves.

Those who lived in a neighborhood where the plague appeared generally fled, helping to spread it around. All the while, night and day, the church bells tolled. The usual sign indicating there was plague in a house was a bundle of straw hanging from the façade. Children who had lost a brother or sister to the disease had to carry a white stick when they played in the streets. Others played games that involved make-believe funerals in which two boys carried a third through the streets, lying on a plank, wrapped in a blanket. A fourth boy led the little parade holding a wooden cross.

OCCUPATIONS

Many household items were sold by itinerant vendors from door to door. From them the lady of the house could purchase candles, wood, ceramic or copper candleholders, candle snuffers, and small lamps that burned rapeseed oil for heat and light. People went to bed early, often just after dark, hence little artificial light was required.

In 1566, occupations in Antwerp, one of the largest cities in northern Europe, were recorded:

169 bakers
78 butchers
91 fishmongers
110 barber-surgeons
124 goldsmiths
300 painters and sculptors
594 tailors and stocking makers[9]

There were, to be sure, some doctors of medicine, numerous clerics and monks, musicians, and actors, traders, and many thousands of laborers, sailors and foreign merchants, and beggars.

Most women were able to spin and make a little extra income, which they did at home. Using wool or flax, they fastened the fibers to a wooden distaff. The fibers were pulled out with one hand, twisted into thread with the other hand, and rolled onto a spindle. Eye glasses were available for those with poor sight.

People who worked for a daily wage lived on the edge. One month, they had a job; the next month, they had nothing. This was especially true of farm seasonal workers when the planting or harvesting were finished. Unable to buy food, they might find a charitable organization in a large city to keep them from death's door, and if not, their only alternative was to beg. Even for nonresidents, the possibility of working as a wage laborer was not uncommon in the seven northern provinces of the Netherlands. Expected to work 12 to 14 hours a day, they were not usually allowed to reside in the same village as their employers and lived in squalor in separate dependent villages.[10]

FISHING

The Dutch designed special ships for the Baltic herring trade, but an edict from Charles V issued in 1519 specified that all ships had to have a license to sail and that only new barrels could be used. Inspectors were appointed to verify proper barreling of fish in all ports. Fishing was at its peak there around 1600–1630, and the many herring factories employed large numbers of men and women.

The Dutch fishing industry, an important part of the economic base of the northern Netherlands, included a type of factory ship called the herring bus that enabled the fishermen to follow the herring to the shoals of the Dogger Bank and other places, far from the shores of the Netherlands, and to stay at sea for long periods. This ship was equipped to salt the fish while at sea. Herring was an important export.

Fishing also attracted its own supporting businesses such as trade in and refining of salt, manufacturing of fishnets, and specialized building of ships. Traders invested the fishing revenues in buying up grain in Baltic ports during the winter months that they transported to western Europe when the ice floes thawed in spring. The income generated from this incidental trade was invested in unrefined salt or in new ships. The fishing fleet was protected by naval vessels against privateers.

TRAVEL AND TRANSPORTATION

With no reliable transportation service available, there was little possibility of sending packages or goods to another party or to another city Instead, people carried their own belongings from place to place in sacks or baskets usually conveyed on their heads or backs or by use of a yoke. Wheelbarrows could be converted into sleighs in winter for traveling over frozen rivers or canals. Rowboats and sailboats were plentiful in summer and were used to carry passengers and their luggage from one side of a river or bay to the other; they were also used to transport grain from region to region around the Baltic Sea.

Horses were a primary means of transport, but sometimes three or four peasants shared one since not everyone could afford a horse.

Travelers without transportation often found it useful to make inquiries in a town to find out if anyone with a horse-drawn wagon was going their way, in which case they might find a ride for a fee. Travel by horse was, of course, safer than walking, but even then, it was dangerous to travel alone. On the open road, behind every clump of trees was a potential ambush where thieves could lie in wait for the unwary.

Travel could be monotonous and uncomfortable, bouncing around in a wagon over rutted paths through a flat landscape for hours on end. There were few people out in the country, away from the towns. The land was often marshy. One would pass a farm now and again and spot a farmer with his oxen plowing or a shepherd with his flock. Cows were not plentiful in open country, as fields were difficult to fence off, and most animals were kept in wooden enclosures behind the house.

CRIME AND RETRIBUTION

The telltale signs of approaching a large city were obvious from both the smell on the wind and the bodies of hanged men or women left to twist slowly on the gibbets—a warning that crime was severely punished.

Many towns had laws regulating activities after dark. In some places it was mandatory to carry a lantern on the streets at night, and to be caught without one was a punishable offense. Walking around with a torch or any other open flame was against the law due to the ever-present hazard of fire.

The punishments for crimes such as stealing could be severe and included whipping, mutilation, dismembering, the loss of an ear (or part of one), the loss of the nose, and branding on the face, so they could be recognized elsewhere since most thieves were then banished from the city. Under such conditions, there was little choice but to attach themselves to the army of vagabonds and highwaymen who roamed the countryside seeking victims. They usually ended up on the gallows.

When a thief or murderer was about to be hanged outside the city walls, people gathered to see the spectacle. Entire families, including young children, came out to watch. The criminals did not fall through a trap door and die quickly of a broken neck; they were often pulled up from the ground by a pair of horses, their hands tied behind their backs, legs jerking and kicking, searching for something solid. Meantime, they strangled to death. People also gathered around when someone was to be beheaded, flogged, or their bones broken on the wheel. A priest would stand by holding a cross and looking on as a person's joints slowly parted on the rack. There were many kinds of tools for inflicting pain during interrogation of a prisoner designed to make him confess to a crime, guilty or not. One such device was an iron shaft with folded down metal leaves. When it was inserted into the anus, a screw was turned that caused the leaves to expand outward from the shaft.

A suspect could not be condemned until he or she confessed. To place a person in the stocks and apply a burning torch to the feet was one way to extract a confession; to tie one down and pour water into their mouths through a funnel until they felt they were drowning also worked, along with weights tied to the limbs and added until the joints gave way was also used. Rope, soaked in water and tied tightly to the arms and legs and left to dry, shrank inexorably into the skin and muscle and gave the victim time to think about his confession as the pain became unbearable. Crowds particularly enjoyed seeing a heretic burned alive.

Punishments varied from beatings to being locked in a cage suspended above the street for days, encased in the stocks to be tormented by passersby, to having a sharp, two-ended fork (one end embedded under the chin and the other in the chest) held in place by a leather strap around the neck so the head could not be lowered or turned. Such punishments were designed primarily for humiliation of the victim.

Excused from torture were doctors, knights, officers, children under the age of fourteen, the old and feeble, and pregnant women. Such procedures and regulations differed from district to district. However, no one was exonerated for certain crimes such as treason, witchcraft, or holding hostages.

For a crime as small as stealing a chicken, the culprit might spend a few days in the stocks. For witchcraft, punishment was death by burning. Aged women, bent-over from a lifetime of leaning over the fire and carrying heavy buckets of water, someone who had outlived their family and friends and perhaps seemed somewhat senile, were often targets of suspected witchcraft.

Other forms of punishment used for convicted criminals included mutilation and dismembering, and fingers, ears, and noses were often chopped off for minor offenses (one of which was blasphemy against God). People witnessed these atrocious punitive measures from childhood and did not lose any sleep over them.

EFFECTS OF THE REFORMATION

The long, intense struggle in the northern provinces for independence from both the Catholic Church and from Spain resulted in a number of Protestant sects in Holland. In the south, Belgium, nearly all inhabitants remained Catholic. While Lutheranism made little headway, Calvinists poured into Holland by the thousands from areas where they were persecuted such as Alsace and France. The degree of toleration in the Netherlands was more acceptable than elsewhere. Catholics could live and work there but were prohibited from religious activities. In 1577, William of Orange granted Anabaptists the right to worship for the first time.

NOTES

1. Simon, 85.
2. Duke, 39.
3. Walker, 383.
4. Hillerbrand (2007), 377.
5. For more on Sea Beggars, see Elliott, 207–213.
6. Poortvliet, 120–121.
7. Ibid., for much of the following.
8. The plague was apparently introduced into Europe from Asia in the fourteenth century by rats aboard trade ships.
9. Poortvliet, 93.
10. Watts, 55.

10

THE FAMILY

MARRIAGE

In northern Europe, family units were centered around a married couple and their children; in the south, the household would often include a husband and wife, their married children and grandchildren as well as surviving grandparents.

A wife was expected to be a companion to her husband but always his obedient subordinate. A husband's right to beat his wife with impunity generally had community approval. For Catholics, marriage was a sacrament and could not be undone except under the most special circumstances such as if it were not consummated or if incest was involved. As a result, Catholic marriages were sometimes loveless (especially those arranged by parents) and supplemented by adulterous behavior. In Italy and Spain, outside the orbit of the Reformation, divorce was practically unknown.

In a time of constant wars, famines, and plagues, the loss of a spouse was quite common, and new marriages were quickly sought and undertaken. Orphaned children passed from relative to relative or into a monastery.

One of the institutions that came under close scrutiny by Protestant reformers was that of the patriarchal nuclear family as the liberator of men, women, and children from religious and sexual enslavement.[1]

Reformers and Marriage

Early on, Martin Luther wrote about marriage asserting that it was an institution in crisis. From the point of view of the reformer, unlike that of the Catholic Church, chastity was unnatural and contrary to God's will, although sexual acts should take place only after marriage. For the

Catholic Church, sex was permitted inside marriage but only for procreation and for no other reason.

Rejecting this view, Luther and other early reformers noted that all forms of life are represented by males and females the way God had designed it, and marriage was its natural outcome. Young women in nunneries were deprived of their natural womanhood, abused by male clergy, and culturally isolated. Luther prevailed upon families to liberate their daughters and take them home to find suitable husbands. Through his encouragement, Protestant towns closed down convents and cloisters.

FAMILY RELATIONSHIPS

Following the teachings of St. Paul regarding the authority of the father, Protestants of Reformation Europe decreed that wives, children, and servants had to obey the master of the house just as Christians obeyed God.

Within the German burgher families, however, the wife held a position of authority deserving equal respect and sharing responsibility. Frequently, she took an active part in the running of her husband's business affairs.

In Geneva, marriages between young women and much older men were opposed, although some felt that an older woman might not be sufficiently subservient to a younger man. Those who brought a large dowry to marriage could also make their husbands feel inadequate. Geneva, where wife beaters were speedily brought before the courts, was known as "the Woman's Paradise".[2]

The Hus-band's Role Thus, the duties of the father were first to control his wife, second to bring up his children, and third to govern his servants who should not lack bread, work, and scolding. The master's "relationship with the servants was not based on justice, but on patronage, as if they were children."[3]

The husband's duty was to protect his family, provide for everyone in the household, and to be a model of self-discipline as well as a wise, moderate, God-fearing person who worked hard. Most important, as master ruling the family and servants, he could not be challenged.[4] He was to be faithful to his wife, and when the Protestant governments put restrictions on houses of prostitution, it was to maintain sexual fidelity within the family.

A Wife's Duties In his *Boke of Husbandry* (London, 1525), John Fitzherbert makes a list of a wife's duties:

'when thou art up and ready, then first sweep thy house, dress up thy dishboard and set all things in good order within thy house; milk thy kine, feed thy calves, sile (strain) up thy milk, take up thy children and array them, and provide for thy husband's breakfast, dinner, supper, and for thy children and servants, and take thy part with them. And to ordain corn and malt to the mill, to bake and brew withal when need is. . . . Thou must make butter and cheese when thou may; serve thy swine, both morning and evening, and give thy pullen (fowl) meat in the morning, and when time of the year cometh, thou must take heed how thy hen, ducks and geese do lay, and to gather up their eggs; and when they wax broody to set them thereas no beasts, swine or other vermin hurt them. . . . And in the beginning of March, or a little before, is time for a wife to make her garden. . . . And also in March is time to sow flax and hemp . . . and thereof may they make sheets, board-clothes (table cloths), towels, shirts, smocks, and such other necessaries; and therefore let thy distaff be always ready for a pastime, that thou be not idle. . . .'[5]

According to the Protestant ethic, a husband should never strike his wife but should treat her honorably. For her part, she should be virtuous, pious, and mature enough to run the household efficiently. Protestantism, however, did not give educated women the same advantages as they had experienced under Catholicism, and engaging in activities outside the home became more difficult. The wife's responsibility was foremost to be faithful and stand by her husband, be friendly, modest, not given to excess, and give the household her first priority. Her role was ordained by God, and through her efforts she exercised her faith and endorsed her salvation.[6] Women who found their roles demeaning were told that submission was required of them to atone for Eve's sins. According to Markham, a contemporary writer, although the woman was theoretically subservient, in fact, she was an "active and indispensable partner in the domestic economy."[7]

Up to this time, for families under severe economic stress and near starvation, sending their children off to monastic life had been one way of reducing household expenditures and giving the child a chance for a future. The alternative for girls from poor families, who did not find a husband, was too often prostitution.

Reformists were determined that children would no longer be forced into a life of involuntary celibacy (some girls and boys went voluntarily) but that they should remain at home unless they married. Protestants, set against the celibate life, deemed the cloister inhuman and antisocial.[8]

VILLAGE, HAMLET, AND FARM

Nearly every aspect of running a household in the countryside depended on the peasant wife's vigilance. She tended the home, the children, and the livestock, made the clothes, washed them in the stream, gathered wild fruit and berries, cultivated a vegetable garden, and collected firewood.

She had her share of remedies using medicinal herbs, fruit and vegetables, and sometimes the entrails of animals when a member of the family had a headache, toothache, worms, bleeding, or other ills. Hemorrhoids, for instance, were treated by taking

> 'the sole of an old shoe worn by a man much used to travel; cut it into pieces, and burn it, yet neither to gray or white ashes, but to a friable and tender coal. Reduce it into an impalpable powder. Take then unsalted hog lard, and work it to an ointment, and anoint the afflicted part often therewith.'[9]

A woman was expected to know about herbs for seasoning in cooking, salads, or sauces; she would know when each herb should be planted and the best time to harvest it. Food was often highly seasoned with both herbs and spice (especially meat that was far from fresh). Herbs were used for making preserves, medicines, and cleaning preparations.

For insect stings, lemon balm was used either by drinking the crushed leaves with wine or applying them directly to the skin. Fruits were dried, vegetables pickled, and meats salted amongst other things for winter supply.

Another wifely duty was to keep clothes clean, and she often used ashes, bread, urine, vinegar, and egg whites in addition to soap and water. Clothes were laid out on the grass to dry in the sun. In addition, she took care of the chickens and bees and milked the cows. She also produced cream, cheese, and butter. In many cases, the wife was also charged with making malt and brewing beer: "the drink by which the household is nourished and sustained since it was both consumed by the family and sold for profit."[10]

A CASE OF BETROTHAL AND MARRIAGE

Before a formal union of marriage, arrangements were normally conducted by the families regarding a dowry and other matters of concern.

Typical of the upper middle class, Felix Platter, son of Thomas Platter, a student of medicine, conducted his courtship of Madlen Jeckelmann in Basel in various stages. First was the formal introduction (although they already knew each other). A luncheon was prepared to which members of both families and friends were invited. Following a walk around the Platter country estate, the formal luncheon was served. Then Felix entertained the guests with music, playing the lute, and dancing.

Later came the official proposal to which Madlen's father consented after some hesitation. The only stipulations he made were that Felix obtain his doctorate beforehand and that Madlen manage her father's house as well as her own during their first two years together.

This agreed, Felix was free to visit Madlen (who was always chaperoned) daily. Otherwise, the engagement was to be kept secret until Felix had completed his studies. When the day arrived for the long anticipated wedding, the two fathers of the couple began arguing over dowry. Madlen's father, a surgeon, offered a quarter of her dowry in cash, the rest to be paid in the form of a trousseau. Felix's father, less well-off, finally agreed. The wedding ceremony took place at the cathedral after a sermon and the exchange of rings.

Next came the banquet, prepared with great care for between 150 and 200 guests. Fifteen tables were set up, and the food was served in four courses consisting of appetizers, fish, roast, and dessert. Once this was over, a choral recital and dancing followed. Later in the evening, they dined again on fowl and various meats including pork, beef, and game. Wine from Alsace was served throughout both meals.[11] Once the speeches were finished, the young couple said their goodbyes and slipped away to the nuptial bed.

When Fynes Moryson wrote his travel memoirs, he had something to say about marriage in the German-speaking **A German** areas of Europe, noting, for example, that cities and towns **Wedding** in Saxony generally appointed a working day for the marriage. Sunday was considered inappropriate since the celebration involved heavy drinking. Before the feast, a colorfully dressed young man rode through town to invite the guests. Beside him, a boy ran from house to house to make sure somebody was home before the rider dismounted to extend the invitation. Two youths attended the bride on her wedding day, carrying torches before her wherever she went.

After dinner, dancing and drinking began either at the house where the feast took place or at an inn, and those not invited to enjoy the food could come and join the dancing. The men stood on one side of the room and women on the other. The boys attending the bride brought the women across the floor and presented them to the men with whom they were to dance. In one incident a virgin maiden refused to dance with a certain

	Midday Meal	*Evening Meal*
MENU FOR FELIX PLATTER'S WEDDING, NOVEMBER 1557		
First Course: Appetizer (*voressen*)	Chopped fish	Chicken liver
	Soup	Tripe
	Meat	Meat soup
	Chicken	Chicken
Second Course: Fish	Boiled pike	Boiled carp
Third Course: Roast	Roast	Roast as earlier
	Pigeon, cock, goose	Black Forest game
	Boiled rice	Stew
	Liver slices in aspic	Fish cakes
Fourth Course: Dessert	Cheese	Pastries
	Fruit	

man, and he gave her a slap on the ear. Taken before a judge, the man was pardoned. He had done her no harm, but she had disgraced him as a person unworthy to dance with her.

A gift of money was presented to the bride and groom just after the feast, and the wealthy were expected to give more than those with less means. Moryson also mentions that in many places he had "seene Cittizens of good quality gather mony of the guests to pay the Musitions."[12]

Barrels of beer and wine were provided, and the groom entertained the men. The bride entertained the women. The feasts were more grandiose in some places while in others it was inexpensive, consisting of smoked herring, raw beans, certain kinds of nuts, along with sliced bread that was salted and peppered to stimulate a thirst for more drink.

CHILD BEARING AND BAPTISM IN GERMANY

During the time a woman was in bed before or after giving birth, anyone who entered the house presented her with a small gift of money to help pay for the midwife and the nurse.

When a child was born in any level of society, there was a celebration that would be of some material benefit, especially to the poor, as each guest was expected to bring a gift. This occasionally took the form of money. For the rich, some of the presents and the ceremony itself, could be very extravagant. An invitation to be a godparent was an honor, and the final choice of name for the child was the responsibility of the father.

Baptism followed soon after birth in the Catholic Church. The baby was taken on a cushion covered in a white cloth to the priest who laid a piece of white linen over its face as a symbol of purity. Godfathers and godmothers were on hand (there could be any number of them) as the child was immersed in the water of a fountain. An exorcism was read to rid the child of original sin.

Children of royalty underwent more elaborate ceremonies. Copious refreshments and the presentation of gifts followed. The duke of Saxony invited the entire town when his child was born, and each person brought a gift.

If a mother were not able to suckle the baby, a wet nurse was hired. Unlike many other places, in Germany children were never sent away from home to be suckled elsewhere.

The nature and benefit of baptism became a controversial issue during the Reformation. At first, adult baptism took place when a person, old enough to know what was happening, was welcomed into the Church. Baptism of infants was conducted throughout Christendom in the Middle Ages.[13] By the time of the Reformation, there were Protestants who were sure that infant baptism occurred in the Bible and should be continued, whereas others, a minority (Anabaptists), were sure it did not, and only adult baptism was valid. Zwingli believed there was no clear evidence in the Bible either way. The argument revolved around an infant's inability to consciously become a disciple of Christ.

INFANTS

Married women were pregnant much of the time, and records show that at least one-third of all children died before age five. Midwives generally delivered the children, but sometimes they were inexperienced or negligent.

Swaddling was encouraged to keep the child warm, and its limbs straight, but on occasion babies were swaddled with their limbs in the wrong place, causing permanent damage. The Catholic Church required abstinence from sex if the mother was nursing a child, so many of those who could afford it put their children in the hands of wet nurses for the first eighteen months of their lives. Problems arose if the wet nurses were unhealthy, unclean, or could not supply sufficient milk. In France, death rates as high as 75 percent resulted when children were sent away to the provinces to nurse. They often died on the journey.

If a nursing mother ran out of her own milk, the baby of a poor family would be given cow's milk, which frequently came from conditions that were far from hygienic.

PARENTAL SUPERVISION

In Reformation Germany, raising of children was considered the responsibility of both parents who prepared them for this and the spiritual world. They should not be overindulged. In the middle of the century, Veit Dietrich, pastor in Nürnberg, berated parents who were too permissive toward their children. Corvinus, a Church man from Hesse, accused noble parents of corrupting their children with materialism and lack of discipline, thereby not encouraging their spiritual and intellectual growth. Erasmus summed up the concern of the Reformists with morals and discipline when he said "human beings are not born, but formed."[14]

In Germany, as elsewhere, most of the responsibility for the child fell on the mother during the early years. Once the child of a poor family reached six or seven, however, he or she came more under the control of the father and was introduced to the working world. The son of a wealthy burgher family at this age would perhaps learn to fence and ride a horse.

One couple's letters to each other give some insight as to a child's requests to his father, a Nürnberg merchant, who traveled frequently. Some of the items he asked for were stockings of various colors, boots, purses, clothing, and spurs. His mother wrote that she was taking care of his education, and when he reached six years, he was ready to enroll in Latin school. The next year, he was taking music lessons after class each day and writing each night.

Other rules for children of the middle and upper class included neat hair, fresh, clean mouth, body and hands, orderly dress, good manners, no yawning, no scratching, no loud laughter or shouting, and no spitting. They should be obedient, and all children should pray regularly to God, not to saints.

According to Erasmus, children should be forbidden to play chess, dice, cards, and go swimming, as these games invoked "private greed." Rather, they should indulge in occupations that encouraged strong character and teamwork such as dancing, running, singing, ballgames, and exercising. In the presence of a teacher, fencing was also beneficial.

Girls learned to sew and embroider, and in England they all had daily tasks such as the handling of wool and flax and carding and spinning wool. In the upper classes, a young girl who was between childhood and marriage was almost always surrounded by women servants. Families of more limited means made sure their daughters remained under the watchful eye of a servant or relative, protecting her from any contact with immodest or wanton behavior that could cost her good name.

In poorer families, girls were taught not to "tap their feet; . . . sit alone with a man . . .; talk too much; . . . change friends too often; . . . spend more than they earned if they worked for wages . . . or . . . drink too much, gorge their food or indulge in light looks or laughter."[15]

Children were disciplined from about seven; and by the time boys were 14 and girls were 12, they had reached an age when they could marry. The Protestants considered that the moral character had been shaped by that time.

Children were especially subject to many different diseases such as measles and smallpox, which killed millions in the mid-sixteenth century.

In peasant families, children were put to work as soon as they were able to follow instructions, about age six or seven. Education for the peasantry was not an option. Girls helped out at home until they were married, or they went to work as servants. The father had full authority with approval of the Church.

MIDDLE CLASS CHILDREN

Male children of merchants and artisans mostly followed in the steps of their fathers. After the age of seven, children frequently lived with families other than their own in order to learn a trade, but increasingly their education became a matter for the school, which began at this time to take the place of the family.

In Germany, children learned about religion and prayer, cooperation with others within the family, and to rely on skill and acts rather than on words in order to get on well in life. Honesty was a key value to success, as were loyalty, obedience, and self-reliance. Well-known and successful schools such as those in Strassburg served as models for both Lutherans and Calvinists.

Girls learned about running a home and at first did not attend school unless it was a small one. Further, they needed a dowry to bring to a marriage, which had to be approved by the parents. In the German areas, geese were often included as part of the dowry of a poor girl.

When both parents worked in a middle class family, children were often sent off to boarding school where they slept in dormitories and ate in a large dining room sitting on benches at long tables. Breakfast normally consisted of bread, butter, and seasonal fruit. The midday meal comprised pottage and occasionally meat pie. On fast days, they ate bread and salted fish accompanied by vegetables such as peas or Lentils with buttermilk to drink. Salads often began the meal, and cheese and fruit ended it. Supper was not a heavy meal, offering bread, nuts, and fruit accompanied by diluted wine or ale. Grace would precede the meal, and often a lively discussion would take place as they ate. Afterwards, each boy would be given a basin of water and a new napkin with which to wash and dry his hands. During all meals, the master watched the boys closely to ascertain that their manners and comportment were correct.[16]

ENGLISH CHILDREN

In Elizabethan England, frequently children of wealthy parents were sent off to become wards of influential friends or family members who could give them a proper, well-disciplined, religious upbringing, as well as provide them with advantages that were not available within their own homes. As wards, they were usually kept busy assisting at the table where they sometimes could listen to intellectual guests conduct interesting conversation.

Boys in a wealthy or noble household might be sent away to a squire's home or a bishop's palace to learn how to become pages, perhaps to one day serve at the royal court. They were given some education in Latin, rhetoric, math, and philosophy. When about 15 years old, they learned fencing, riding, swordsmanship, and the art of war. Many would become high-ranking soldiers; the others would serve the king or enter the Church.

In almost all cases, and at all levels of society, the husband and father had the last word in family affairs.

CATHOLIC CHILDREN

Some differences occurred in the raising of Catholic children. For example, they were acutely aware of sin that required confessing. In the rituals of the Church, children were disposed to believe in miraculous events and saints. Good Catholic parents reinforced these beliefs. The sacrament of confirmation administered in early adolescence firmly anchored the child to the Church.

DIVORCE

In Protestant regions in which marriage was not a holy sacrament and divorce could be obtained, marriage courts made an effort to bring reconciliation and harmony back into the household of separated couples. When the estrangement could not be overcome, when no hope remained for reunification, a divorce was granted, and the couples were free to remarry. Incompatibility was not the only reason for divorce however. If a husband and wife were forced to live apart due to exile of one or the other, and religious persecution would follow if one followed the other, a divorce could be obtained. In one known case, an Italian wife refused to live in Calvinist Geneva where her husband went to reside, fearing persecution in Italy. Under such conditions, forced to live apart, a divorce would be granted.[17]

There were other pathways to free women from abusive husbands that included bigamy, adultery, impotence (the purpose of marriage was to have children) abandonment, and cruelty that threatened life.

WIDOWS

A middle class woman needed a dowry that would often provide help for a young man of ambition to establish his own business. This might consist of money, jewelry, household goods, or land. A contract drawn up before marriage would include a clause giving the terms of the dower rights of the bride in case of widowhood. Widows sometimes waived those rights in favor of returning to their parents' house or by remarrying.

Young widows were sometimes looked after by their families, who immediately began the search for a new husband. Margaret Dakins of Yorkshire's first husband was killed in war. She met and subsequently married Thomas Sidney with whom she had fallen in love in spite of the machinations of the family to try to marry her off to someone else whom she disliked. After three years, she was again a widow, and this same young man plied his suit once more. As with many women in this situation, she gave in after much pressure from her family.

A lower class widow had little opportunity of making a decent living unless she had been left a shop or business by her deceased husband. A woman in the upper middle class who had property needed to be protected by her family against fortune hunters. Widows needed to show piety and modesty in England if they were to avoid slanderous gossip.

FUNERALS

No church bells were rung for the dying or the dead in Saxony. As with weddings, people were invited to funerals by a horseman and a lackey going from door to door. The bier was set down in the street the day before the burial, and notice of the dead was given by the preacher from the pulpit. They were usually buried in coffins with windows over the face to be opened and shut as the mourner wished. In most places people were not buried in a church yard but in some walled ground outside the city that contained a cloister around the wall and a little chapel. The cemetery was called Gottsacker or God's acre. The wealthy reserved places under the cloister for themselves and their family. Others were interred in a field. The monuments had painted or engraved crosses. The preacher would make a short sermon, and the Lutheran witnesses would remain silent in some towns or sang a psalm in others.

If a hospital patient in England died, burial normally took place the next day. A procession of friends and relatives followed a few musicians who accompanied the body to the graveyard. For a woman, a wreath of flowers and herbs was carried in front of the coffin by a close friend, a glove placed at the center of it symbolizing virginity. Mourners often laid rosemary, bay leaves, or other evergreens on the coffin to symbolize the soul's immortality. Both Protestants and Catholics wanted a fine sermon preached for the deceased after which elaborate refreshments were served back at the house. If the bereaved were wealthy, this was sometimes followed by days of feasting and drinking. The poor also had funeral feasts, much of which was contributed by the guests. Sometimes mourners were engaged to walk in the procession, their food and clothing for the occasion being paid for by the family.

Among the chief mourners, the women covered their faces with white linen and the men with black so they had to be led by a servant to the site. Funerals were frequent, and ministers were paid for their prayers.

At the death of a prince, more ostentatious practices took place. Moryson witnessed the funeral of the Elector of Saxony as well as the ceremonies in Dresden where he died. There the body was laid out with the face exposed for two days for all to see. The body had a velvet cap decorated with an expensive jewel. To be buried with him was a gold chain around the neck, a tablet of the fellowship between the Protestant princes of the union, three rings on his fingers: a diamond, a ruby, and a turquoise; two bracelets of gold on his arms; and a gilded hammer in his right hand. His coat of armor, his rapier, spurs, and diverse banners lay nearby on display. After two days, the body was enclosed in copper and sent from Dresden to Freiburg (a day's journey), with bells ringing in all the churches along the way. He was eventually buried with great pomp in the main church of the city. The Latin inscription (rendered into modern English) read:

Has here been deposed what so ever was mortal, his soul immortal in joyous eternal happiness with God. You, mindful of human frailty, prepare thyself to follow him in the same steps of true piety, and faith in God, in which he has gone before you.

Along the route, memorial coins minted for the purpose, were scattered among the crowds.[18]

INHERITANCE

In some places as in England and France, primogeniture was strictly adhered to, whereby the first son inherited everything. In Germany, however, inheritance was more equally divided between all the children, although the first son still received the major share of not only money and estate but also of educational opportunities. Under the rule of primogeniture in England, the older boy was expected to care for his parents in their old age. If he had brothers, he was responsible for their welfare and to see they received training to become courtiers, diplomats, lawyers, or serve in the military, so they could follow distinguished careers. In fact, the younger siblings often fell subject to neglect and abuse. Too, if there were many brothers and sisters, the burden on the oldest son could become intolerable.

NOTES

1. Ozment (1983), 6.
2. Ibid., 208, n. 79.
3. See Ariès, 396–397.
4. Ozment, op. cit., 50.
5. Markham, 1.
6. Ozment, op. cit., 68.
7. Markham, xxvii, 5.
8. Ozment, op. cit, 24–25.
9. Jennifer Heisse, from Salmon, W. *The Family Dictionary* (1986).
10. Markham, xlvi, xlix, 180.
11. Ladurie, 318–331.
12. Moryson (1967), 329.
13. Seccombe, 76.
14. Ozment, op. cit., 135–136.
15. Pearson, 109–113.
16. Ibid., 179–180.
17. Bainton (1952), 260.
18. Moryson, op. cit., 337.

11

LEISURE AND THE ARTS

GAMES AND SPORTS

Throughout Europe, boys wrestled and took part in mock fights: they ran, leapt over obstacles, competed at archery, threw the javelin or stones, and engaged in tug of war, or whatever tested their strength and prowess. Games for girls and boys included blind man's bluff, hide and seek, riding hobby horses, spinning tops, hitting shuttlecocks back and forth, and leap-frog. In cold weather there were snowball fights, sledding, and especially in Holland, young people skated by tying bones to the soles of their shoes.

Wooden hoops or wheels were bowled along with sticks. Tennis and croquet originated in France at this time. Punch and Judy shows began in Italy in the sixteenth century and made their way across Europe to England as marionettes or puppets. Some children had a jack-in-the-box, the Jack often being an admiral on a stick or a Punch with a horrible face.

Peasant children, such as those who lived in the Swiss and German mountain areas, played at riding wooden horses; tossing rocks, quoits, and rings; blowing the horns of shepherds; and jumping rope. They also had toys that included puppet soldiers, dolls, balls, stilts, marbles, kites, and tops. Along with the adults, they played skittles and chess.

In sixteenth-century Scotland and elsewhere, children often made their own toys, such as paper windmills and little boats. By the time of James VI, dolls, rattles, and whistles were being imported.[1]

Curling was well established by this time in Scotland and the Netherlands. The Scottish played the game with large, smooth stones called granites, held and sent on their way by means of a handle attached to the top. The earliest known stone that was used for curling dates from

Children's Games, Pieter Brueghel the Elder, 1560. This painting depicts some 200 children engaged in various activities including many individual games. (Kunsthistorisches Museum, Wien oder KHM, Wien.)

1511. The first depictions of curling in the Netherlands are found in the mid-sixteenth century paintings by Brueghel. It is thought that early Dutch and Flemish players used lumps of frozen earth or ice with a wooden handle frozen into them.

The first book on the game of checkers, was written in 1547 by Antonio Torquemada. Although the game was probably well known from ancient times, it was more sophisticated than earlier board games.

In Scotland the rich took part in archery, hunting, hawking, and golf.[2] In 1576, the imprisoned Mary, Queen of Scots, lamented that her billiard table had been taken away. Mary may have learned to play the popular game in France, whence it was imported into England. It was played with only two balls that were hit with the end of a tool that resembled a hockey stick. The table, covered in a green cloth, had cushioned sides that were packed with pieces of felt. Some tables had pockets, others had obstacles such as hoops, pegs, or miniature military fortifications on the cloth.

FRANCE

Upper Class   The royal court and the grand nobility of France spent much time and money on entertainment. The lavish balls at the royal palaces, such as the Louvre in Paris and

Ice skating on a lake in winter, Pieter Brueghel the Younger, 1568. (Museo Nacional del Prado, Madrid.)

nearby Fontainebleau, often in costume, accompanied by sumptuous dinners, spared no expense. These Bacchanalian affairs involved drinking, eating, music, dancing, gambling, plays, and flirtations.

Tournaments were also popular but had become more pageantry than battle. Jousting was still practiced, but resulted in few fatalities although King Henri II, a participant in a joust, was fatally wounded on June 30, 1559. By the end of the century, noblemen were tilting their lances at wooden targets rather than at an armed opponent.

Other aristocratic pastimes entailed dice, cards, chess, and tennis in which the ball was hit with the palm of the hand (*Jeu de paume*). There were also bowls, fencing, hunting, and a brutal type of entertainment entailing fights to the death between animals. The royal spectators enjoyed watching lions, tigers, and bears tear each other to pieces or mastiffs pitted against bulls in mortal combat.

The common people had their own forms of entertainment. Folk drama, jugglers, and ballad singers flourished in the festivals and fairs of country and city as **Lower Classes** they had since early medieval times. There were celebrations in honor of the parish, the guilds, the lord of the manor, his wife, the worker, for births, marriages, Communion, a visit of the king or queen to the city and the numerous Church holidays such as Christmas, Easter, and saints' days.

Parisians especially loved bonfire displays that lit up the public buildings or city hall to commemorate some past event when everyone came into the streets to dance, sing and drink. On June 23, eve of the day of Saint-Jean, a tall tree was placed in the Place de Grève surrounded by a large pyre on which hung sacks full of cats. The official executioner had the privilege of erecting a grandstand around the pyre and renting the seats. At seven o'clock trumpets sounded, artillery fire resounded throughout the town, and fireworks were set off. Municipal magistrates and the provost arrived, their heads crowned with roses. Having walked three times around the pyre with a lighted torch, and if the king was present, the provost on bended knee, handed him the torch to light the pyre. The fire soon consumed the tree while the audience with great jubilation shouted and clapped drowning out the horrific and pitiful cries of the animals burned alive. Many festivities called for the torture and death of animals not unlike those humans accused of certain crimes. Similar fires took place at the same time in different quarters in the squares in front of major churches and the celebrations, accompanied by bread and much wine, continued until dawn.[3]

Bookshops and Stalls
There were nearly 400 book outlets in Paris at the end of the sixteenth century. For those who could read, diverse subjects were available such as astrology, astronomy, travel stories, works of famous Greek and Latin authors, natural events including floods, comets, supposedly miraculous happenings, crimes, politics, and battles. Michel de Montaigne was one of France's most influential writers, and his works sold well, as did the poetry of Ronsard, duBellay, and others. There was a good deal of forgery, copying of works, and black market Protestant material. A number of books and pamphlets were secretly imported from the presses in the Netherlands, but the city council kept a sharp eye out for subversive ideas.

THEATER

Mystery plays, that is, medieval religious dramas based on the Bible, continued to be performed during the Renaissance and Reformation in public squares, châteaux, upper class homes, and in some abbeys throughout Europe. Comedies, farces, ballets, and reproductions of Greek and Roman classics became more popular. In France, the upper classes sat in the boxes overlooking the galleries often paying nothing. They imperiously announced their name and went to their box. Their servants did the same.[4] Below sat or stood the commoners, workers, pages, clerks, and thieves. These people came to the theater around noon although the performance did not begin until two o'clock. They fought over seats and often turned the place into a rowdy brawl before the play began. Playwrights were careful about what they wrote: a satire on a prominent figure or the Church might delight the crowd but land the author in jail.

The nature of stage plays began to change during the Reformation. Instead of depicting stories of heroines who preferred death to losing their virginity, dramas concentrated more on the benefits of marriage and family life. The medieval passion plays, the dramatic presentation depicting the trial, suffering, and death of Jesus and the resurrection, continued to be performed at Easter, but other mystery plays dedicated to miracles, the flood, and other biblical stories that were sometimes staged by the various guilds, waned in popularity in Protestant areas.

Felix Platter's memoirs mention theatrical productions in Switzerland. In Basel, attending was free of charge, and the plays were performed in venues such as the fish and grain markets and at the university gymnasium. Their subject matter included religious themes taken from both the New and Old Testament, such as the conversion of St. Paul and Christ's Resurrection, as well as the "Ten Ages of Man" about European culture, and a play entitled "Hamanus" that propagated Lutheran beliefs. In Basel, Latin comedies by Plautus and Terence were also staged.[5]

In England, actors were regarded with suspicion by the authorities who considered them worthless. After 1572, actors had to have a license. Plays were generally put on in market squares. In 1576, the first theater was built by James Burbage. Those who could afford the best seats were shielded from the weather, but most stood in the open air. Boys played women's parts, and there were no female actors.

Elizabeth I was a patron of arts and literature and loved watching plays, masques, and other dramatic performances. She had her own company of actors, The Queen's Players, who often performed for her and her courtiers.

ENGLAND

There was much literary activity at this time with writers such as Shakespeare, John Milton, and John Bunyan. After the advent of printing in 1476, books became cheaper and reading popular among the educated.

Elizabeth I also enjoyed hawking and hunting and would hunt deer and stags with her courtiers, and when the unfortunate animal was caught, she would be invited to cut its throat. In 1575, the French Ambassador reported that she had killed "six does" with her crossbow. The queen and her courtiers would often have a picnic in the forest while hunting.

Like the rest of Europe, the Elizabethans had no concept of animal cruelty, and enjoyed a whole manner of violent animal "sports," such as bear-baiting (where dogs were trained to attack a bear chained to a post), cock-fighting, and dog-fighting.

The queen also enjoyed watching a game of tennis, especially if one of her favorite courtiers was playing. Once she even dressed up as one of her ladies so that she could secretly watch Robert Dudley compete in a shooting match, and afterward, she surprised him by revealing her identity.

Elizabeth had a love of learning and reputedly studied two or three hours a day. She read books in Latin or French and translated classic works into English. She also wrote poetry, and a few of her poems are still extant. Embroidery was a popular pastime for women, and the queen sometimes spent an evening embroidering with her maids of honor and ladies in waiting. There were also games they could play on rainy days or winter nights, among them backgammon, chess, and cards. Darts was also enjoyed by the nobility.

Christmas, an elaborate occasion in England, was celebrated with strong ale, feasting, and a carnival atmosphere. In poorer houses, games such as shoe-the-mare were played, in which a girl was chased around the house by those attempting to shoe her.[6] Some young men played a version of football with few rules. Goal posts were set far apart, and the field often included woods and streams. Injuries were common.

Holidays The holiday period extended to the twelfth night after Christmas, a time when lord, lady, servants, and workers mingled freely as equals in the same halls and took part in the same games. The poor visited the great houses and begged for ale, which was freely given.[7] A huge yule log was dragged into the house and set alight in the fireplace to ward off evil spirits, mingling its light with the many candles on the sideboards. As the log burned, family, friends, and domestics consumed quantities of yule dough, cake, and boiled wheat in milk flavored with sugar, spice, and raisins. After Christmas, dancing, masked balls, bowling, and children's games carried on the festivities. Among poor houses, plays were performed by door-to-door troupes of traveling actors and musicians.

New Year's Eve was celebrated by feasting and drinking one another's health, and New Year's Day was celebrated by an exchange of gifts in the home. In cities people went to neighbors' houses at midnight to wish them good cheer.

Other feast days with quantities of food for the wealthy were Easter, followed by May Day when flowers were gathered, queens elected from the common people, and maypoles erected bedecked with flowers. Young women gathered morning dew to apply to their faces as a charm to protect them from blight. People came out dressed in their best, performed Morris dances, and took part in pantomimes.

Other Cele-brations In the tradition of the old pagan rites, June was the month when Midsummer's Eve was celebrated. Fires were lit at midnight in the cities and on the hilltops to commemorate the passing of the sun god through the highest point of the zodiac, summer solstice; and parades, merrymaking, and pageants abounded. Pickpockets were also out in force as were the police to maintain order. Queen Elizabeth helped to temporarily relieve the unemployment problem by hiring workers to build the wagons for the parades, to construct stages and stands, to collect wood for the bonfires, and later, to clean up the streets of the city.[8]

The harvest was celebrated on September 29, Michaelmas Day, and the family who could afford it satisfied their appetites with a sumptuous dinner of roasted goose, cakes, and puddings. On the eve of November 1, All Saints (Hallowe'en), outdoor fires were kindled; and drinking and dancing went on through the night. It was believed that this was the night when witches and goblins came to do their mischief.

November 11 was Saint Martin's day when the goose was again the centerpiece of the bountiful table; and this was followed by Saint Catherine's feast, a day of rejoicing along with a good deal of cider as it coincided with the apple harvest.

The Fight between Carnival and Lent, Pieter Brueghel the Elder, 1559. The painting shows the contrast between enjoyment and drinking (the Inn, left) and of serious religious observance (church, right). Carnival is represented by the fat man on a barrel, with a pie on his head and with a pig's head on a spit. (Kunsthistorisches Museum, Wien oder KHM, Wien.)

CARNIVAL

The annual carnival in most southern cities of Europe held just before Lent was the most important of the popular festivals. Men, women, youths, and sometimes even priests, put on masks concealing their identity and cavorted around the towns. They played tricks on one another, made a lot of noise, and mocked the municipal officials and even church rituals. This was the time to forget the restraints of daily life. Floats drawn through the streets in procession often featured giants of gargantuan proportions or awe-inspiring figures such as bears, dragons, and a variety of farmyard animals. Participants enacted pantomimes on street corners or on the floats. For example, a man acting the part of Noah's wife made it clear that she, not Noah, was in charge of the ark.[9] Plays were staged suggesting the rich and powerful were incompetent fools. Magistrates were ridiculed for their decisions and lust for money. People of high position might be shown as asses. Authorities, subjects of farces, were expected to laugh at themselves, and perhaps better serve the community in the future.

Anti-Catholic incidents were common in many German-speaking cities during Carnival. Effigies of the pope, cardinals, and bishops were especially ridiculed with such things as the devil's horns and tails. Interaction between social events such as carnival and Reformation was evident in Wittenberg on December 10, 1520. That morning at the university Luther had burned the papal bull condemning him, and in the afternoon about 100 students staged a carnival. A float was prepared full of young men with mock papal bulls stuck on the end of sticks or on swords.

Accompanied by music, they boisterously passed through the streets drawing laughter from the crowds. They carried books by Luther's enemies such as Eck, gathered wood in the city, rekindled the fire where Luther had burned the papal bull, and burned the books. One dressed like the pope threw his tiara into the fire.[10]

In some carnivals men dressed as monks pulled plows through the streets; and women, imitating nuns, walked behind carrying babies. Certain towns prohibited satirizing the pope; others supported it. Mock hunts of monks, nuns, priests, and the pope delighted the citizens, sometimes ending with all trapped in a net.

MUSIC AND DANCING

Music   Music was popular in England during Elizabethan times, and songs were often accompanied by an eight-stringed lute. On formal occasions, madrigals were sung that entailed several voices and guests were invited to join in. Church and instrumental music continued to be enjoyed and after 1560, Puritans sang psalms in their homes

Peasant Dance. Pieter Brueghel the Elder, 1568. A festive scene of peasants dancing, drinking, and eating. The painting depicts a couple kissing, a young girl being pulled to join in the dancing, and children imitating the adults. (Kunsthistorisches Museum, Wien oder KHM, Wien.)

sometimes accompanied by an instrument. It was not uncommon for a servant with a good voice to sing for the family.

Many villages had their own choir and bell-ringers, and the royal court made use of high-quality choirs for the pleasure of guests or the family. Sometimes, young boys with fine voices were taken from their homes and forced into a choir.

Families liked to show off their daughters' accomplishments by having them play the virginal or harpsichord for guests. Both instruments were household treasures and would often be highly decorated with paintings. Musical instruments were also used as decorations in the home. A wealthy family might display cornets, flutes, viols, violins, recorders, and even an organ to impress company.

Dancing provided pleasure, and variations were many. The upper classes danced the slow pavan; the faster galliard, which entailed leaping into the air in time with the music; and the volta in which the woman was lifted high above the floor. Lively dances also were the coranto (or courante) and the Spanish canary.[11] Morris dancing, a type of group folk dancing, was popular with all levels of society.

Elizabethans loved music, and the queen was no exception. She played the virginals and the lute, enjoyed musical entertainment, encouraged musicians and composers, and was especially fond of dancing. She danced the difficult and demanding galliard every morning to keep herself fit. She also loved to dance with her courtiers and was fond of the volta.

Wandering musicians were looked down upon by upper class patrons; but if they were good, they might on occasion play for royalty. It was customary in taverns to demand music with the meal. The best inns had a lute, a bandore, and sometimes the virginal to soothe and entertain the guests.

In Scotland, music was becoming popular in the homes by the beginning of the sixteenth century; the harp, fiddle, lute, spinet, and various other instruments were all used domestically. Groups of musical people sprung up, especially in the towns, where both players and singers enjoyed getting together.

The Swiss, Felix Platter, studied the lute when he was eight years old. When other boys also learned to play the instrument, they formed a sort of musical circle. Although in other parts of Europe the lute was considered an instrument of the court until the seventeenth century, it was pervasive among the middle and lower-middle classes of Switzerland. Also popular at this time were the clavichord, harp, viola, Jew's harp, dulcimer, and spinet.[12]

Religious Music

Unlike some religious fanatics, Luther viewed music with high esteem. He himself was an accomplished musician and composed hymns. He further believed that music should be taught in schools as part of the training of young men entering the priesthood. He advocated that common people needed to hear the Word of God and to sing His praises in their own languages not, as before the Reformation, only in Latin as it was sung by church choirs. German pastors writing hymns based on the psalms were advised by Luther to use the most simple, common words but keeping to the meaning of the psalms as closely as possible. In Protestant churches, Luther dispensed with the choir and allocated singing to the congregation. Johann Sebastian Bach, a Lutheran, taught his students that music was an act of worship. He said all musicians should commit their talents to the Lord Jesus Christ.

ART AND THE REFORMATION

Religious art thrived throughout the middle ages, and the popes were often its patrons. Papal support continued in Catholic countries after the Reformation. Protestant countries, on the other hand, did not construct large cathedral buildings for their simplified religious activities. They denounced ecclesiastical painting and sculpture and shunned religious trappings.

David Teniers, 1633. Music in the kitchen. (Museo Nacional del Prado, Madrid.)

The Reformation initiated a new tradition that redirected artistic efforts into secular forms such as landscape and portrait painting. Religious art continued much longer in Catholic countries. Iconic images of Christ, the Virgin, the saints, and scenes from the Passion as subject matter became less frequent as biblical portrayals of contemporary life with moral overtones became preferred subjects. Some works displayed sinners accepted by Christ, in sympathy with the Protestant orientation that salvation comes only through God's grace.

The Reformation prompted a surge of iconoclasm since many Protestant sects regarded religious paintings and sculpture as idolatrous. Zwingli and Calvin took all religious images from the churches, while Luther permitted them to remain as long as the congregation was made to understand that such imagery was simply symbolic and of little significance.

Since one of the principal theological differences between Protestantism and Catholicism concerned transubstantiation (or literal transformation of the Communion wafer and wine into the body and blood of Christ); Protestant churches often selected altar piece scenes portraying the last supper, a reminder to the congregation of the purely symbolic message of the Eucharist. Catholics, wishing to stress the actual transformation of the bread and wine into the body of Christ preferred to see crucifixion scenes above the altar.

Perhaps more than Catholics, Protestants took advantage of printmaking in northern Europe to mass produce visual images of religious opponents and their beliefs in the form of caricatures that were often violent, vulgar, and defamatory.

Peasant Feast by Pieter Aertsen, 1550. (Kunsthistorisches Museum, Wien oder KHM, Wien.)

Among Protestants, portraits of reformers were in demand; and their likenesses were sometimes painted into biblical scenes. After the first years of the Reformation, however, Northern European artists concentrated less and less on religious art.

The great genre painter of his time, Pieter Brueghel of Flanders, was employed by both Catholic and Protestant patrons. He devoted much of his paintings to landscape and to sixteenth-century peasant life in Flanders. His *Wedding Feast*, depicting a peasant wedding dinner held in a barn, does not refer in any way to events of religious, historical, or classical import. Brueghel's work gave impetus to many future northern landscape artists who painted in a similar genre.

In Catholic Italy, the painting of the Last Judgment by Michelangelo in the Sistine Chapel came under attack during the Counter-Reformation for nudity, for a depiction of a clean-shaven Christ standing, and for including the pagan figure of Charon.

THE COUNTER-REFORMATION AND ART

Protestants, in recognizing that the division between sacred and secular was artificial, felt they could approach God directly without the use of intermediaries; Catholics, on the other hand, maintained the tradition of separation, seeing a need for intermediaries. In so doing, they showed reverence to images. The art produced at this time by each side focused on such differences, especially in the case of artists in Catholic countries who were forced by the Church to adhere to the medieval tradition of turning out only paintings with religious themes. Artists in Protestant countries, by contrast, generally painted ordinary people. Subject matter thus provided the main distinction between Reformation and Counter-Reformation art.

At the time, portrait painting became popular in northern Europe; and Protestant works showed more realism. In the south, during the Counter-Reformation, artists were still bound to the glorification of Catholic traditions, graphically portraying immaculate-looking saints undergoing martyrdom or Christ and the Virgin Mary.

To encourage piety, decrees emanating from the Council of Trent demanded that art provide an accurate account of a biblical story or the life of a saint. In 1563, the Council instructed that paintings should not include anything profane or lustful and could not be placed in churches unless approved by the bishop.

The reforms resulting from the Council set the tone for the Counter Reformation, and pictures of Christ were now promoted that only showed Mary on bended knee before her child. She no longer was permitted to be shown swooning at the foot of the cross; in scenes of the last judgment she had to be portrayed sternly sitting beside Christ. There was no room for artistic imagination.

The Venetian artist Paolo Veronese was summoned by the Inquisition to explain why his Last Supper, a huge canvas designated for the refectory of a monastery, contained, according to the inquisitors, "buffoons, drunken Germans, dwarfs and other such scurrilities" as well as extravagant costumes and settings. Veronese was ordered to change his painting within three months. He only changed the title to *The Feast in the House of Levi*, still an event from the Gospels but less central to doctrine, and the matter was closed.

As the Counter-Reformation progressed in strength, the Catholic Church grew more confident; and Rome again asserted its universality in nations around the world. The Jesuits spread the "true" faith sending missionaries to Asia, the New World, and Africa and made use of the arts to spread their message, all of which had a profound impact.

In producing secular art, the Reformation artists glorified God by portraying the natural beauty of His creation. Catholics of the Counter-Reformation did not share this view, believing that art must have a didactic religious content.

NOTES

1. Warrack, 131.
2. Op. cit., 125.
3. Erlanger, 202 ff.
4. Op. cit., 209.

5. Ladurie, 93–101 for plays performed in Basel at this time.
6. Pearson, 550.
7. Op. cit., 546–548.
8. Op. cit., 536.
9. Watts, 175.
10. Scribner, 72.
11. Pearson, 524.
12. Ladurie, 82–83

12

CLOTHING AND FASHION

Wherever the Reformation became entrenched, fashions changed, often reflecting the Protestant ethic with less flamboyant styles than those worn in the Renaissance. At the same time, while the Catholics stressed imagery and ceremony, the Protestant view was that faith should be expressed privately with more emphasis on the spiritual than the material.[1]

Class differences were primarily shown by the style and quality of fabric, and the influx into the towns of a large variety of people from other lands and different levels of society permitted the citizenry to evaluate and judge one another's relative wealth and status as reflected in their dress.[2]

Poor people throughout Europe wore clothes of coarse cloth, and this did not change much during the century. But fashion for those who were better off was very diverse. The dramatist, Thomas Dekker, reflected on the clothes worn by friends:

> 'his Codpeece is in Denmarke, the collar, his Duble
> and the belly in France, the wing and narrow sleeve
> in Italy: the short waste hangs over a Dutch Botchers
> stall in Utrich: his huge Sloppes speakes Spanish:
> Polonia give him the Bootes.'[3]

SPAIN

In the middle of the sixteenth century, many western European countries, both Protestant and Catholic, adopted the styles of the Spanish nobility. The cut of the clothes and their rigid and formal elegance, along with perfect distinction of line caught the attention of everyone interested in fastidious dressing. Red, green, and yellow were popular colors, although the symbol of the elegance of Spain was always black. Italy and France, in particular, took on the predilection for black.

Women   Spaniards believed woman was the instrument for seduction, and that besides her face, the principal symbols of temptation and sin were the signals of her fertility, her hips and breasts. These were kept well covered, although the face remained exposed. Skirts fell right to the ground and shoes, made of wood or cork with high soles, were worn, so the skirts would not drag in the dirt.

Women's clothes included hooped supports under the skirts, a style that was not abandoned until the middle of the seventeenth century, long after the rest of Europe had ceased to wear them. With these farthingales (or *guardinfantes*), the wealthy wore tight-fitting bodices combined with ballooned sleeves with decorated cuffs. Near the end of the century, the neck ruff was fashionable and continued to be worn even after 1623 when Felipe IV banned them in his sumptuary laws.

Gloves, crucifixes, and jewelry were much in evidence, and the fan took special importance being used not only to keep cool but also in flirting where certain movements sent a message, especially to potential lovers. Lace handkerchiefs now came into their own. Some kind of cloth hidden in a pocket had been used for a long time for blowing the nose or wiping away perspiration; but in the sixteenth century, it became an open accessory, attached to the clothing or carried in the hand. By the end of the century, every lady and gentleman carried one. Mantillas were used by all classes and loose outer cloaks sometimes covered the body from head to foot so as to make the wearer feel and seem anonymous. Hair was drawn back severely and coiled at the nape of the neck.

Men   Men wore tightly fitting doublets that emphasized the slimness of the waist as the century progressed, neck ruffs became higher and higher, holding the head up high. Short pantaloons and socks were sometimes stuffed or quilted, worn along with large, prominent codpieces.[4]

Women of the lower classes wore loose clothing that enabled them to move freely, while the men generally dressed in brown shirts and knee-length woolen trousers. As in the rest of Europe, children wore similar clothes to the adults.

ENGLAND AND SCOTLAND

Repeated sumptuary legislation attempted to set out what should or should not be worn by each level of society. Clothes were to be used to indicate the wearer's social status and to provide a visual boundary marker via the value of the material worn and the amount used to make

Alonso Sanchez Coello. The Infantas Isabel Clara Eugenia and Catalina Micaela, the young daughters of Felipe II and Isabelle Valois. This painting illustrates the practice of dressing children in the same manner as adults. Here, the girls wear jewelery and their dresses, like those of grown women, show tight bodices and sleeves with ruffs and hooped supports under the skirts. (Musco Nacional del Prado, Madrid.)

the garments. The laws were unenforceable and mostly ignored. The legislation did not affect the poor, as they could not afford expensive materials to begin with.[5] During the Elizabethan period, the queen herself had a wardrobe of some 3,000 dresses, many of which were trimmed with expensive lace, fur, embroidery; and the wealthy aristocracy, following suit, clad themselves richly, demanding every kind of luxury and excess.

Fashion played an important role for the wealthy who alone could afford high quality wool, silk, cotton, and richly embroi- **Upper** dered materials. Dyes were mainly vegetable based, such as **Classes** woad for blue and walnut for brown, and were fixed with a chemical known as a mordant. The most expensive dyes were red and black, the latter very costly.

Upper Class Men

Men wore a vest cut short at the waist, the edges laced with strips of leather or ribbon, showing a shirt both above and below. Germany and Switzerland had much influence on these styles that frequently had slashed and puffed sleeves, which in time, grew very large and elaborate, some outfits even equipped with interchangeable sleeves, each pair attached with lacing.

The style adopted by Henry VIII included long, fitted, silk stockings, shoes with square toes, and an elaborately stitched tunic held at the waist by a belt. The tunic was usually open in front, showing off decorative ruffles on the front of the shirt and at the wrists. On the ruffles were black embroidery combined with gold and red. An embroidered and jeweled codpiece was worn, as was a dagger that was normally attached at the waist. The king's handkerchiefs were made of Dutch linen or lawn with Venetian gold fringes around the edges. They were embroidered in red or white silk.

Men and women wore heavy jeweled necklaces, chains, pendants, jeweled buttons, and rings on both hands, especially on the thumbs. All carried embroidered and perfumed gloves.

In the 1550s, it became fashionable for men to have short hair, a clipped beard (sometimes terminating in two points), and a mustache. On the head a velvet beret was worn often with a feather or a felt cap ornamented with jewels.

Once Felipe II of Spain married Mary Tudor, Spanish influence again began to be seen in England; and men's hats in black velvet had narrow brims, trimmed with silk, wool, lace, plumes, or chains of gold. Short capes with stand-up collars had a notch where the collar joined the front.

By 1558, when Elizabeth came to the throne, Spanish influence was still more entrenched with the slashed and embroidered peasecod bellied doublet with a long, pointed projecting front. A small, detachable collar, called the partlet, was worn by both sexes.

Venetian-style men's breeches were now full at the top, narrowing at the knee, while French breeches were tight with padded trunk hose. The latter were puffed, covering the thighs, and often made into one garment joined to the stockings. These were seen also in Germany and had pockets in the lining. Stockings, usually made of wool or silk that joined the breeches at the knees were known as netherstocks, while the breeches themselves were upperstocks. Sometimes they were embroidered in gold and silver thread at the ankles. Garters made of ribbons were tied just below the knees. Capes were worn for traveling and the short, Spanish version, made of perfumed leather was the most popular.

Many Englishmen wore swords, rapiers, or daggers sheathed in velvet or embroidered linen; but according to Moryson, this encouraged duels. In 1580, a law was passed restricting the length of these weapons.[6]

Women's cloaks had similar collars to men's and were worn over double skirts. Cloaks and capes were often of fur, but the kind of fur was dictated by rank and wealth. Perfume enhanced not only gloves but also shoes and fans of which the most popular were leather mounted on carved ivory.

Hoods were smaller, and dresses became much more simple with higher necks and (usually white) collars made of silk or linen, sometimes wired at the edge. Hair also was simpler and although puffed in front, was parted in the middle and knotted in the back. A jeweled girdle was worn with a mirror or rosary at the end, and bouquets of flowers often tucked into the bodice at the neck. Underneath, a brocaded or embroidered skirt of velvet was visible as the top skirt of contrasting color flared open.

It is known that Anne Boleyn wore a nightgown of black satin trimmed with velvet of the same color. At this time, men and women both began to wear velvet nightcaps.

During the Elizabethan period, both a fan-shaped collar or a pleated and wired Spanish ruff accompanied copious amounts of jewelry. False sleeves as well as separate ones were laced to the armhole. Noble English-women wore bodices with a square, low neck and sleeves that had wide cuffs made of colored velvet, fur, or net. At times, the bodice opened over a stomacher, a decorated triangular-shaped panel that could be laced up. Ruffles from the chemise were visible at the wrists. A steel corset with hinges on one side and hooks on the other was covered with velvet, often a design was perforated into it. Another corset of buckram, laced tightly, went underneath.

On their heads women wore elaborate diamond-shaped headdresses, later followed by what was known as the French hood, which left the hair on the forehead uncovered. A bonnet made of velvet or satin was put over a small embroidered cap of white linen or gold net. Women's hats often had a plume and bands or necklaces around the crown. Caps made of lawn were worn close to the head. The "Mary Stuart" cap with a dip over the forehead had a frame and was made of cambric and lace.

Up to about 1626, pins to hold clothes together were imported from France (after that, they began to be made in England). Since at first the pin was fairly expensive and considered a luxury, the term "'pin money'" was introduced for the money given to the women by their husbands expressly for this purpose.

The preferred color of hair was red (like Elizabeth's). Wigs, as well as false hairpieces, were decorated with jewels, glass, or feathers. Powder and rouge were applied and perfume hung from the waist in small silver or gold pomanders. A fan and mirror were likewise transported. All accessories were perfumed and clothes were fumigated with herbal scents, as in fact few people took baths. The odor, caused by rotting teeth, was disguised by breath fresheners.

Alexander Hay Ritchie. Engraving, c. 1852. Mary, Queen of Scots. (Library of Congress.)

The queen introduced leather and velvet shoes with high heels and cork soles. They were often stamped with a design or embroidered. Red hose were frequently worn with embroidered red or blue shoes and had lace and jewels; they were tied with shoe roses, and red heels were popular. Chopines or clogs were used in England, as they were on the continent; and slippers with cork soles were worn over the shoes of both men and women when outside. Sometimes the chopines had stilts on them as high as seven inches. It is said that Elizabeth was the first woman in England to wear silk stockings, and following suit, women then began wearing hand-knitted silk stockings usually decorated with gold, silver, and colored designs.

In 1589, an Englishman, William Lee, invented the first knitting machine, but he was ignored in England, so he went to France where he stayed and worked until the end of his life. After Henri III was assassinated, Lee's workers returned to England with the machine to make stockings.[7]

After Elizabeth's death, people began wearing lighter colors and richer materials. Fynes Moryson lamented although the materials were fine, there was no sense of style.[8]

For the lower classes, clothes had to be hard-wearing and practical. Men often wore a leather jerkin or a tunic that was easier to work in than the doublet. On their legs **Lower Classes** were woolen hose and sometimes shorts under the breeches. Woolen caps were worn on Sundays. For women, smocks of linen or wool usually had nothing underneath; a two-piece dress of coarse, rough brown wool was put over the smock, detachable laces held the sleeves in place. An apron and sometimes a linen cap called a coif was used for work.

After the Reformation, very plain clothing without any of the trimmings was favored by extremists who tended to wear **Puritans** sober colors of gray, black, and white with green woolen stockings.

Men's jackets were plain but sometimes the sleeves were of dark red. Breeches were either full and tight at the knee **Puritan Men** or cut straight with a simple frill or ruffle at the end. No lace edges were used for the cuffs or the collar, which was tied with plain strings attached to a neckband, fastening in the back. This style of collar was eventually used by the professional class.

Puritan men tended to cut their hair fairly short, scorning the long curls of the aristocrats; their moustaches were well trimmed.

Shoes had square toes and boots, made of soft leather, without laces at the top. Hats with broad brims and high crowns were used by both men and women, and men's were frequently adorned by a ribbon and a buckle.

Women wore sheer linen caps covering the hair, wide collars, and cuffs. There was no lace edging at all. Those who **Puritan** were less zealous tended to wear a full skirt that, hooked up, **Women** showed a petticoat that was sometimes quilted and of a contrasting color. These women also wore a cap, collar, and cuffs that were often embroidered.

A large beaver or felt hat was worn over a cap in summer and over a black hood in winter. Cloaks were ample, and muffs were used to keep the hands warm. Shoes for women had square toes and small shoe roses. Not much in the way of ribbons were used, and most materials were in subdued tones.[9]

FRANCE

Clothing was somewhat different across France, depending on the region. A bourgeois in Roussillon, for example, might wear a hat and cloak embellished with silver, a gray coat with green sleeves, and blue breeches. His wife would have a dress of blue, with silver and green around the edges. Her sleeves and cape could be crimson with silver or gold relief, and her hat could be the color of gold. Another woman from elsewhere might be seen wearing a white, striped bonnet, a shawl, and a black cape with perhaps some silver or gold embellishments. She might also be wearing a white apron. Her shoes would be high and adorned with alternating white and gold zigzags.

Men   A priest could be seen in a white silver-embossed surplice over a black garment and crimson stockings with silver relief.[10] When the Abbot Locatelli went to Lyon in the early seventeenth century dressed in the Italian style that included a 'sugar loaf' hat and colored hose, he was greatly mocked, especially by the children, and hastily changed to the French style of black stockings, a shorter cassock, narrow shoes with buckles, and a narrow-brimmed hat. In these clothes he did no't feel like a priest any more, but rather, thought he looked like a scholar or doctor.[11]

Spanish influence was still apparent, especially in the style of short boots, which came in light colors and were made of soft leather. The tops were turned down, and spurs were attached for both indoors and out. The high red heels and red soles continued to be fashionable. Hooks and eyes replaced ribbons for fastenings, and breeches were fairly full and tied with ribbons below the knee.

The cravat, which was popular after 1636, began as a piece of fine white material with lace on the ends. At that time it was folded and tied loosely around the neck. From this period on, a 'well-dressed' man always used a cravat, scarf, or tie.

Interested in investing in French industry, Henri IV encouraged factories in Lyon to produce brocades, velvets, and silk and those in Tours to provide heavy taffeta for the markets. Other beautiful materials were imported from Italy and Spain, and from the Far East came perfumes. When Henri died in 1610, the French middle class began, for the first time, to show an interest in fashion.[12]

Under Louis XIII, France became a major influence in the world of *haute-couture*. In 1625, Richelieu banned the importation of certain luxury clothing goods such as silver and gold material, and in 1633, another ban was passed against gold, silver, or embroidered braid for decoration. In short, clothes were now made from fabric produced in France and more simplicity of design was stressed as well as more neutral colors. At this time trimming of lace and ribbon became popular.

Women wore a chemise, a corset, and several skirts or petti-
coats over a hoop that was much smaller than the farthingale.   **Women**
On top of all this went an outer skirt that was looped up or
sometimes drawn up at the sides along with a low necked bodice with a
moderate ruff or collar and pale colored sleeves of satin or similar
material. Finally, a lightweight outer coat, open at the front with slashed
sleeves, displayed the contrasting colors worn underneath. In winter,
capes were worn, but once gowns began to be lined with heavier fabric,
the capes were not always necessary.

When the hoop disappeared, the corset became looser. High-waisted
bodices began to have wide collars and cuffs and sometimes were laced
at the back. Aprons trimmed with lace were used on occasion.

From Austria came a headdress with a fringe across the forehead, the
sides of the hair cut short with ringlets hanging over the ears, the rest of
the hair knotted at the back. Stylish aristocratic women went bare-
headed outside, but bourgeois women wore veils, hoods, or hats similar
to the men's with wide brims and plumes.

Women's long, narrow square-toed shoes were often adorned with
large shoe roses with jewels in the center.[13] Shoes were made of satin or
leather from Morocco and worn with pink stockings. Slippers had flaps
in front and red velvet patterns on them. Soles were thick and made of
cork. Long gloves and muffs of fur and perfumed leather gauntlets were
popular. Perfume was now available in liquid form, cosmetics were freely
applied, and the fan was used by both men and women.

As France became established as a leader of fashion, the doublet
evolved into the vest, the jerkin into a jacket, and the cloak became today's
overcoat.

HOLY ROMAN EMPIRE

In the first half of the sixteenth century, Germans tended to use slashing
in their clothes. This style was begun by Swiss soldiers in the late fifteenth
century when they repaired their uniforms with strips of material from
tents, banners, etc. left behind by the enemy. Slashing and puffing was
very popular with the Germans, and the style spread to the rest of Europe
especially between 1520 and 1535. Clothing of all kinds, including gloves,
shoes, and hose, were made in this fashion using puffs of variously
colored fabrics.

Men elected to have a broad, square look and wore large hats
over a cap, their hair in waves or ringlets. Hats were often made   **Men**
of felt, and sometimes on holidays, they were adorned with feathers. Brims were slashed and frequently a string held the hat in place.
Shoes were wide with square toes, swords, and daggers in elaborately
decorated cases hung from the belt.

The Germans began weaving linens and cottons as well as gauze and fine muslins. At this time, too, heavy, rich materials in wool and brocade were used for tunics and robes.[14]

Women

Women had high, tight waistlines, narrow shoulders, with extra fullness over the stomach achieved by aprons with materials that often hung in heavy folds. The petticoat was of a different color and material and had embroidered bands under which several linen underskirts were worn. A shirt went underneath, next to the skin.

For formal outerwear, the colors were usually black and white. Veils were worn as were white collars and hairnets of satin. Hair was drawn tightly away from the face and concealed by a cap or embroidered hats that were decorated by ostrich feathers or jewelry. Hats were frequently made of fur and were pointed, square or flat. No cosmetics or perfume were used at this time. Accessories included gold and silver brooches and buckles, and a small dagger was often carried along with an ornate bag hanging from the sash. Pearls and mother of pearl were very popular; rings and heavy gold necklaces were worn by both sexes.

Before 1550, dresses had high waistlines and rounder shoulders, seen in portraits and paintings by such artists as Holbein, Dürer, and Brueghel. Later waistlines became longer, and high puffs appeared at the shoulders. Wool was greatly utilized, skirts tended to be long (the overskirt reaching to the ground), and women of all classes drew them up at the sides if they needed to.

Hair was generally kept up and covered much of the time, although young women wore their hair down in ringlets or braids. Upper class German women followed the latest fashions; and although the basic model of dress was similar to the style worn by the lower class women, the materials were of fine, high-quality wool, brocade, velvet, and silk that was additionally used for accents. Sleeves, sometimes laced, were again fairly tight from elbow to wrist and had several puffs on the upper part. Colors were varied and included red and black (the latter especially for aristocracy and nobles). Gold and black embroidery was popular and jewelry included gold chains, pearls, rings with precious stones. Earrings were not popular in Germany.

Many plumes decorated their hats, but aprons were not regularly worn unless they were embroidered and used for decoration.

Hats were of various shapes and included flat ones with large brims made of straw, wool, or velvet decorated variously with plumes, jewelry, and pleated ribbons. Belts were of leather, cord, or cloth and had keys, a purse, or a knife (for eating) attached to them. They were occasionally decorated. Lined woolen cloaks, with or without a hood, were worn.

Shoes were of leather with flat or low heels. They were sometimes slashed and of black or some other solid color and worn with colored or striped hose made of cotton or wool with patterns on them.

A German noble might be seen in a red hat decorated
with a white feather, a striped jacket with slit upper sleeves **Upper Class**
in orange with gold embossing, and white with silver
decoration. The lower part of the sleeves might be crimson light and dark
striped, with silver relief, and his breeches also crimson with silver on
them. The stockings would be orange and white stripes, trimmed with
gray fur. His wife might wear a red cap, a neckband of orange with gold
embossing, a dress of red and silver with black edges, and a shawl of
white and silver. Her gloves would be white, and the laces of the bodice
and the purse would be grayish green.[15]

For the lower middle class, bodices sometimes had
high necks with a mandarin type of collar as in a doublet. **Middle Class**
Sleeves regularly had slashes and were fitted from elbow
to the wrist. Materials were probably finer than those used by the lower
class, including low quality brocades, velveteens in deep green, dark blue,
or plum colors. The aprons for these women were more decorative than
utilitarian. Materials of all colors were of wool, brocade, and velvet with
silk or satin decoration. Necklines were embroidered or smocked, and
slashing and puffing were used. Gold chains, strings of pearls, and fine
slashed leather gloves accompanied a cloak.

Lower class German women wore simple clothing of
sturdy and durable material such as rough wool, which **Lower Class**
was often old and worn as they lived and worked in it.
Normally the dress consisted of a bodice with square or round neck.
Sleeves tended to fit from the elbow to the wrist, and skirts frequently
hung in several layers. An embroidered or smocked apron was normally
worn over the skirt.

NETHERLANDS

The same clothes were worn as long as possible by many people in the working class, after which they were turned into rags **Men**
or mops for scrubbing the floors. Ragmen collected used clothing
and sold it to the very poor. There was always the danger of plague-
carrying fleas in the lining of these garments if the person had died of that
disease; but there were many poor and handicapped people in need of
clothes.

The shirts men used for work was also slept in. When they awoke in the
morning, they slipped into stretch stockings that pulled up to just above
the knee and fastened them with a garter. They shaved with a straight
razor and without lather. The shirt was tucked between their legs in the
front and the back, and the pants pulled up over the top. Pants were short,
reaching down to the stockings and bulged out on all sides giving a
balloon effect. They came in several varieties. There were the simple,

working man's pants, fancy, puffed pants for the middle class man, and the so-called plunder pants that were often brightly colored and had slits in them. No under garments were worn, but a codpiece was attached to make room for the male organ so that the wearer looked manly. A doublet had the pants tied to it with strings. A ruffled collar, tied in front by ribbons, was added that showed above the doublet.

Men did not usually go into the streets wearing only the doublet; instead, either a jerkin was worn over it or a coat with long sleeves and holes for the elbows through which, for more flexibility, the entire arms could be extended.

Shoes were fastened on with leather shoelaces and were completely flat without supports under the heels. A slip-on served as an overshoe to traverse the muddy streets. Wooden shoes were generally worn in winter. When weather permitted, country people usually went around barefoot.

Berets came with or without ear flaps, but on the streets many different kinds of hats could be seen. Poor people sometimes wore a stocking on their heads. A fine suit of clothes could cost about 10 guilders; but a worker earned only about one-third of a guilder per day. As people liked to call attention to themselves, some would wear a spoon or comb on their hats, or a badge representing, for instance, a pilgrimage, such as the scallop shell of Saint James. Some badges had pornographic symbols on them.

Peasants wore similar but more old-fashioned clothes. The doublet came with or without sleeves. A pair of stockings, some with leather for the foot, stretching to the waist, took the place of pants, and the shirt again was tucked between the legs and covered by an overgarment. There were few or no pockets, so a belt was worn with hooks to hang things on. Knives were carried behind; their dimensions were set by the village or city council. Young boys made their own daggers out of wood, and these could be of any length. A sword, worn on the left side, was almost mandatory for going out at night into the unlit streets.

Women
Women also slept in a long nightshirt with the head covered; and the same shirt was used as an undergarment during the day. Stockings were fastened by garters; and an under bodice, closed with a lace in front, was separate from the skirt. From around the neck a scarf hung down to the waist where it was tucked under the bodice. Decorative colored sleeves were then pulled up over the sleeves of the shirt and pinned to the straps of the under bodice. Hair was generally braided and a cap worn over it. Sometimes a hat was worn on top of the hood of a cloak made from worsted cloth. Some had a peak extending over the forehead.

Slippers were worn in the house, but a leather buckled shoe was used out of doors. Party shoes could be of velvet and have embroidered slits.

An upper class woman generally wore a black head-
dress with gold trim and a gold necklace. Her upper **Upper Class**
garment was crimson and silver with blue-gray edges **Women**
and gray fur might be found along the bottom and lining
the armholes. A white veil would have had a lot of gold relief-work on it.

Jewelry included fancy hook fasteners for cloaks; spiral rings often had
proverbs engraved on them and were worn on the third finger of the left
hand (called the gold finger). An engagement ring usually had two
clasped hands on it.

Children looked like small adults, dressed in the same manner as their parents. A boy might wear flat shoes and doublet **Children**
made of leather. When outside, he wore a jacket or coat with
a full skirt to it. A girl wore a kerchief on her head (except on Sundays
or holidays when she wore a cap), and a long nightshirt for underwear
during the day.

CHANGES IN THE MID-SEVENTEENTH CENTURY

Throughout Europe, men's jackets became shorter, and shirts bloused
beneath them as well as the sleeves below those of the jacket. A camisole
was worn underneath to keep out the cold. A coat, buttoned and reaching
the knees, had shorter sleeves. Heads were shaved to accommodate the
full, long wig; and collars grew smaller. From Holland came the tubular
breeches, and often lace ruffles were worn just below the knees. Later,
ornamented petticoat breeches of various styles were used; but after the
1570s, these only survived in the livery of footmen.[16]

Later in this period, small jeweled buckles appeared on the square-toed
shoes. As boots went out of fashion, jeweled buckles grew larger. Men's
clothing became more and more elegant and included sashes with fringes,
lace, and tassels. Handkerchiefs were draped from shirt pockets. Snuff-
boxes and ornamented walking sticks were carried as well as muffs. Cra-
vats had strings of lace tied under the chin.

Women's clothes were gradually changing, too. The bodice, worn over
a corset, was getting tighter, and the low neck decorated with a deep falling collar was introduced by Anne of Austria. Collars and cuffs had
embroidery or lace edgings. Reaching the floor, full skirts were worn over
bell-shaped hoops, and they frequently opened in front to reveal other
skirts of different colors. They were often looped toward the back. Accessories also became more flamboyant and included multicolored ribbons,
striped and hand-painted fabrics, much lace, especially on the sleeves,
and even trains, which were carried over the left arm (except in the presence of royalty when they were left to trail on the floor).

Feminine hairstyles had the sides cut short, reaching the shoulders in ringlets, and short, wired curls called "heartbreakers" over the forehead. The rest of the hair was knotted at the back.

Shoes made of brocade, satin, and soft leather were pointed and had high heels. Buckles were jeweled and rosettes continued to ornament them. White or pale-colored gloves were elbow length; and fans made entirely of lace were in vogue along with fringed parasols, pearl necklaces, and other jewelry covered with diamonds and other stones. Artificial jewelry and the abundant use of extravagant buttons also became very popular.[17]

NOTES

1. Richardson, 15.
2. Turner-Wilcox, 118, ff.
3. Braudel, (1979), 321.
4. Anderson. 169–182.
5. Richardson, 111. (Sweetinburgh, Sheila "'Clothing the Naked in Late Medieval East Kent.'"
6. Pearson, 576.
7. Turner-Wilcox, 120–134.
8. Pearson, loc. cit.
9. Turner-Wilcox, 158–159.
10. Weiditz, 52.
11. Braudel loc. cit.
12. Turner-Wilcox, 138.
13. Ibid., 145.
14. Ibid., 77–78.
15. Weiditz, 55.
16. Turner-Wilcox, 168.
17. Ibid., 162–64 for a fuller treatment.

13

THE MILITARY

MERCENARIES

European armies were normally manned by two classes: the aristocracy who bought their officers' commissions and the enlisted men who came from the unemployed and poor sections of society who joined the army in return for food, a little money, and most important of all, the opportunity to plunder.

There were also men from the middle class, and even the petty nobility, who as the second, third, or fourth child in the family had no chance of inheritance and joined the army to seek their fortunes.

Throughout the early modern period mercenaries formed a significant part of any European military force. Professional armies needed to be equipped and paid full time during peace or war and hence were expensive to maintain. Mercenaries, on the other hand, could be disbanded after a war. Battle between nations could turn out to be one between two different groups of soldiers of fortune.

When countries or states went to war, mercenaries were recruited by a captain who received funds to outfit a company and find conscripts from town, country, and sometimes even prisons, usually landless young men with no established trade. In the main, a soldier had to supply himself with clothes, arms, and food. These things could be obtained by pillaging or from military entrepreneurs for a price.

Commissions were a kind of subsidy for the officers who were naturally hostile to opportunities for military advancement offered to the lower classes. Their pay was not great, but they benefited often by paying

Halberdier on horseback. Engraving by Barthel Beham, 1500–1540. (Library of Congress.)

their men as little as possible and by collecting the pay of the dead or of deserters for their own pockets. Officers could sometimes extract ransoms for captives and keep the money for themselves. Many impecunious, younger sons of the nobility, unable to buy commissions, enlisted as simple men-at-arms or infantry men with the hope of making their fortunes; although the richest ransoms and best plunder went to the officers.

Armies made up of mercenary companies had their own specializations: eastern Europeans were used as light horse; Scots and Gascons were often employed in the infantry; pike companies were the national industry of the Swiss; and from the German states came both Landsknechts and cavalry pistoleers. Patriotism was not a consideration for most men unless they were fighting for their own town.

The quintessential fighting men of Europe belonged to Spain, which is thought to have been the first modern European country to have a standing army in the sixteenth century. The successful tercio, a large infantry regiment, contained pikes, some sword-and-buckler men (at least earlier in the century), and light firearms. Spain recruited these men and kept them prepared through part-time military training. After fighting in the campaigns in Italy and the Netherlands, they became a formidable enemy, confident and experienced, and with a high esprit de corps.

It was always a problem for governments to raise money and to get it to where it was needed in order to pay the troops. When pay was irregular, discipline became lax, and mercenaries of all nationalities would desert when it fell too far in arrears. Frustration about money and the wretched circumstances under which they conducted long sieges, could lead to the worst repercussions, as in the sack of Antwerp in 1576 by out-of-control soldiers. When the army disbanded, the countryside was flooded with unemployed, often socially maladjusted armed men. Between the French civil wars of religion, brigandage was rampant.

Among the best paid mercenary soldiers were the Landsknects, primarily of German origin, from all parts of the empire. These soldiers of fortune were recruited at public fairs, in inns and taverns, or in a village square where the recruiting officer offered them a contract to fight for the duration of a particular war in progress. Often, the new conscript had no idea who he would fight for or where, but promises of pay and booty were strong inducements to sign up. Mercenary troops fought in all the major engagements in Europe during the sixteenth century and up to and beyond the Thirty Years' War. At times they fought against the Turks when the latter made incursions into the frontier lands separating the Holy Roman and Turkish Empires.

Landsknects and Swiss Pike Men

The regiments were flexible and could vary in size from several hundred to a force of thousands depending on the campaign and the financier, money was the crucial factor. The lord who had the most resources could recruit the most soldiers. They wended their way across the countryside walking, riding, or traveling in carts helping themselves to whatever they wanted when en route to their destinations.

Maximilian I gave the Landsknechts the privilege to wear whatever colors and clothing they desired. This translated into a colorful force of troops, garishly dressed, with large feathered hats.

The development of the Swiss pike square ended the dominance of the mounted knight. Armed with 18-foot pikes, aligned in a square formation, disciplined pike men could bring a cavalry charge to a quick end. For a time, they were considered essential to a sixteenth-century army.

Ensign, Drummer, and Piper. Engraving by Hans Sebald Beham, 1543. (Library of Congress.)

Such regiments came from the Swiss cantons making up the bulk of the French army's infantry as well as those of the Italian city states. When they were not on good terms with the Swiss, the kings of France used the Landsknects as did other countries. Raised from coreligionists in Germany, the Landsknechts formed a large component of the Huguenot armies; but the proven battlefield capabilities of the Swiss with the pike made them the most sought-after mercenary troops in Europe.

As technology improved, and firearms and artillery became more efficient; however, the Swiss pike men lost their advantage in battle.

A large proportion of Scots, fleeing from the law or seeking fame and fortune, earned a living as soldiers in the service of every **Scots** dynasty in western Europe during the sixteenth and seventeenth centuries, and especially during the Thirty Years' War of 1618–1648. In addition, the armies of France, Holland, and Sweden all benefited from their many outstanding commanders who came, sometimes accompanied by complete regiments that served with distinction.

The Scottish mercenaries' weapon of choice was the six-foot-long two-handed sword known as the Slaughter Sword, which proved to be more than a match for any adversary.

Families or clans, living along the border of Scotland and England known as Reivers, raided both sides of the marches with **Reivers**[1] impartiality. They came from every social class; they were guerillas, rustlers, and fighters whose exploits were legendary for their violence and destruction. Their lawlessness was fostered by a tribal system, rather than English versus Scots, and neither government was able to control them.

After centuries of feuding and attacking, they had evolved into fine soldiers and expert riders, taking their swift horses into skirmishes or battle. The horses, in fact, were descendants of the Frisian horses brought to Britain by the Romans. These shaggy animals developed into hardy ponies, called hobbys, who needed little attention, survived by eating anything, and who were equipped with amazing stamina. In addition they were very sure-footed and could manage well in the difficult, boggy terrain around the border.

The Reivers served as mercenaries in both the English and the Scottish armies, sometimes forced to do so under threat of death to their families. Thus, although hated in times of peace, their services were avidly sought in war. In 1540, the Border Horse regiment was recruited by the English under Henry VIII, who considered them to be the best light cavalry in all of Europe.

Their behavior, however, left much to be desired. Often they robbed and looted, claiming to be Scottish or English as it suited them. Frequently, they refused to obey orders, and no one really knew how trustworthy they were. There is a story that during at least one battle, it was seen that the Scottish and English Reivers only pretended to fight one another, but were ready to change sides to ascertain they ended up on the winning side.

Their word reflected their honor; however, and the act of spitting and shaking hands meant any agreement would not lightly be broken.

Reivers usually wore light armor or a 'jack,' a quilted leather coat with plates of metal or horn sewn into it, along with helmets of metal. They were sometimes called the "steel bonnets". They used lances (sometimes as long as 13 ft), shields, and on occasion longbows or small crossbows. They always bore a sword and a dagger; and later in the century, they carried arquebuses and pistols.

Hackapells were light cavalryman whose name comes
Finnish Light from the Finnish war cry *hakkaa päälle*, most commonly
Cavalry translated, "Cut them down!" These troops were fast,
their horses strong, and their attacks were ferocious in
spite of the fact that they only carried two pistols and a sword.

Hackapells were used by King Gustavus Adolphus of Sweden during
the Thirty Years' War and in small regiments by German city states.

The use of pike men was the first major threat to the
Tactics and armored knights of the middle ages; and from the begin-
Weapons ning of the sixteenth century, they were often used alongside men of the infantry who were armed with crossbows,
longbows, or muskets.

At the same time as firearms (muskets and hand guns) took the place of
pikes and bows, military units became more effective as the front ranks of
soldiers fired and then kneeled or stepped back to reload, while the next
rank fired their weapons. Although the effective range of firearms was
only about 100 yards, this technique created a continuous and deadly
field of fire in front of the formation. The infantryman, however, was
highly vulnerable to cannon shot containing steel balls, bits of rock and
metal, nails, and other lethal substances. Cannons could demolish city
walls, changing the nature of siege warfare.

MILITARY MEDICINE

Wounds suffered by the soldiers also changed along with the weaponry,
and many more injuries to the limbs occurred. Wounds from traditional
weapons such as pikes and swords, in general tended to be relatively clean,
so the odds of recovery were fairly good. Compound fractures, once rarely
found in battle conditions, were now commonplace due to the force of a
bullet striking a bone. Unsanitary conditions and surgeons probing
gunshot wounds with unclean fingers usually led to infection and death.
The shattering of bones resulted in the need for amputatation, which often
resulted in death from shock.

Many other soldiers succumbed to dysentery, typhus, smallpox, malaria,
plague, syphilis, and trench foot whereby they lost part of the rotted foot
or toes as they took off their boots for the first time in months. In addition,
constant heavy shelling led to what might be called today traumatic stress
disorders.

In times of war, civilian physicians and barber surgeons were often
forced into the army for the duration of a campaign in order to treat the
enlisted men. The barber surgeons were trained through apprenticeship
and experience to perform surgical and other military medical tasks.

Medical manuals were published in the sixteenth century and used by
the doctors and barber surgeons. With the printing press, knowledge

Ambroise Paré operating on a soldier wounded in battle. (National Library of Medicine.)

became more widespread, having the effect of standardizing procedures since medical personnel all over Europe could now consult the same references and deal with the terrible wounds.

In spite of advances in medical knowledge in the seventeenth century, treatment of disease and infection progressed slowly. One of the main problems was the lack of a scientific method to research medications. Many remedies were tried to help patients; but more often than not, they proved to be useless, causing more harm. Apothecaries frequently sold salves and powders that had no benefit whatsoever.

The French military surgeon Ambroise Paré was responsible for major advances in the treatment of wounds incurred on the battlefield[2]. Previously, it had been thought that since the patient often died of infection, the lead in the bullets poisoned the wounds. Paré tried a new treatment and instead of cauterization when he ran out of oil one day while treating gunshot wounds, he concocted a dressing made of raw egg whites, oil of roses, and turpentine which, he discovered reduced infection, gave the patient some relief from pain and speeded up recovery when applied.

Infection was also the result of burns from exploding cannons and muskets. In 1537 during the Turin campaign in Italy, a boy fell into a caldron of boiling oil. En route to treat him, Paré stopped to obtain medicines from an apothecary. There, an old woman told him to use a dressing of crushed onions and salt, which she said would reduce the blistering and scarring. When Paré came to treat the boy, he followed her advice by putting onion paste over some of the burnt flesh, while using the traditional remedy to treat the rest of the wound. The next day he discovered that the part treated with the onion paste was free of blisters, unlike the rest that was covered in them.

Paré also introduced better methods of battlefield amputation using ligatures that reduced the chances of heavy bleeding. It was learned about this time that this helped to prevent gangrene.

Another innovative pioneer of battlefield medicine was William Clowes, a barber surgeon who served under the Earl of Leicester in the Netherlands in 1580. He became an expert in treating battle wounds claiming that many deaths in battle or afterwards were caused by the incompetence of the surgeon. Low pay and possible danger kept many of the best surgeons away from military duty.

Hygiene and Hospitals Military field hospitals for wounded soldiers were first established in Spain under Queen Isabella during the conquest of Granada in the last decade of the fifteenth century. Six large tents equipped with medicine, bandages, and beds were moved from siege to siege as Muslim cities fell one by one. The queen also converted a royal building in Sevilla into a hospital for incapacitated soldiers who had served the crown.[3]

Disease could spread easily throughout army camps; but some commanders tried to do something to avoid it. The Earl of Leicester, for example, when in the Netherlands, insisted upon places being set up for soldiers to relieve themselves. He also designated specific places outside the garrison where animals were to be butchered andtheir entrails to be buried. On pain of death, the stream beside the camp was not to be polluted.

Those commanders who were not strict on hygiene often suffered the consequences of epidemics, and the Spanish and other initiatives were not employed by other countries even when they were known about. The government of Elizabeth I, for example, ignored proposals by Thomas Digges, an English astronomer, to create a pool of carriages and drivers for ambulance services in war time.[4]

The first military hospital outside of Spain was established by the Spanish duke of Alba in the Netherlands in 1567 where combat wounds, disease, and battle trauma were cared for and supported by the Spanish government. During the early seventeenth century, more hospitals for wounded soldiers were beginning to appear. In 1638 the Swedish government used a former monastery for such treatment. During sieges, makeshift field hospitals came into existence in other parts of Europe that were generally respected by both sides of a conflict.

SIEGE WARFARE

Feudal castles or medieval town walls could be knocked down fairly easily by cannon, but as military engineers quickly replaced high walls with thick, squat, star-shaped fortifications with bastions, cannon were less effective.

Since towns were of economic importance, sieges became a major strategy. This required larger armies since the besieging force had to surround a town and fortify their own camps in order to protect themselves against attacks from the rear.

Soldiers occupied in warfare often spent weeks or months encamped outside a town's walls, and many died from disease brought on by malnutrition and lack of supplies when the local area had been stripped of food.

COSTS OF WAR

Paying for ever-larger armies taxed the treasuries of states engaged in warfare. Some wars were settled more by financial pressure than by actual military means. It was not uncommon for a victory to melt away because the army disbanded afterwards for lack of pay. The need to continue a war and occupy enemy ground often led to a rise in taxes and various schemes for obtaining steady income for the royal treasury. In France, this often meant the creation of more government bureaucracy by selling administrative and judicial offices to the highest bidder. Competence was not a necessary factor. The unpopularity of Henri III's regime was primarily caused by his need to raise money to finance wars that were entering their third decade.

Apart from the guard that traveled with the court, permanent garrisons were posted around the more troublesome borders between the Valois kingdom and Habsburg territories (the north and east). Not only did the citizens pay higher taxes to support armies from which they reaped no real benefits, but they saw their sons go off to war often never to be seen again or to return maimed and incapable of work. A terrible price for a farmer was to see a needed son go into the army.

Soldiers were expected to live off the land; and campaigns generally took place between March and October when the weather was better, and the land was more bountiful. Some communities set up warning systems of armies on the move, so they could abandon their farms and hamlets and make for the nearest fortified town. Such measures took a toll on farm production especially during planting or harvest time.

The little pay soldiers received was unreliable. They seized what they needed from peasants or conquered towns. Pay could be months and even a year in arrears. Lack of money helped account for high desertion rates, often rebellion among the troops, and intense sacking of the local environment. Foraging parties stole anything movable. For most common soldiers, army life was not glorious but miserable. Sometimes systematic destruction of a given area, including towns and villages, was ordered to prevent enemy use when troops were withdrawn. Agricultural production might be lost for years. When pay did arrive at the front, the money lenders who had advanced cash to the soldiers, swooped down to collect their payments at outrageous interest rates. Officers, too, participated in these usurious practices.

Governments were unable or unwilling to quarter soldiers in the countryside between battles and inflicted them on the local towns and villages. Soldiers commandeered peasant houses and farms, requisitioned what they wanted, and had the weapons to back up their demands. At their own expense, the peasants were obliged to feed them and their horses and work for them such as doing laundry and cooking. If soldiers wanted meat, the farmer's pigs and cattle were slaughtered. In short order, the farmer's livelihood could be ruined and his family left hungry.

Fighting between peasants and soldiers or between army units at the local taverns was common. When all had enough drink, arguments ensued, knives unsheathed, and killings occurred. Hatred between troops and peasants was palpable.

CAMP FOLLOWERS

Camp followers were motley groups that formed an integral part of the army. They included provisioners, carters, odd-job men, peddlers, gamblers, and women who tended the sick and wounded, did the laundry, carried soldiers' goods and camp amenities on their backs, and also sold sexual services.

While wives and children often accompanied the campaigns, most camp followers were prostitutes and knaves looking for easy money. Women and gambling often led to disputes among soldiers and even the occasional murder. These military hangers-on also had to eat and shared in the plunder of farms and shops when rations and pay for the soldiers were not forthcoming. By the time a town had been thoroughly sacked by an enemy army, little remained, except remnants of walls. Often half or more of the population lay dead and in some cases, the site abandoned.

KNIGHTS

Along with the growing importance of gunpowder in the field of battle, the heavy cavalry of knights, once protected by their armor, became obsolete; at the same time, the strategic importance of their castles, now subject to cannon fire, diminished. Their self-indulgent lifestyle used up most of their income and as costs of living continued to rise, many took it upon themselves to exercise their ancient right of plundering the countryside by means of highway robbery and ransoming prisoners in order to squeeze what profits they could out of their territories.

At the beginning of the sixteenth century, open pillage by knights was sanctioned as an honorable pursuit. Belligerent relations between knights and towns whose wealthy citizens were waylaid and robbed along the trade routes leading to and from the cities were taken as a matter of course. Although knights and the town patricians were continually quarreling, the knights were often in debt and attacking the merchants, holding them prisoner in their castles until they extracted a ransom.

Knights' social privileges had been based on the assumption that they owed service in war when called by the king. In exchange they received land (and its tenants) that supported their way of life. Knights paid no taxes, but nor did they receive pay. They provided their own horses, trappings, and support troops; but by the end of the century, as firearms came into use, the heavy lance they used had disappeared. This move from the lance to firearms progressed irregularly. Heavy lances were used by the Spaniards throughout the century, while Henri IV's army in France did not use them at all.

If the knights were kept fighting for very long, they often left the field of their own accord, especially if their own property was in danger, or if the collection of ransoms and plunder was not going well.

In the early part of the century, foot soldiers with firearms were brutally treated if they were unlucky enough to be captured by knights who felt that these low-born men with their long-distance weapons could kill their betters without the decency of face-to-face combat. By the end of the century, firearms had become the normal fighting weapons.

A leader of robber-knights in Germany, Hans Thomas was known to rob even the poorest people and to maim and cripple his victims. In June, 1522, he hacked off the right hand of a wretched craftsman, although the man begged him not to destroy his means of earning his living.

The following August, Hans attacked a Nürnberg tanner and a cutlery repairer, whose hands were similarly removed, gathered up, and sent to the burgermeister of Nürnberg with a warning that Hans Thomas would deal with everyone who came from the city in a similar manner. In spite of their mutual antagonism, the princes, as overlords, did not hesitate to shelter knights; so strong was their opinion with regard to the inviolability of the privileged noble class, no matter what they did. It was felt by many that a knight must live in a style befitting his rank; and if he had to resort to robbery, it must be respected as his only resource and was a legitimate means of livelihood for an aristocrat.

In 1524 when, spurred on by Luther's teachings, the Peasants' War broke out, German Protestants were divided along class lines between peasants and Protestant aristocrats. The peasants began taking over farms and mines owned by nobles, but Luther sided with the aristocrats who only wanted clerical not social reforms. He demanded the peasants put down their arms and surrender their farms. Radical peasants believed Luther had betrayed them.

Luther expressed his views on war in 1526 stating in effect that the sword was instituted by God to punish evil and protect the good; therefore, God directed everything connected with war. Luther had no problem with mercenaries, considering their service to be like any other occupation. He thought, however, that many soldiers were inspired by the devil.[5]

DESERTERS

Often commanders took attrition into account when calculating numbers of soldiers needed to fight, but the appalling conditions encountered during war often became unbearable so that sizable units abandoned their positions to the enemy, which was preferable to starving, being maimed, or both.

In 1576, the Spanish army, fighting in Flanders, lost some 50,000 men to desertion. Such men flooded Europe as rogues and bandits, robbing farms and villages, often with impunity. Some made it back to their homes where they were either accepted or driven away.

NOTES

1. See MacDonald Fraser for more detail on the Reivers.
2. Ring, 105 ff.
3. Anderson, 253.
4. Cunningham, 135.
5. Ibid., 140.

14

MEDICINE

Treatment of disease and other ailments had advanced little in the sixteenth century from ancient times. Galen, a highly-revered second-century medical practitioner, believed disease resulted from an imbalance of the four humors that were thought to be responsible for a person's temperament. This view, going back to the ancient Greeks, prevailed among doctors to the sixteenth century.

Luther did not seem to have much faith in the physicians of his time, believing that a preacher would have more effect on spiritual disorders. Further, in the case of physical sickness, one would do as well to follow a good diet and go to bed early rather than see a doctor. He did not object to doctors, per se, but felt that the devil sometimes caused one to be ill, and only with God's help could the patient be cured through prayer and faith. Luther's view of medicine was typical of the time when he stated: "Experience has proven the toad to be endowed with valuable qualities. If you run a stick through three toads, dry them in the sun, and apply them to any pestilent tumor, they draw out all the poison and the malady will disappear."[1]

HUMORS AND VAPORS

The four main bodily fluids, or humors, were embedded in the belief that human beings and their food were composed of the elements that constituted the universe, that is, air, fire, water and earth.

Within the body, these elements formed four corresponding humors: blood, yellow bile, black bile, and phlegm; each one displayed two of the four primary qualities: hot, cold, wet, and dry. When they were out of balance, the best cure was to prescribe substances with opposing qualities. For example, a fever could be cured with ice water and herbs considered cold (such as hemlock), while those herbs or plants thought to be hot, peppers, for example, should be given to someone who was listless and unresponsive.

Element	Humor	Temperament
Air	Blood	Sanguine (hot and dry)
Fire	Yellow bile	Choleric (hot and dry)
Water	phlegm	Phlegmatic (cool and moist)
Earth	black bile	Melancholic (cool and dry)[2]

CAUSE OF DISEASE

Unsanitary conditions, especially in the cities, promoted the spread of disease. Domestic waste (human and animal) contaminated everything, and the rise in the numbers of rats, fleas and body lice brought epidemics that took the lives of the old and the young in particular.

THE PLAGUE

The scourge of the plague that appeared in different places at different times was a major concern for everyone, high or low, on the social hierarchy. Diseases such as this were accepted by all, including physicians, as God's will and as a punishment for the sins of mankind.

It was recognized that the plague was highly contagious, but how it was spread remained a mystery. All doctors were aware that corpses of victims of plague should be avoided, that their houses should be closed, and that possessions should be burned. Because people believed no one could be infected while attending a religious service, they crowded around burial pits at funerals. One of many treatments for the plague consisted of holding a plucked chicken against the sores to draw out the poison. For the plague, like other diseases, it was thought that the cure lay in bringing the humors back into balance.

OTHER COMMON DISEASES

Tuberculosis took a high toll in the Early Modern Period, but other diseases were also common that partially accounted for the loss of life. Influenza, dropsy (the swelling of soft tissues caused by the accumulation of excess water), smallpox, dysentery, diphtheria (a bacterial infection that spreads quickly and easily among people living in crowded or unclean conditions), typhus, and syphilis through sexual contact were always present dangers. The latter, a debatable New World disease with purplish eruptions on the body was sometimes mistaken for other ailments such as the plague. Under such circumstances medical practitioners could do little more than bleed the patient and call on the blessings of the saints.

CONSULTATION

In their examinations of patients, doctors consulted not only medical texts but also books on astrology, numbers, and the Bible to project the length, severity, and eventual outcome of an illness. They often wanted to know the patients horoscope and sometimes gazed at the planets to determine if the time for treatment was auspicious.

DIAGNOSIS AND TREATMENT

Most physicians rarely touched a patient physically, unless taking a pulse or checking a fever. Instead they relied upon the examination of excrement looking at consistency, odor, and shade. An 'informed' physician could identify more than a score of different colors and densities of urine and describe the significance of each. To the well-trained physician, such nuances might indicate lack of vitality, the presence of a melancholy humor, digestive disorder, or dropsy.

The ground-up penis of a boar was believed to act as a cure for pleurisy, grease was applied to burns, pigeon dung was used for irritations of the eyes, and powdered animal bone was supposed to cure deafness. It was believed that a wart could be removed by placing a dead mouse on it. Another cure advised using camphor in vinegar to rid the patient of scaly skin.

Although some treatments included chemicals such as zinc and arsenic, these often damaged the patients. Most popular were natural treatments such as herbs, and although they sometimes worked, no one knew why. For fevers in general, some of the remedies included mixing an egg yolk with aqua vitae, which was then taken by the patient. Fever caused by a wound involved the application of hot oil to the injured part to bring the fever down. To induce sweating, a few bruised aniseeds were mixed with hot posset ale (spiced milk curd made by pouring hot milk into ale) and drunk each time the patient began shaking. If he or she sweated too much, linseed and lettuce had to be beaten together and applied to the stomach and replaced every four hours.[3] Other basic remedies included roses or lavender for headaches, roasted onion put inside the ear for earache, wormwood, mint and balm for stomach ache, and licorice and comfrey for lung diseases.

TOBACCO

Tobacco was thought to have many medicinal uses; smoking was supposed to prevent catarrh, alleviate fatigue, be a gentle laxative, and to fortify the stomach. Application of the green leaves to the skin was supposed to cure leprosy, kill lice, and heal wounds. Tobacco juice was also used to make a dressing for cuts, bruises and burns, gunshot wounds, and to cure the bites of venomous creatures when mixed with olive oil, turpentine, wax, and verdigris. For colic, rectal injections of tobacco smoke were employed.

RURAL MEDICINE

People in villages and small towns continued to visit local men and women who practiced medical skills and cures handed down by example and word of mouth through the ages. There was generally someone, even in a hamlet, that had some knowledge of the benefits of herbs and spices that figured largely into their remedies. Some ingredients could be obtained locally; others were imported. In cities, apothecaries often blended plants for the desired medicine that might consist of pepper, cloves, ginger, and China root, the latter for gout. Imported ingredients could be expensive and unavailable to the poor. For injuries such as a broken leg or arm the local blacksmith or barber was called upon to set the injured limb.

BLEEDING

For rich and poor alike, bleeding was done to help rid a patient of evil fluids in which disease flourished. Those who could afford the process, sometimes had themselves bled four times a year. Others, much more. A bleeding holiday was not unusual in which families and friends went in groups to the public baths where surgeons opened their veins and allowed the blood to flow.[4] Taken from the elbow, chest, or from the basilic or temporal vein, it was the most common treatment for releasing toxic humors. Every sickness had its own specific vein. Letting of blood was thus used as a panacea since most illnesses were thought to be the result of unclean substances in the body, the bleeding casting them out to restore the natural equilibrium.

THERMAL WATERS

Others had great faith in the benefits of the waters of thermal springs to be drunk at the source if possible. There, the patient would be purged and then combine rest with bathing and drinking some two to three liters of water daily.

HOSPITALS

Not many people went into hospitals, which were considered mostly as places for the homeless and somewhere to die. Care was far from adequate and sometimes as many as six people with a variety of illnesses, were put in the same bed, which was seldom clean. In the sixteenth century, there were five epidemics of the plague, and those who contracted it were not admitted to hospital in England, for example, unless there were special houses to confine them. Hospitals, themselves, usually financed by a charitable patron or the town hall, were places where disease spread easily.

THE CATHOLIC CHURCH

Many doctors thought they would have more chance of success in curing the patient if they prayed before administering their treatment. The Catholic Church in Europe continued to promote Galen's anatomical ideas as infallible, and its control over medical practice and training in the universities remained strong. However, as the Renaissance took hold in Europe, and inventions such as the microscope appeared, leading doctors began more and more to investigate the anatomy and physiology of the body. Classical theories were put to the test of thorough investigation for the first time. The ideas of Galen were hard to overturn, however, since his theories had been the accepted wisdom of the medical world for more than a thousand years. Even when he appeared to be wrong, many doctors would doubt or ignore their own observations and adhere to the time honored views.[5]

A scholar who questioned old ideas, such as those of Galen on the human body, went against the commonly accepted views and would acquire many enemies. Nevertheless, there were a few men who found new paths forward in the fields of medicine and science. Change was slow in the use of new drugs such as the chemicals (e.g., mercury, antimony, and quinine) in the treatment of disease.

DISSECTION

In the sixteenth century, dissection of the human body became more common. Previously, the only dissections that had been permissible were those undertaken on the corpses of criminals, and these had been carried out purely to support Galen's theories. By the sixteenth century, the main pressure to maintain the general ban on dissection came from senior university professors, who were afraid that the ideas of Galen (who experimented only on animals) would be challenged by new discoveries. Andreas Vesalius, who distrusted the teachings of Galen, made his own observations when he became professor of surgery at the University of Padua in 1537. He taught his students using the dissection of human corpses to illustrate anatomical facts. The tradition that dissection should only be done while a professor read aloud the theories of Galen was dropped. In the pioneering atmosphere of the Renaissance, dissection was accepted as a means to develop new ideas and explain these to students.

GERMANY

To combat diseases in Germany, people followed the oral traditions including a purging calendar (published in Nürnberg, 1496). Physicians tended to think of medicine and their services as divinely inspired. For all but a few, faith and prayers were the most important remedies for ill health; but when all else failed, God allowed one more possibility, consult the doctor. Many physicians, devout as any clergyman, considered plague to be God's curse on the wicked.

Physicians also gave sensible advice in many cases, alerting people to the fact that disease was spread by physical contact and cautioned people to avoid the afflicted, their houses, clothes, bed covers, and so on. Ventilation was important in closed spaces, alcohol should be avoided, a clean house maintained; one should eat lightly, bathe frequently, and stay warm in winter with a continuous fire in the hearth.[6] Like most people, they believed in talismans such as sapphires to be worn in the streets to ward off disease.

The English traveler, Fynes Moryson, having fallen ill in Leipzig, recounts that German physicians were very honest and learned. They never took money until the cure was complete; and if the patient died, they expected no pay. Apothecaries were few in the city; only those permitted by the prince could practice. They sold drugs at a reasonable rate, and were careful not to sell spoiled medicines. To prevent any fraud, imperial laws and local decrees demanded that once a year physicians visit the apothecary shops and destroy all out of date drugs no longer fit to be used.

QUACKS

Throughout Europe, medicine men roamed the countryside stopping at hamlets, farms, and local markets to peddle their elixir promising it as a panacea for just about everything.

Moryson noted that in Germany as in Italy, there were quacks who professed to have special salves, oils for most ailments, and who carried testimonials under seals of princes and free cities that attested to the cures they had performed. These were mounted on walls and stalls in the market place where they lectured on their skills in applying them. They pictured drawings of cures, gall stones they had removed from patients, and teeth they had extracted.[7]

FRANCE

In sixteenth-century France, Montpellier's School of Medicine was internationally famous and highly respected. It was here that Felix Platter, at age 15, was sent from his home in Basel to study. Felix was a Protestant; and Montpellier, although known as a haven for Protestants, still witnessed some violence and persecution as he noted when Bibles found in a bookshop were publicly burned. German-speaking Protestant students generally stuck together, as did the French-speaking Catholic students.

He attended four to six lectures daily. The first autopsy he saw was on the body of a boy whose death derived from a stomach absess. A professor presided, and the surgery was done by a barber-surgeon. A large, attentive audience witnessed the event including some monks. At the conclusion of his studies, Felix returned to Basel to become the foremost physician in that town.

ENGLAND

The state of medicine and the diseases doctors endeavored to manage or cure were no different than those on the European continent. There as elsewhere, the major cause of disease was the absence of sanitation. London and other cities had open sewers in the streets that also served as garbage dumps, and animals and sometimes people defecated wherever they pleased. Typhoid was spread from contaminated shared wells. As elsewhere in Europe, the vast majority of people could not afford good doctors who, at any rate, would not attend patients with plague, typhoid fever, and other highly contagious diseases. Housewives kept on hand certain herbs and potions for family use that were often the only remedies for illness among the poor. Not only were sewers unhealthy places, but rivers and streams were often blocked by rotting garbage and attracted multitudes of rats and mice. Again, as elsewhere, every household, rich and poor, had its share of lice and fleas.

BARBER SURGEONS

Most barbers filled other functions besides cutting hair and shaving beards. They also pulled teeth and performed surgical procedures, occasionally including amputations. They treated trauma, set broken bones, cauterized (sometimes with the use of a red-hot iron) or stitched up bleeding wounds, and bled patients. If their services were not required by humans, they often took care of sick animals.

Paoli Magni. At the Barber Surgeon's. 1854. A satirical engraving illustrating the many tasks performed by barber surgeons. One could have wounds treated, blood let, teeth pulled, and hair cut. (Bibliothèque Nationale de France, Paris.)

Wounds were cleaned and washed with salted water as a first aid measure. Splinting and traction were employed in the treatment of fractures. In injuries of the mouth, which rendered the intake of food difficult or impossible, nourishment was administered by means of nutrient enemas.

Barber surgeons were not doctors and needed only on-the-job training, not a university degree. They were looked down upon by physicians whose education was better and whose services were much more expensive.

ANESTHESIA

Anesthesia was primitive and often not used at all. When amputations or other procedures were performed, a patient's hands and feet were tied to the table, and various methods were tried to render him unconscious including putting a helmet on him and delivering a solid blow to it with a wooden hammer. Another procedure used sponges soaked in mandrake and belladonna pressed against the mouth. In both cases, the odds of killing the patient, instead of merely rendering him unconscious, were high. Shock and infection frequently killed most of those who survived the surgery anyway.

DENTISTRY

In England, tooth decay was rampant among the upper classes who consumed huge quantities of sugar, used in almost every dish—sweet or savory. A large number of people, including the queen, had black teeth in a seriously bad state of deterioration.

To combat this, many would dip their fingers into powdered alabaster or ashes of rosemary leaves, which they rubbed onto the teeth. Other methods included rinsing them with a solution of honey and burnt salt or with a quart of vinegar and honey and half a quart of white wine boiled together. Sometimes the teeth were rubbed with a mixture made of powdered pumice stone, brick, or coral. This frequently removed stain, along with the enamel.

Copious use was made of toothpicks, which came in various shapes, sizes, and metals and were often worn in the hat as a decoration.

Various implements made of metal were employed to scrape the teeth, after which nitric acid was rubbed on in an attempt to whiten them. This frequently resulted in the teeth dropping out. Sir Hugh Platt warned that such treatment could be calamitous for after a few applications a lady may "be forced to borrow a ranke of teeth to eate her dinner."[8]

One cure for toothache was to rub urine on the gum; if that did not work, the tooth was knocked out using a hammer and chisel. Throughout Europe, mouthwashes were concocted and recommended for bad breath, Some believed that roasted turnip peel put behind the ear could get rid of it. Recipes to freshen the breath included a mixture of spices such as cinnamon, cloves, mint, nutmeg, anise, caraway, and fennel. A gargle made from tobacco was supposed to cure toothache, and tobacco was also used to fill a hollow tooth.

Going to the dentist was painful and dangerous; people sometimes died from loss of blood and pain caused by the instruments that were used. They included pliers, instruments with claws (for dislodging a tooth from the socket), and an implement that pulled out the roots.

For toothache, Markham suggests a handful of dried daisy roots be pounded, then half a nutshell of bay salt be sprinkled over them, after which a clean cloth is used to strain the mixture. Add some grated herbs and mix well together with the juice of the roots; then put in a quill and snuff it up into the nose.[9]

At this time, fillings began to be used, the most common materials being gold leaf, molten lead, or scrapings of silver. But often a tooth was just removed and replaced with a good one from a poor person in need of money. Unfortunately for the donor, they would lose one tooth after another as the dentist strove to find one that would fit the mouth of his patient. If no one was available to supply a tooth, those of sheep, dogs, goats, and corpses were used.

When false teeth eventually were constructed, they came from sources such as animal bones, ivory, silver, porcelain plaster, or inflammable vulcanite and celluloid. It seemed that whatever course was followed, it was usually perilous for the patient.

NOTES

1. Luther, 424–426.
2. Anderson, 263.
3. Markham, 13.
4. Ozment (1986), 119.
5. Simon, 165.
6. Ozment, op. cit., 114–17.
7. Moryson (1967), 10.
8. Brears, 10. Platt, an innovative domestic historian and agriculturalist, was author of *Jewell House of Art and Nature* (1594) that expounded on everything from recipes, making parchment transparent, candles, gathering wasps, and a variety of other subjects including beauty tips, curing and pickling.
9. Markham, 16.

15

EDUCATION

BEFORE THE REFORMATION

Throughout the Middle Ages, most literate people were clerics who were required to know Latin for religious ceremonies. The Catholic Church endowed schools to teach Latin that were attached to cathedrals, monasteries, and parishes to train future clerics and administrators. Secular town councils and even great nobles or the king sometimes founded their own schools for the betterment of their subjects, officials, and managers. Nevertheless, prior to the Reformation, schools and universities throughout Europe were firmly in the hands of the Catholic Church who had the only literate teachers to run them.

By beginning of the sixteenth century, grammar (or Latin) schools for young male subjects were well ensconced in most European countries.[1] At the most fundamental level of reading and writing, the Church conducted classes in chapels and monasteries within the parish. At a higher level, Latin was taught in monasteries and cathedrals. Girls could find a little religious education from the sisters in convents that held libraries but generally only if they lived there. Guilds of artisans and merchants also had schools for young men prepared to follow the trade. On occasion a peasant boy might find some elementary education at a monastery if the parents could pay the fee. In general, the Catholic Church was little interested in educating the masses; it was enough to educate the clergy who would then lead the masses to salvation.

VALUE OF EDUCATION

With the coming of the Renaissance and Humanist ideas, the concept of the individual took on more importance. More attention was paid to the here and now and less to a life hereafter. Under such circumstances, education began to have more significance.

GIRLS' EDUCATION

While tutors taught upper class girls social refinements including foreign languages, those of the middle class received a little basic education in reading, writing and arithmetic from family members, or from the parish priest. A merchants' daughter often learned to run her father's business.

CATHOLIC WOMEN

Some of the new religious orders of women in Catholic Europe offered schooling for girls, many of whom boarded at the convent for a number of years. Courses taught included good manners, singing, and sewing. When a girl left, she was expected to be virtuous and ready to get married. Those who made the decision to stay on and become nuns themselves often continued with their education.

LOWER CLASSES AND MIDDLE CLASSES

A vast number of both urban and rural young men did not attend school at all. Born into a commercial family, they might receive a seven-year (or shorter) apprenticeship in order to learn a trade. If it required reading and writing, they would learn the rudiments from the local priest or the master. In towns where there were teachers, the sons of the bourgeoisie might have had a little schooling in their early years, but the study of Latin required in higher grades was considered much less important than becoming an apprentice and learning a trade. There were craftsmen who could read and write, but very few laborers were ever given such opportunities.

For the majority of people, the peasants, formal schooling was not an issue. Their education came from their fathers and grandfathers and consisted of how to manage the planting and harvesting, take care of the animals, and participate in the trade of the local markets. Girls were taught household chores from making butter, mending clothes, preparing food, to caring for babies, from their mothers.

DISCIPLINE

In Tudor England, in Germany, and elsewhere infringement of the school rules could lead to corporal punishment. Such methods of control were sanctioned by the medieval Church that also encouraged self-flagellation as a disciplinary activity. Even today in Catholic countries such as Spain, self-flagellation, at least symbolically, can be seen among participants in Holy Week parades.

It was not uncommon for disorderly boys to be struck on the buttocks or on the flat of their hands with a stick.

WEALTHY FAMILIES

Sons and daughters of well-to-do families were sometimes taught by tutors in the home or received their first admission to education in a school for young children. Boarding schools for both boys and girls were introduced in many cities in the sixteenth century as students often had to come from afar. Girls were taught music, reading, writing, and needlework. A girl's merit lay in her attainment and success in these matters rather than in academic studies.

Catholic Church officials served as part-time teachers while performing other ecclesiastical duties, but in Protestant cities teaching became a full-time profession for some men that were trained as clerics before adopting the Protestant persuasion.

Wealthy families also believed that young girls should not be idle. They were allocated some playtime but otherwise were put to work on tasks deemed suitable by their parents and the priest. The education of girls was thus mainly for the privileged and the rich. Its aim was to produce wives schooled in godly and moral precepts. It was not intended to promote independent thinking.

TEACHERS AND SCHOOLS

More often than not, the local parish priest served as the schoolmaster. There were also schools that taught basic arithmetic for the sons of merchants and traders, so they could keep accounts. The elementary school was closely associated with the Church as was the secondary or grammar school whose students were generally admitted about age seven and trained to go on to university to become clerics, lawyers, or doctors. The quality of teaching, however, was often poor reflecting the mediocre education of many priests.[2]

By the end of the sixteenth century in England, it had become fashionable for the rich to found schools and endow universities and students; and most towns could boast of a secular grammar school no longer under the control of the Church. Religious instruction still played a large part in the curriculum, and at many schools, was even more important than Latin or Greek.

REFORMERS' IMPACT ON EDUCATION

Major reformers agreed that schooling was important, it should be available to everyone, and religion should be included in the curriculum. An open letter sent in 1524 to town councilors in Germany by Luther made his view clear. He stated in part:

> 'If Christianity is to rise in its power we must surely begin with the children ... Family education must be assisted by the school ... For the sake of the Church we must have and maintain Christian schools ... Let everyone then send his children to school. It is only the devil who desires the people to remain dull blocks.'[3]

He added that it was the business of rulers to compel their subjects to educate their children. If they could force a youth to go to war, they could most certainly make them attend school. Luther also promoted the teaching of the sacred languages (Latin, Greek and Hebrew) and claimed that without them and the Bible,

> 'Germany has sunk so low that her wretched people, like poor dumb cattle, can neither read nor write good German, and have well nigh lost the sense of their natural reason.'[4]

Music, said Luther,

> '... is the best of all the arts, it dispels the sorrow of the breast. If a schoolmaster does not know music, I have nothing to say to him. Music is a beautiful divine gift of God, and next to theology.'[5]

UNIVERSAL EDUCATION

A remarkable man who promoted education was Erasmus, perhaps the most highly educated man of the period. Professor of Divinity and lecturer in Greek at Cambridge University, his views on education promoted not punishment for the lazy child but stimulus to arouse his interest. No threats, blows, or scolding, but only praise, smiles, and encouraging words were the key to learning. He also believed that girls as well as boys should be educated instead of shutting girls up until they reached a marriageable age. Other Protestant scholars agreed with this assessment.

Calvin turned the city of Geneva into a center of learning (along the lines he desired). He promoted education for everyone, as did John Knox in Scotland.

It was becoming more common in the schools to dispense with the rod. At the school in Elbing (now in Poland), a regulation forbade the use of the stick to beat the children; however, they could be slapped and their hair, ears, and noses pulled.[6]

In spite of such ideals, most children never entered the doors of a school. Boys and girls from poor families were expected to start working and contributing to the family income at an early age.

CATHOLIC EDUCATION

By the time of the Council of Trent, Catholic leaders were also interested in increasing educational facilities. At the forefront were the Jesuits who established universities and colleges throughout Europe and the world. Thus, by the time of the Counter-Reformation, the Catholic Church was gradually changing, raising the standards of education of the clergy, more and more of whom were attending university. Both the Reformation and the Counter-Reformation succeeded in creating more learned men of the Church, both Protestant and Catholic.

Founded by the Basque, Ignatius Loyola in 1540, Jesuits were well trained; and part of their success lay in the fact that instead of flogging the children to force them to learn, they preferred to stimulate their interest, as did many Protestant teachers. In addition, they made the curriculum more interesting by promoting competition and giving prizes for excellence. Students in Jesuit schools were required to attend Mass on a daily basis; and by the time they left and went out into the world, they were not only well educated, but they were also well indoctrinated in the faith. These kinds of efforts helped Catholicism survive the Reformation.

Jesuit schools were, however, primarily for the well born and wealthy.[7] They played a large role in preserving Catholicism in Spain, France, Italy, southern Germany, and Poland, as well as making converts around the world. Jesuits were warriors in the forefront of the Counter-Reformation, spreading the message of the Council of Trent.

Understanding the advantages of a good education as a means to power and prestige, the Jesuits approached the problem with zeal. They soon bypassed the Protestant educational system in organization and discipline. Their system was uncompromising. Every minute of every day was delegated to a certain task, and students were encouraged to spy on one another and report any infractions of the code. In attempting to monopolize education and for other political interference, the Order has at one time or another been expelled from most European countries but always found ways to return.

PROTESTANTS

Luther strongly advocated the compulsory education of both boys and girls, and the churches did offer some free instruction in Sunday Schools, while Bible study at home was encouraged. But in the main, he felt children should be educated in public schools in order that the young be guided in matters of religion and the arts by public officials. Elementary schooling of at least one hour daily was also to be given to girls, some of whom would become teachers, if not in the classroom, at least at home to their children.[8]

In Strassburg Johann Sturm's Humanistic gymnasium was a model for the new Protestant persuasion (both Lutheran and Calvinist), and primary schools in Nürnberg offered a very good education.[9]

IMPROVEMENTS IN ENGLAND AND FRANCE

Originally, all classes in England took place in a single room, with the students divided into small groups and taught by a single master. Low-ranking schools still had one master take care of several classes at a time. For educators such as Erasmus it was obvious that bunching students together hindered intellectual growth. The use of separate rooms came into force showing a realization that there were various categories of children to be considered, involving age development and learning capacity, and they should not all be lumped together. As early as 1501, some cities such as Paris, Liège, and Strassburg saw to it that each class had its own room.[10]

MANNERS

One of the purposes of education was to teach children how to take their place in life. Everyone was aware of the importance of good manners. Students were made aware that they could move up and flourish within society if they were well behaved; and part of everyone's education came to embody the knowledge of good manners and how to be courteous and refined.

Young men of high birth found they were no longer limited to the king's retinue, the civil service, or the military. Before, to be called a gentleman, one had to have a coat of arms awarded to the family; but after Henry VIII, the military and the medical profession were penetrated by the ambitious, no matter what their class. Even children of low birth began to realize that they could advance socially.

One respected educator, Richard Mulcaster, who had an ambitious school program for the English middle-class, took into account a child's intelligence as well as his physical abilities. He advocated physical and mental training and encouraged schools to have vocational programs to help the children make use of their innate talents. Mulcaster wanted girls educated by women, and believed that it was during the first three years in school that the basic foundations were laid.

For people to rise and succeed within the social system, then, education was the answer, and as parents' hopes and expectations for their children rose, more and more of the middle class Puritans began sending their offspring off to higher education. If they had enough money, Puritans preferred to send their sons to university, rather than putting them out to be apprentices. Their daughters, too, attended public grammar schools.

There was sometimes a possibility for poor boys to be given scholarships to the university, but they had to be exceedingly clever, for such an education remained a privilege and was available to only a relative few.

PURITAN VIEW OF EDUCATION

Education for the masses was a goal of the Puritan communities at least to the extent that everyone would be able to read the Bible.

Puritan sects also wanted educated pastors who could read and interpret the Bible in its ancient languages such as Greek and Hebrew and scholarly treatises written in Latin. Young men, but not women, were encouraged to attend a university.

Adhering to the teachings of St. Paul and Old Testament prophets that a woman's place was in the home, Puritans thought that it was dangerous to educate women too much, or they would become harder to control. Housewifery was still primary because most girls' futures depended on their getting married. In short, a little education was fine for girls, reading and writing, but not beyond that.

AN ENGLISH BOY'S DAY AT SCHOOL

A schoolboy in Elizabethan England had a long, arduous day. He left home around 6:00 a.m. and once he arrived, he studied until the 15-minute 9:00 recess, after which he returned to his desk for a further two hours study. He was permitted a couple of hours for a meal, which he ate either at school or at home. Another two hours of study followed, combined with recitation, and then after a last recess, he worked until 5:00 p.m. Before leaving for home, the master read the Bible to the class who then sang a psalm if this was a Puritan school. A prayer for dismissal was said before leaving. In winter, when going to the school and returning home, students often had to carry lanterns to light their way. Elizabethan law required that the catechism had to be learned by all young people under 20 and that they should be taught this every holy day and Sunday both before and after evening prayers.[11]

EDUCATION ON THE CONTINENT

Public schools took over education in many places in Germany after Luther had urged magistrates to provide compulsory instruction for both boys and girls. Lutheran children had at least one hour of formal schooling daily.

Children from families with means completed their studies at home under tutors or in the local public schools endowed by the city or a patron by age 12 or 13, after which they entered service, apprenticeships, or continued on to higher education. Young men pursuing university and professional careers in law, medicine, or theology usually enrolled between the ages of 13 and 17. A course of last resort was to enlist in the military.

ITINERANT STUDENTS

Schools were established by Church organizations, by private individuals, and by the municipality through charitable endowments. In the countryside, the village priest or the sacristan sometimes provided some rudimentary education like reading, writing, catechism and arithmetic. Many hamlets did not concern themselves with children's education. Such was the case of Thomas Platter. Born into a large family in a village of the Valais, Switzerland, the family was left penniless after the death of his father. By the age of eight Thomas was an experienced goatherd living in the mountain heights with animals in his charge. Hoping he would become a clergyman, his mother sent him off to live with a relative, a priest, who was to give him the rudiments of education. Thomas was not willing to endure the priest's brutality, remarking that he was beaten horribly and lifted off the ground by his ears. Realizing he had learned nothing useful when a cousin of his, an itinerant student, passed through the village by chance, Thomas left with him. Together they traveled around Europe from city to city attending classes and living by their wits. Like many itinerant young men of the age, half would be students and half would be vagabonds; they worked odd jobs, sang in the streets for money, stole geese or raided chicken houses, and begged. In Munich, at 16 years of age, Thomas slept on grain sacks in the market, snatching bones from dogs in the street to survive. He then made the decision to leave his cousin, setting off on his own and finally reaching Zürich where he tried in vain to persuade established students to give him lessons. His time on the road had taught him little; at 18 he still could not read. Leaving the city, he ended up in Schlestadt, Alsace, where he stayed for awhile and acquired a little education, courtesy of a schoolmaster who allowed him into a class of about 900 students where he was placed with the small children. In class he felt like a mother hen surrounded by his brood. Soon he had to leave for lack of money. Returning to his native Valais, he received some rudiments of learning at a small local school established there as well as from relatives, and by age 19 he could read and write.

In 1522, after hearing a dynamic sermon by Zwingli, Thomas became a zealous partisan of the Reformation. He returned to Zürich where he boarded with the schoolmaster Friedrich Myconius, a friend of Zwingli and Luther. Not unlike many young men of the time, upon hearing a persuasive, energetic speaker on the Reformation, Thomas became convinced of the inherent iniquities of the Catholic Church. He became a dedicated disciple, and in just a few years learned Latin, Greek, and some Hebrew. He earned a living by giving private lessons. Returning to Valais, he opened a school. Travel from place to place always searching for greener pastures and someone to teach them and often living off the land, was typical of many impecunious students of the time. Others with a better start in life and unencumbered by lack of money did not undergo these privations.[12]

Lucas, a young boy from Nürnberg, went to live in Altdorf at ten years of age, in order to embark on his formal **A Boy from** education. He spent 10 years there, from 1597 to 1607, **Nürnberg** attending a gymnasium studying (in Latin) philosophy, ethics, law, politics, history, and the classics. Interested in music, he became an accomplished musician by the time he graduated. Altdorf was close enough to Nürnberg that he was able to remain in touch with his family, sending his laundry home weekly to his stepmother who washed and returned it, usually accompanied by a treat of some kind. By 1608 he had left home again, this time to study at the universities of Poitiers and Angés with a view to learning French.[13]

Sons of wealthy families in Nürnberg frequently traveled to Venice where they stayed in the German House, an entry into Italy for students, apprentices, and merchants. Others went for their legal education to Louvain in Belgium. Travel to other countries was a rite of passage for burghers' sons before they were ready to begin adult life. Daughters were not permitted such a privilege.

UNIVERSITIES

Students criss-crossed Europe, some from well-off families, riding horses or in carriages; others of less means walking or hitching rides on merchants' wagons, all on the way to their chosen university.

As traveling scholars, many earned a precarious living by begging or 'professing' medicine, assisting the illiterate for a small fee, or reading horoscopes.

The rapid spread of the Reformation in a given region depended on whether or not it was under the jurisdiction of a free city ruled by city councilmen, a territory ruled by a nobleman, or one under the authority of a bishop. The presence of a university was important since religious reform was often propagated by university teachers.[14]

German Universities

There were abundant universities in the German-speaking lands and with the waning of imperial and papal power, most princes and free cities founded one. There were generally professors of divinity, medicine, civil law, and one or two of mathematics, physics, history, rhetoric, logic, natural philosophy, astrology, and sometimes, one of Hebrew. When a space fell vacant it was filled by someone who was recommended by the professors and approved by the prince of the realm.

Professors also chose the deans of the different faculties and the rector. Both teachers and students wore cloaks and hats. Professors, rector, deans, and assistants and a public notary made up the university senate that ran the institution and punished students for breaking the rules by fines or, in the worst cases, with banishment. Students swore an oath to be observant of their superiors, to show favor toward the university, promote religion, and to be thankful to the college of their faculty. They promised to obey the statutes, not to resist lawful arrest or banishment and refrain from seeking revenge by violence for any wrong done them.

Professors worked year round without vacations and their pay could increase or decrease depending on merit. Lectures were read slowly and clearly and the students wrote them down word for word. If something was said that was not intelligible, the students pounded on their desks until the professor repeated it in a clearer manner.

Examinations

Examinations for a degree might last three days. Two professors and two assistants were chosen to examine a student, but anyone could participate and ask questions. Moryson discusses the German custom whereby both the examiner and the examined drank to each other with nearly every question from pots set beside them. In at least one instance, the session degenerated until both dropped off to sleep.

Conferring of Degrees

Solemn speeches and great festivities, music, and pomp accompanied the conferring of a doctor, masters, or bachelors degree.

Physicians gave an oath to practice with knowledge and not with old wives' recipes, not to destroy any children in the mother's womb, and not to give any deadly poison or bad medicine to a sick person. During the ceremony, those who earned the doctor of philosophy degree moved to upper seats and were given a purple hat (to distinguish them), along with a ring to indicate their marriage to philosophy. They were given an open book as an invitation to read and a closed book signifying contemplation with reading. The doctors of civil law in some universities were given a military belt to indicate their obligation to defend the law.

Ceremonies took place in a church and upon their conclusion, the graduates were led up to the high altar by the chief professor of divinity and the vice chancellor where they fell on their knees and prayed. Each received a pair of gloves; and other gloves were tossed to the audience who snatched them if they were able. At the end, graduates and professors retired in a specific order to the public house of the city to enjoy a feast.

The graduates paid for their degrees and the money, in some places, was divided in half: one half was divided again and went to the rector, the dean, the notary, examiners and the beadles; and the other half went to the Public Treasury for repair of public buildings, alms to the poor, and other matters.[15]

German students spent the night drinking heavily and visiting prostitutes, walking through the streets with naked swords, hitting them against stones and making a lot of noise. Such disturbances were forbidden in most German cities; but students paid little heed, and their exuberance was generally tolerated.

According to Fynes Moryson, Germans despised those who took degrees in Italy where, ignorant of their subject, they simply paid for them. The Italians had a saying: **Foreign Degrees**

'Wee take mony, and send an asse in a Doctors habitt into Germany.'[16]

In Spain, students attending university lived more or less isolated from the rest of society. Early in the sixteenth century the influence of humanism began to make some headway, but those professors teaching these precepts frequently found themselves before the Inquisition. Questioning the Catholic religious orthodoxy was not tolerated. By the end of the century, universities had become training grounds for careers in the government bureaucracy or the Church.

At the oldest and most prestigious university, Salamanca, lectures were delivered by a professor dressed in his doctoral robes from a lofty pulpit that towered above the students. No one was permitted to speak in the classroom, although questions might be asked outside after the lecture was over.

Successful graduation was a splendid affair, and sometimes the entire town took part in the costly celebrations paid for by the student and his family. For those who failed, however, the medieval practice was followed whereby the candidate had to leave by the back door of the cathedral where he was being examined. There, he was met by an unsympathetic crowd and underwent the humiliation of having rotten fruit and vegetables thrown at him, as well as much ridicule. There is a story that in Salamanca, the back door led directly to the river, and the failed student's studies came to a watery, but not fatal, end. Higher education for women was not available until the latter part of the eighteenth century.[17]

The Sorbonne University in Paris, founded in the thirteenth century, ranked until the Reformation as the leading university of Europe, especially

Martín de Cervera. A university Theology lecture. (University of Salamanca (Spain) Sala de manuscritos de la Antiqua Librería.)

in theological studies. Authority to judge doctrinal questions was vested in the Sorbonne faculty who, in 1521, condemned Luther's propositions. The university collaborated with the parliament of Paris to ban certain books, but the inefficient policing of trade routes and bookstores allowed numerous traders in forbidden material to sell these items in France.

NOTES

1. For education in the sixteenth century, see Rank, J., "Latin School," in Fass, Paula S. J. *Encyclopedia of Children and Childhood in History and Society.* New York: Macmillan Reference USA (c2004).

2. Elton, G. R. ed. (1965), 415–417.

3. Payne, 37.

4. Ibid., 38.

5. Loc. cit.

6. Ibid., 44.

7. Walker, 377.

8. Ozment (1983), 153.

9. Ibid. (1999), 215.

10. For more on schools, see Ariès, 177–187.

11. Pearson, 177.

12. For more on Thomas Platter, see Ladurie.

13. Ozment (1999), 7–8.

14. Wiesner, 8.

15. See Moryson (1617), 308–315 for much of the above. The fee paid by doctors was 37 gold guldens and by a master of arts 8 silver guldens.

16. Ibid., 315.

17. Anderson (2002), 239

16

FOOD

For people of all classes, the most important time of each day was the hour when the family came together for their main meal.

Meals, for most people, were eaten in the kitchen, the warmest room in the house. Parents sat at the table or by the fire; their children sat nearby on benches or stood at the table. Guests were received in this room, and farmers and day laborers ate their small fare there at the end of a day's work. Sometimes chickens and ducks sheltered under the table, and dogs sprawled in any warm spot they could find.

As new foods from the Americas began to be introduced, such as potatoes, tomatoes, and sweet potatoes, and caught on in much of Europe, it took almost another century for them to be adopted in England. At first they were eaten either by animals or the very poor, but once it was realized that potatoes were resistant to most disease and could grow in any soil, they became very popular. Several other new vegetables included maize, spinach, chili peppers, asparagus, artichokes, string beans, and kidney beans; the latter was primarily eaten by the poor.[1] Turkeys from Mexico and Central America were much in demand, and after the middle of the century, were regularly to be found in the markets of London.

Merchants traveled far and wide from France, Germany, Netherlands, Spain, Greece, and Italy to attend the great fairs held in such cities as Lyon and Beaucaire, where they purchased spices, saffron, cloves, cinnamon, ginger, sugared almonds, sugar, sweet wine, rice, dried currants and figs, as well as salted fish for Lent such as tuna, porpoise, cod, and anchovies. Since the sea route to the East Indies had been discovered by the Portuguese, the cost of spices had come down, putting them within the reach of the middle class. In the eastern part of Europe, especially in Germany, there was still a taste for strong seasoning, but once the price and prestige had fallen, there was less demand.[2]

FRANCE

Many of the French scorned vegetables unless well cooked with the exception of truffles and artichokes, the latter thought to be an aphrodisiac. Some, such as cabbage, were toted as a cure for conditions of baldness, asthma, rabies, and paralysis. Fresh fruits, for example, peaches, pears, and cherries were eaten with many varieties of cheese, Brie being the favorite, that formed part of the diet. Fresh apples were also used to perfume lingerie. It was considered bad form to eat apples on Christmas Day; however, since it was a reminder of the sin committed by Adam and Eve.[3]

To serve a meal, French wealthy people used plates of gold and silver, often with a small notch in them for salt, and dishes of earthenware and glass. Cups made of earthenware (known as Cistercian Ware) were used for beverages, and the best wine and beer glasses came from Venice. Presentation was important, for instance, flowers were used as garnish for salads.

France had its pottage, eaten by all classes. For the well-off, it accompanied or contained meat and was sometimes very rich with different vegetables and bread (to thicken), herbs, and various cereals, including rice. By the beginning of the seventeenth century, pottage was known as soupe in France—referring to the "sop" of bread that was put on the bottom of the bowl before the liquid was added. Pottage was a whole meal for the poor and usually consisted of cereals such as barley, wheat, rye, or oatmeal, along with vegetables and sometimes a small piece of boiled meat.

Serviettes were used by the upper classes and were placed on the table folded in the shape of fruit, animals, or birds. They were attached like a bib and since most food was eaten with fingers, were changed with each course. Even the tablecloth was changed before dessert was served.

Each place at the table was given a soup spoon. and a few knives were shared by all. The host would say a prayer from the head of the table, whereupon bread was served, accompanied by a bread knife. A prayer of thanks would be said afterwards.

If spoons were used, they were made of silver or pewter for the rich and of wood for the poor. When the fork was introduced in the sixteenth century, it was condemned by a German preacher who called it a "diabolical luxury" since "if God had wanted people to use such an instrument, He would not have given them fingers!"[4] Plates and dishes of gold and silver that had been in the family for generations were generally kept in safe places to be produced at important banquets. There was always the fear

David Teniers. Peasant Festival. The illustration shows peasants dancing in front of a barn (and a wall). (Museo Nacional del Prado, Madrid.)

that the owner's position or financial situation might decline or that a king in need would requisition them.

Glass drinking vessels in France were put on a buffet; and if required by a diner, a servant would fill it. The same glass was always used by the same person for all drinks. There was often much toasting. It was unforgivable not to raise one's glass in response.

Wealthy families in France usually followed an order of serving that consisted of a first course of stew, minced meats, or salad. On special occasions a large bird, such as a swan or a peacock, might be presented along with all its feathers, its feet and beak gilded.

Fish and seafood included salmon, shrimp, and oysters. More exotic dishes served were of frogs, snails, grass snakes, hedgehogs, and turtles.[5]

ENGLAND

The upper classes ate copious amounts of flesh (such as venison, beef, pork and lamb) but not much in the way of vegetables, as most considered that food from the earth was not as healthy as meat and fish. Most English people looked at raw fruits and vegetables with great suspicion, although dried fruit such as raisins, currants, prunes, figs, dates, almonds, and walnuts, were imported in large quantities.

In England, Fresh fruit was considered edible only if cooked, put into pies or tarts, or if preserved or candied. Sugar was extremely expensive in most countries, so one had to have money to buy crystallized fruits, syrups, or sweetmeats of any kind. In England it was also used in seasoning meat, fish, and vegetable dishes.[6]

Rose water often appears in English recipes, while the petals and sometimes the buds were put together with sugar to make candy. Along with butter, eggs and flour, rose water was also used in pies and to flavor cakes to which could be added anise, coriander, and similar flavorings. In upper class households, butter and sugar were often carved into exotic shapes.

Upper Classes and Nobility   Wealthy houses would have had several entire buildings devoted to storage of food, wine, and beer as well as some where baking, roasting, and boiling took place in kitchens with large fireplaces. These buildings accommodated not only the daily requirements of the residents but also could deal with the massive amount of food needed if the court decided to visit. In this event, a clerk of the kitchen, who answered to the Lord Chamberlain, had control over a staff of some 1,600 people, each of whom in turn had their own specialties. For example, the person in charge of bread had someone to maintain supplies of corn and flour, others to transport these supplies, and still others to bake it. The dairy was the domain of women; the kitchen was the domain of men.

Equipment for the kitchens included knives, whisks (made of blanched twigs), bowls, and colanders. Heated by charcoal, the temperature of the stove could be controlled to a fine degree.[7]

In 1557, Queen Elizabeth and her entourage spent three days visiting Lord North. It is said that for this short period of time 140 bushels of wheat, 67 sheep, 34 pigs, 4 stags, 16 bucks, 1,200 chickens, 363 capons, 33 geese, 6 turkeys, 237 dozen pigeons, fish and wild fowl of all varieties and horse loads of oysters were consumed. About 2,500 eggs and 430 pounds of butter were required by the cooks.[8]

Tarts and pies were popular and often presented in animal shapes or with coats of arms or other designs on the top crusts. Several varieties might appear at a single meal, all of which would have been large, containing great quantities of ingredients including meat, whole chickens, various vegetables, and fruits.

For banquets, pies have been reported measuring as much as nine feet in circumference with a weight of some 165 pounds. Such a pie would have used about two bushels of flour and at least 24 pounds of butter. It would have been stuffed with various animals such as goose, rabbit, pigeon, and fowl, the latter usually a pheasant or peacock, was often cooked whole and presented to the guests complete with feathers.[9]

One dish that appeared on the royal table when the guests were to be especially impressed was a tart filled with live birds. When it was cut open, they flew out (having been put in just before serving).

When the court went on a hunting expedition, the accompanying entourage included butchers; fishmongers; sellers of fruit, vegetables, and wine; and bakers. If the hunt was conducted on meatless days, fast horsemen would be there to ride to the coast in order to bring back fish or shellfish for the repast.

In 1553, Elizabeth I of England had Parliament proclaim that fish was compulsory for Wednesdays, Fridays, Saturdays, and during Lent. This law helped boost the fishing industry and contributed to bringing down the price of meat.

One popular dessert was trifle, enjoyed both at home or out on a picnic by families of all classes and means.

TRIFLE

Take a pint of the best and thickest cream, and set it on the fire in a clean skillet, and put into it sugar, cinnamon, and a nutmeg cut into four quarters, and so boil it well: then put it into the dish you intend to serve it in, and let it stand to cool till it be no more than lukewarm: then put in a spoonful of the best earning [rennet], and stir it well about, and so let it stand till it be cold, and then strew sugar upon it, and so serve it up, and this you may serve either in a dish, glass, or on another plate.[10]

Lower Classes People of lower social standing including merchants, artisans, and professionals, used pewter plates and dishes instead of gold and silver. Often children served the food and generally attended to the table. In the poorer sections of cities, laborers, street cleaners, water carriers, and those in other menial jobs used wooden plates and bowls.

In some areas, peasants ate nothing before they started work at sunrise and only a snack later, which had to last them until supper. They usually produced their own food. Bees supplied honey used for sweetening instead of sugar; meat was cured and salted; and bread and beer, staples of the diet, were made at home. Herbs were used in the kitchens of both rich and poor. The busy farmer's' wife made pickles and jams and preserved vegetables grown on their plot. If permitted by the landlord, her husband hunted and fished to supplement their diet.

The best produce was sold at local markets, and the family took what was left. Itinerant merchants brought various seasonings for sale, as well as news of the world outside the village.

The Poor The diet of the poor was monotonous, and the peasants were constantly undernourished. Bread, cheese, and onions sufficed in the morning; and for their one cooked meal per day, they stirred grain in with boiling water, cooked it slowly until the grain softened, and then added boiled roots and vegetables to make pottage that was scooped up by coarse bread made of barley or rye. A little meat or a slice of bacon would be a luxury.

Peasants' food included eggs, milk, and home-grown vegetables such as leeks, cabbage, turnips, peas, beans, and garlic. Herbs were widely used for everything.

There are many different recipes for pottage; but most seem to be variations on the theme of broth made of vegetables and herbs augmented with meat. One of these is given below:

POTTAGE (after Gervase Markham)
Take some meat bones or a strip of bacon, wash and boil well, skimming off any fat that comes to the top.
When cooked, strain and put the meat aside.
Using the same broth, add a couple of handfuls of cereal such as oats, barley or rye, along with some sliced onions, lettuce, carrots, turnips, spinach, cauliflower or cabbage.
Return the meat to the pot and add parsley, rosemary, a pinch of mace and 1/2 teaspoonful of sugar.
Boil all together, then cover and simmer about 3/4 hour or until done. Taste to adjust the seasonings.
Put a slice of bread in the bottom of a soup dish and cover with pottage.[11]

SCOTLAND

The Englishman, Fynes Moryson, whose travels took him to Scotland in April 1598, discussed the Scottish diet, noting that they ate a lot of kale and cabbage but not much fresh meat. When they ate mutton and geese, it was salted (which Fynes hated), and beef, venison, grouse, and fish, mostly salmon, were restricted to the wealthy. Porridge, stovies (a potato and meat stew), and various cheeses were consumed by almost everyone.

They drank pure wine, although at banquets comfits (sweetmeats made of fruit, roots or seeds, and preserved in sugar) were added. Wine was also taken by the wealthy in the morning and during the day. Brewed ale was a favorite drink.

Fynes attended a dinner at the house of a knight whose servants brought meat to the table set with plates of broth in which the meat was soaked. Those sitting at the main table, however, had chicken with prunes instead. He did' not think much of the cooking.

GERMANY

The free cities had a year's supply of victuals put away in the public houses to feed people in case the city was besieged. Moryson found the diet of the Germans to be simple and modest, apart from their heavy drinking. They were content with a morsel of meat and bread, preferring their own produce, and little was imported.

Commonly served at the table was sour cabbage (crawt) and beer boiled with bread (swoope). In upper Germany, veal and beef were served in small quantities, but in lower Germany the meal contained bacon and large dried savory puddings. In addition, dried fish, dried apples, and pears prepared with a cinnamon and butter sauce were popular. The Germans used many sauces, and one that particularly appealed to Moryson was made from cherries, served with roasted meat. In Saxony, he experienced a meal consisting of an entire calf's head complete with teeth. He said it looked like the head of a monster. Nevertheless, he enjoyed it because of the sauces accompanying it.

The Germans ate little cheese or butter, and Moryson mentions only one cheese he found palatable that was made from goats' milk. Another was prepared with a round hole into which was poured some wine. It was eaten when it was sufficiently moldy along with the maggots as "dainty morsels." Cheeses were strong and salty to stimulate the need for drink.

Breakfast was seldom eaten at the inns except by those setting out on journeys who would generally take a little ginger bread and aquavit. Moryson tells us that Germans never left the table until everything was consumed no matter how long it took, and the worst complaint that could be made was that there was not enough to eat. Some cities passed laws that guests could not sit more than five hours at the table.

Invited to a wedding feast in the house of an important citizen of Leipzig, Moryson described the supper more or less as follows: first, he was served hot and cold roast beef with a sauce made from sugar and sweet wine. This was followed by fried carp, then roasted mutton, then dried pears prepared with butter and cinnamon. Next came broiled salmon and herrings and finally a kind of bread-like English fritters with a little cheese. Bread, sprinkled with salt and pepper was provided to promote thirst. Barrels of wine were steadily consumed throughout the meal, and once it was finally finished, the drinking went on until no one could stand. Moryson seemed impressed with German drinking habits as he mentions them again and again. He tells us, for example, in Saxony, in the evening, men reeled from one side of the street to the other, stumbled and fell in the dirt, jostled every post, pillar, and person while trying to walk, and the gates of the city seemed too narrow for them to pass through. Yet it was no shame to be so drunk, nor to urinate under the table at the inn or in bed. It was not uncommon to fall out of the saddle when trying to ride under the influence of too much wine or beer.[12]

On special occasions, in a German city such as Nürnberg, it was customary to invite family and friends for a prodigious feast. On December 10, 1549, for example, at the baptism of Paul Behaim II, 36 pints of mead, 48 pastries,

A German Baptismal Feast

La Cocina Pobre ("The Poor Kitchen"). Pieter van der Heyden, 1563. (© Biblioteca Nacional de España.)

10 pints of new wine, and 7 of superior dark red wine were served along with more pastries and dates; three days later, two tables of guests were served 17 boiled and salted fish, a rabbit, 2 chickens, 24 geese, 2 ducks, 2 doves, bacon, 2 capons, white bread, fruit, 7 pints of new wine and 7 of year-old wine. Six weeks after the birth, neighbors and laborers were sent gifts that included pork, venison, other wild game, lard cake, wine, and (for some) expensive Westphalian ham. The reason for this last benificence was to proclaim that the mother had now recovered and returned to administration of the household.[13]

THE NETHERLANDS

For a main meal, sliced artichokes, beans, cabbage, cauliflower, carrots, onions, peas, and other vegetables, along with stale bread were made into a stew or hodgpodge. When the pig was killed in the autumn, the meat was sold or salted, and some was made into sausages. Mustard was a favorite sauce eaten with sausages and tripe. Wealthy people ate wild fowl and venison, others consumed fish, a staple food, purchased in the market or from a fishmonger making the rounds of the neighborhood. Fresh fish was not always as fresh as claimed, but the housewife could

La Cocina Rica ("The Rich Kitchen"). Pieter van der Heyden, 1563. (© Biblioteca Nacional de España.)

usually find dried cod and smoked herring or mussels. Bread, butter, and cheese were eaten by everyone, and specialties included mushrooms, frogs' legs, and oysters.[14]

Breakfast was generally not eaten except by children who might devour a piece of bread before going to school or work. The bakers' antiquated ovens were unreliable, and bread was not always ready at a given hour; only when the baker blew his horn, was fresh bread ready to be bought. When buying bread, a cloth was taken to carry it, and before cutting it, the wife would make the sign of the cross and then carve one into the loaf.

Gentleman's bread was white, made of wheat; this was also the bread given to someone about to be executed. The less well-off ate black bread, made from rye. In the country, people made their own rye bread adding salt, pork fat, raw onions, and cheese to improve the taste.

Small birds were often caught by placing a board, raised at one end by a stick, under which a few seeds were sprinkled. The stick was attached to the house by a string, and the birds were trapped when the string was pulled and the board crashed down on them. In addition, pots hung from the gutter of the roof for nesting birds, generally starlings, and when the young birds were nearly ready to leave the nest, they were gathered up and cooked.

The table set up for dinner usually had a tablecloth, wooden bowls, a salt dish, another for mustard, and a wooden or pewter spoon. Children stood to eat, and everyone ate with their fingers. No one touched the food before grace was said. Two meals a day were sufficient, and beer was the usual drink.

The Dutch version of the French Sop Jacobine used local sugar and cheeses instead of bread.

JACOBIN SOUP

Debone a roasted chicken; cut a good cheese into thin slices; cut wheat bread, into squares and place in the bottom of the dish so the food won't burn; arrange some of the cheese to cover and place some chicken meat on top sprinkled with sugar; then add another layer of cheese and another layer of chicken and again a layer of cheese; add some broth from fresh beef, put the dish on the fire, and let it come to a boil; serve hot.[15]

Waffles were part of the diet in the Netherlands, and, according to custom, if the waffle iron was borrowed from a neighbor, the last waffle produced was left on it for the loaner's benefit.[16]

SEAFOOD

Buyers of fish needed to be vigilant as often the gills were smeared with pig's blood to make it look fresh, when in fact, it could be old.

Many Netherlanders worked in the fishing business using boats called *buizen* in which the fish were not only caught, but also gutted, salted, and put in barrels on board. Other Dutch ships then picked up the catch and took it to market so the *buizen* could remain at sea.

People who lived near a river or the sea were able to eat fresh fish; but, because of difficulties in transporting food at this time, those residing in urban areas, away from the source, ate theirs salted, pickled or dried. The North Sea and the Baltic provided fish in huge numbers. Seafood included eels and herring which were put in pastry, stews and soups, as well as cooked in beer.

BREAD

Bread was an absolute staple in all European countries, and everyone ate it—the quality depending mainly on what kind of flour was used. Wheat had great importance since much bread was made from it. Other crops for making bread included rye, barley, and buckwheat, which did not require such good soil. The rich ate the best, which was left for a day after baking since it was considered unhealthy if eaten fresh.

The working methods in bake houses in England of this period may be seen in the Ordinances of the York Bakers Company. First, the grain was measured and milled, then sifted to remove any bran. The fine flour was swept up with a broom and the wing of a goose, after which it was kneaded with salt, yeast, and water. It was then shaped into small round loaves and weighed, pricked, and left to rise.

The next best bread was of whole wheat, the bran having been removed. Other whole wheat breads included some bran, while brown bread was sometimes mixed with rye to make a loaf of mixed grains. Froth from ale was often used to leaven the bread. Laws were passed to regulate size and quality of each category of loaf.[17] Poor people's bread was made from barley or rye.

The beehive-shaped oven was very hot, and once the fire was raked out, the bread was quickly slipped in by means of a long oven slice. The oven door was then sealed with mud which was not broken until the bread was ready to be removed, after which it was left to cool.[18]

In France, bread prices were regulated by the government and people had less to eat when times were bad. In the worst years, bread was made not from wheat but from oats, barley, millet, peas, chestnuts, or acorns. In Germany, the bread was mainly black and made from oatmeal porridge and rye, peas, and sometimes beans. In the poorest areas peasants were often forced to eat bread adulterated with grass.

BEVERAGES

Water was considered unfit to drink; children drank milk and other people consumed ale or wine. By the mid-sixteenth century ale was the favored drink, and in the south of England, although hops were still being imported from Holland, people were starting to grow them as beer took on a greater role. It was sold in three strengths: single, double, and double-double[19], the latter selling at the highest price. In 1560, Queen Elizabeth prohibited the production of double-double, considering it too strong. In addition, resin and salt were sometimes added by the brewer in order to preserve the ale longer. The flavor was not to everyone's taste. Many people produced their own beer. Numerous varieties were the result as people added various herbs such as sage, mace, and nutmeg to their brew.

French wine was imported into England and that from the Bordeaux region was especially favored. For cooking, Claret was probably the most popular. From Crete came a sweet, aromatic wine; while Italy, Portugal, Greece, and Germany also exported to England. From Spain came the strongest wine, Sherry, which was, in particular, a favorite. Hot, mulled wine and cider made from apples and pears was popular.

Wine was mainly drunk by the affluent in England due to import costs. However, whisky was already being distilled in Scotland by the sixteenth century and was thought to have medicinal properties. By the seventeenth century, the Scottish parliament started taxing whisky produced in private distilleries.

Besides copious amounts of wine, the French drank beer made from barley; although in Normandy where apples were abundant, apple brandy was coming into favor, and cider was widely consumed. By 1550, absinthe was produced from equal parts of dried wormwood leaves, sweet wine, and distilled water. It was believed that cordials made of distilled water kept the heart healthy.

The cacao seed was introduced to Europe by the Spanish shortly after the discovery of the New World in about 1520. It later became very popular as a drink. The first commercial shipment to Europe was from Veracruz to Sevilla in 1585. The Mexicans put chili peppers in the drink, but Europeans found this too bitter and replaced the chili with vanilla and added milk and sugar. Chocolate was at first drunk in a very thick, viscous state, helped along with a glass of water. By the end of the sixteenth century, it was a luxury item among European nobility, commonly drunk for breakfast, and its popularity filtered down to all classes. By the mid-seventeenth century, chocolate was consumed all over Europe, and the first chocolate houses were opened in London and Amsterdam at that time.

Coffee arrived in Europe by the middle of the sixteenth century; and in England, the first coffee house was opened in St Michael's Alley in Cornhill. Women were banned from coffee houses in England; in Germany, they were not.

The first shipments of tea to appear are thought to have come from China to Holland in 1610. Its use spread to France and England some time later, becoming very fashionable in England ca. 1657.[20] Initially, it was only drunk by the wealthy, being too expensive for most people.

SUBSISTENCE LIVING

Workers in Geneva in 1630 seldom earned enough to provide a good diet for their families. Those in the silk industry, for example, earned about 2 sols a day, while bread cost 5 sols a pound. As a result, the city council arranged for wages to be supplemented.

In the Netherlands, about 200 kilos of grain per person, per year minimum was needed for an adequate diet; but this would have required more land to be used to produce it than was available. In addition, with any variations in weather, prices would be greatly affected, so much that grain regularly had to be imported. The peasant majority of the population mostly lived on the brink of subsistence. As the population grew, and the land they worked diminished, they began to lose the ability to feed themselves. As the process of land fragmentation increased, more and more people starved in times of crisis; although in Antwerp, where food was more readily available to ordinary workers, most people lived close to the brink.

The type of crops grown depended on climate and soil; in southern Europe, olives produced oil, whereas further north, grapes flourished, and wine was made. In more northerly regions dairy cattle enabled the production of butter and milk. During winter when there were no fresh vegetables or fruit, it was even harder to follow an adequate diet, and salted or pickled meat and fish were used as much as possible. Under great duress, even putrified meat was marinated and used to the detriment of a family's health.

In some regions of France, the peasants were continually undernourished, existing on poor-quality vegetables and pottage. Many sustained themselves on cereals that were mostly made into bread; in Brittany buckwheat porridge was consumed, whereas in Burgundy maize was used in porridge and rye in bread.

Famine, always a possibility everywhere, was caused by weather and poor harvests, population rises, disease, and war as well as by the hoarding of profit-seekers. There was a major famine in 1594–1597 in which the weather was a primary factor, as was the plague in Spain, Italy, and Germany. The lower classes who lived in the cities could sometimes find relief for their hunger by begging. There was no such help in the rural areas, and people turned to carrion.

In England, in the late 1500s, famine, especially in the north, caused many deaths. Thus, while one portion of society lived luxurious lives and ate well, other members of the population barely survived if at all. Farmers would often find themselves out of work as landowners gave their land over to pastoral use.

Bread riots took place regularly throughout Europe and in Geneva in 1628, where many were constantly undernourished, one of the pastors told his flock the reason they were starving was due to their sinfulness, thereby enraging his audience.[21]

NOTES

1. Ozment (1977), 126.
2. Braudel (1979), 222–223.
3. Erlanger, 198.
4. Braudel, op. cit., 205.
5. See Erlanger, 197–202, for upper class dining rituals and food.
6. Brears, 8–9.
7. Ibid., 15.
8. Salzman, 85–86.
9. Pearson, 550.
10. Markham, 102.
11. Ibid., 76.

12. Moryson, iv, 24–34.
13. Ozment (1990), 85–86.
14. Moryson, op. cit., 60.
15. Poortvliet, 121.
16. Ibid., 122.
17. Sass, 27–28.
18. Brears, 13–14.
19. Sass, 29.
20. Braudel, op. cit., 249–51.
21. Kamen, 35–38.

17

TRAVEL

A visit home to a country estate for a noble living in the city, a merchant
making the rounds of villages to show his wares, a student going home
from university to another town during holidays or, indeed, anyone who
needed to travel often found it a difficult undertaking. Choking dust, lack
of shade, and swarms of flies, gnats, and mosquitoes in the hot summer
months made travel an unpleasant experience. A journey in winter, especially in the northern countries, amounted to another kind of ordeal: icy
wind, snowdrifts blocking the route, rain causing swollen streams, and
floods all contributed to slow-going, especially when the horses sank into
the mud and had to be hauled out, often by a pair of oxen owned by a
local farmer.

Most roads were dirt tracks at this time. Long-distance travel was by
foot or horse, either one's own or hired, and carriages used by the affluent.
On rough roads, without springs, traveling in these vehicles was anything
but comfortable and seemingly endless; for instance. it normally took a
week to go from London to Plymouth. The journey from Calais to Paris
by horse and carriage might take two to three days.

Packhorses or covered wagons were used to transport goods, and the
wagons sometimes carried passengers as well. Whenever possible, the
preference was to move goods by water. England had a coastal trade by
which commodities such as coal were moved from one part of the country
to another. In France, the rivers were widely used to transport goods and
people as were the canals in Holland, and rivers in Germany. A major
river artery, the Rhine, was exploited extensively to transport goods
inland from Rotterdam to Germany, France, and Switzerland, and the

other way, to board ships bound for England, Scandinavia, and other Baltic regions. Toll stations along the rivers collected revenues for the princes who had established frontier barriers that had to be crossed, a fee paid, and sometimes the baggage searched. All this added to the expense of a journey.

INNS

The main roads were used for most travel, and inns, such as they were, had their place along the route. For people in a hurry and with money, post horses could be hired for each stage. The principal highways were sometimes risky enough but to take a back road, even though it might be shorter, was distinctly dangerous. People on the move, such as judges making their circuit rounds, traders, ambassadors, royal couriers, pilgrims on their way to shrines, and occasional tourists, normally elected to follow the main roads. There were some respectable inns where a traveler might expect a form of entertainment such as music accompanying the meals, reasonably clean bedding, and a knock on the door in the morning to arouse him from slumber. Some hostelries could accommodate several hundred people and during fairs in the vicinity, were packed to overflowing.

Luther and his companions, on his one and only visit to Rome, walked 800 miles from Saxony to the Holy City. Since they were monks, they found shelter at night in various monasteries or in humble homes, and thus were not required to carry much money.

Inns of a different caliber were available to those who could ill afford expensive lodging. The rooms above the stables were small, dingy, and dirty, the linen seldom changed, and fleas and bedbugs abounded. Drinking, shouting, and noise from unruly patrons went on all night. Even the finest inns provided only chamber pots for the guests, and in the more sleazy ones, unwashed people slept naked, often several to a bed.

In Germany, when a coach arrived at an inn to pick up passengers, the servants brought a cup of wine, and the maids brought some flowers, all expecting their *drinckgeld*. According to Fynes Moryson, the coachman himself was often rude and would not wait even one minute if a passenger was not at the door ready to go. On route, if someone needed to alight from the vehicle to do urgent business, he was simply left behind if he could not run fast enough to catch up with the coach. At the end of the journey, the driver demanded a substantial tip as his right.

The best inns in Germany were known by the coat of arms on the gate or hanging in the dining room. These were often given to the owner by patrons who wished to show they had been there. Guests sat where they pleased and ate on various square tables in one room. Men ate and drank sometimes with their doublets open to a naked chest.

Fynes found many guests friendly. It was the custom to dip bread into a sauce with the point of a knife. All classes sat at the same table. As they drank to each other they were liable to kiss their neighbor and make bargains, promising anything before they staggered home where their wives squashed their lavish ideas and largesse. Women stayed away from public houses where wine and beer were sold.[1]

Perhaps the most surprising custom that travelers came across in the German lands was the *Schlaffdrincke* or sleeping drink. After dinner, when the table cloth was removed, everyone had to rise immediately and leave or go to bed. If they did not, there was a price to pay. A sip of the cup (from which one had previously been drinking) after the removal of the table cloth required the imbiber to pay an equal share of those who continued to drink all night, even though he went straight to bed after that last sip. For the unwary, the bill in the morning could be a shock.

Merchants staying at an inn generally found the staff unhelpful. They waited on the tables but did little else. They did not pull off one's boots (which was customary elsewhere) and were so rude that if they were asked for something, they would say "get it yourself!" Even though the sheets on the bed might be filthy, they still demanded their *drinckgeld*, and if someone left the inn without paying a tip, they followed him and demanded it.[2] Few ordinary people traveled far from their villages, and most walked, covering at best in a full day about 20 miles.

More inns opened in England after the religious houses, often shelters for travelers, were suppressed in 1539. Many of these had a kind of bunk bed whereby the master slept on top and the servant on the lower part. There is a story about a Scottish Laird who spent the night at an English inn and, being given a room with a four-poster bed in it, assumed he should sleep on the canopy part above, and his servant on the bed below. Needless to say, the Laird slept poorly, and the servant had the best night's sleep of his life![3] In Scotland, upper class travelers relied on hospitality from people of their own echelon, and rarely used the wretched inns.

In France, where the inns were generally of the lowest order, the weary traveler (after a strenuous day on the road), crowded into the inn at night along with vagrants, poor woodcutters, and laborers, who drank themselves into oblivion with cheap wine or ale. A more refined person would spend the night on guard in the dirty room, without fire or light, sword on the table that had been placed in front of the door to make it more secure.

In 1532, a group of monks journeying through Spain complained that they lodged like pigs in filth and dirt and that horses were treated better. The mystic, Santa Teresa, traveling in Spain in 1575 stayed at an inn near Córdoba in a room that previously housed pigs. Replete with vermin and atrocious odors, it had a ceiling so low she was unable to stand up straight. The bed was filthy and uncomfortable, and the shouts and curses of the other guests kept her awake. The next night she and her companions camped in the fields.[4] Most accounts of the time agree that Spain was the worst country for European travelers; but France was not far behind.

At night, in the Netherlands, where it was essential to find an inn, they were few and far between in open country. There, one ate whatever had been cooked that day; there was no choice. As many as five persons slept in the same, large bed, and there was no expectation of finding it to be clean or free of fleas and bugs.

BANDITS

For the student going to a distant university, a lawyer with business elsewhere, or a journeyman looking for work and traveling from city to city, every dark wood, valley, or ravine offered refuge for a robber to strike the unwary. It was always best to keep to the main road in spite of the insects, dust, deep ruts, or ice-covered pools and mud in winter. Even there it was imprudent to travel alone but with enough armed men to deter highwaymen. The bandits were sometimes younger sons of noble blood who had missed out on the family inheritance or impecunious knights. Many were discharged soldiers who could not settle into a routine life of farming or shop-keeping. Matters were made worse by innkeepers who, in collusion with robbers, informed them of any guests lodging in the establishment who appeared to have money. It was also expedient for drovers and herders to pay off the bandits to protect their flocks of sheep or herds of cattle.

Although a few ambassadors, military planners, and some merchants had guide books that were printed in the sixteenth century, the majority of travelers had to rely on paid village guides to reach their destinations. No roads were signposted or otherwise marked as to directions and pitfalls. It was easy to get lost in the dark forests and even in open country when paths diverged; bandits were always on the lookout for such people. A country person who knew the roads and the dangers might refuse to act as a guide unless a party was well armed and paid handsomely because he still had to return home again. Village people and farmers traveled little, but if it were necessary to go beyond the reach of help, they preferred to go on good sunny days since sometimes floods and washed-out bridges caused them to detour on back roads, much to the highwayman's delight.

When one gentleman was out walking alone in the countryside, so the story goes, he spotted in the distance three unsavory-looking characters approaching. Having heard in the last village that there were highwaymen about, he quickly tore his fine clothes into shreds, except the small patch sown into the lining that contained his money, and walked toward them with nothing but rags hanging off him. When he came face to face with the armed scoundrels, he held out his hand and begged for money. They obliged, and gave him enough to pay for his dinner that night.

THE DARKER SIDE OF A MERCHANT'S LIFE

A young Nürnberg merchant, Balthasar Paumgartner, wrote numerous letters to his wife Magdalena when he was away from home.[5] He became a seasoned traveler between Nürnberg, Frankfurt, and Lucca in north central Italy. From Lucca where he spent much time he shipped merchandise to the fairs at the other two cities. His worries and insecurities are noted in his letters as the transportation of merchandise from Italy to northern depots was never certain. He found both Frankfurt and Italy inhospitable places and on one occasion worried about the delay in departing Frankfurt with the merchants' convoy.

He was especially concerned about the routes that were known by his colleagues as murder road. Merchants carefully kept an eye on reports of highwaymen, soldiers, or wandering mercenaries along their routes as well as weather conditions. When it seemed favorable, they set off in their convoys along the tracks going from village to village toward their destination. In some towns suspicious people would close the gate to strangers fearing bearers of disease. A life of traveling was unpleasant in other ways; Balthasar wrote of his hands swollen and cracked after weeks of riding in winter weather. Colds and flu' were a constant problem, and he ran out of handkerchiefs. Intense heat in summer months brought travel to a halt.

An aspect of the trade that Balthasar disliked the most was when the fair was over and buying and selling stopped, and it was time to demand payment. At this point the most arduous work began with the exchange of money and the haggling, screaming, and cursing that accompanied it. Balthasar was perhaps not of the temperament to be a merchant, finding competition and bargaining most unpleasant.

FRENCH ROYAL COURT

The French king, François I, seemed to be perpetually on the move and seldom remained long in one place. Accompanying him, his court comprised a retinue of about 12,000 horses, 3,000–4,000 men and women, a large troop of gentlemen of the household, courtiers, guards, officers, and ladies. Hoards of clergy, craftsmen, laborers, and specialty cooks moved through the countryside staying here and there at a nobleman's chateau, in a city palace, or sometimes camping in an open field, as the king wished. The court brought along its own merchants with the special rights to supply the courtiers, greengrocers, butchers, bakers, wine merchants, and a host of others along with suppliers of hay and oats for the horses and mules, a string of servants to care for the hunting dogs and falcons and horsemen who were ready to ride at the king's bidding to far-off coasts to bring back seafood for meatless days.

The sovereign's large tent and the kitchen utensils were carried on the backs of sturdy mules while the king himself went on horseback or in a litter, the latter used also for the older women of the court. Younger and stronger women rode horseback; others were packed into wagons for long, bone-jarring rides. River barges, when used, were no doubt a relief from the bad roads. Like a small army, the court moved out in its specific order with the quartermaster far ahead, scouting out the next place to lodge.

Mariano Giustiniano, ambassador from Venice, wrote home in 1535 that during his 45 month tenure at the French court, it did not remain in the same place for more than two weeks. When it approached a town or village, the church bells rang, the priests and common people rushed to see the king ride by and perhaps stop for awhile. He must have enjoyed all this. From coronation to death, he continued his rounds of the country.[6]

BENEFITS OF TRAVEL

Travel was considered beneficial for financially well-off young men, allowing them to gain some knowledge about other countries. In Elizabethan England, for example, they studied languages such as French or Spanish and were often sent to those countries accompanied by a tutor who would find experienced teachers there for the boys. By the end of the sixteenth century, government positions required facility in foreign languages as did an entrance into high society. Even in the lower classes that worked in the crafts and trades, parents attempted to provide practical experience for their sons through travel, which often led to study in foreign universities.

Oftentimes young men without connections in the new country lived in private houses; but if they became ill, trouble could easily ensue. If he were Protestant and living in a Catholic home, no one would look after him unless he converted. In addition, no doctor or even servants were permitted to take care of him. This caused great anxiety for parents whose children were studying in Catholic countries and they usually made every effort to see that their son traveled with a good, moral tutor and that they were housed with friends or relatives.

Fynes Moryson traveled mainly on horseback in Europe, and on his way to Italy, he pretended to be a Frenchman lest he be liable as an Englishman to imprisonment in Spanish territory in Italy. In Rome, he felt safe once he proved he was not a spy.

Henry Wotton, traveling to complete his education, followed a similar route to Moryson. He arrived in Italy in 1591 pretending to be a Catholic German, as he would have been incarcerated as a spy if discovered to be English. He stayed two years in that country and in later years, working for the government, his fluent Italian helped, as feigning to be an Italian, he was able to warn the Scottish king of an assassination plot.[7]

According to Coryat, it was hard to meet anyone in society in Germany who had not been to England, Italy, France, or Spain and gained some educational advantage from this. But Coryat, an avid traveler himself, comments that when one has finished traveling, it is better to return to one's own country and learn about that. It was necessary to understand what it meant to travel and not just to gloss over the surface of foreign countries:

> But we will say that he is the man that visiteth forreine Kingdomes and doth truly travell . . . travelleth for the greater benefit of his wit, for the commodity of his studies, and the dexterity of his life, who moveth more in minde then body, who attayneth to the same by the course of his travel, that others doe at home verypainfully and with great study by turning of bookes.[8]

But there were other benefits, too:

> . . . But what shall I say of the other fruits of travell? Where shalt thou more happily and studiously attaine to all the liberal sciences then in Germany, which doth excell the auncient Egyptians in the study of Geometrie, the Hebrews in Religion, the Chaldaeans in Arithmeticke, the Grecians in all arts, the Romans in discipline, and in variety of mechanicall trades, constancy and fortitude, all other nations.[9]

While boys were often permitted to go to other countries to study, girls remained at home to prepare for marriage. Some, who were more ambitious, followed a classical literary course of study, but these were rare.

Felix Platter (son of Thomas Platter), who set off to Montpellier to study, traveled on horseback. En route, he and his companions ran into a storm and, seeking shelter, found an inn in the village of Mézières which, unbeknownst to them, was a haven for bandits and murderers. The inn

> . . . was kept by a woman, who could find
> space for us only on the ground floor, in a room
> open to all the four winds. In this room was
> a long table, at which sat a number of Savoyard
> peasants and beggars, eating roasted chestnuts
> and black bread and drinking cheap wine.[10]

Although not keen, they decided to spend the night there rather than continue in the bad weather, and since there was no room for them, joined the men sitting at the table who were drinking heavily and who eventually staggered out into the adjoining room to sleep by the fire. Platter's guide overheard them plotting to kill and rob them by waiting for them in the forest, so after the men fell into a drunken sleep, Felix's group left quietly for Geneva before daylight. There, he heard Calvin preach to a large group of people and met up with a new traveling companion. En route they saw bodies of men hanging from the trees, and on entering the town of Lyon

> ... met a Christian [Protestant?] who was being led out to be burnt outside the gate; he was in his shirt with a truss of straw fastened on his back.[11]

On his way to visit a friend, he had to cross the river in a small boat run by a woman. When they reached the middle, she demanded the fare, threatening to throw Felix overboard if he didn't pay immediately. Not having the exact money, he overpaid her since she refused to give him change. When he returned to Lyon later in the day, he went via a bridge, although the journey was longer.

In all, it took him 20 days to travel 95 miles and reach Montpellier.

NOTES

1. Moryson (1967), 339–340.
2. Ibid., 345–346.
3. Warrack, 163–164.
4. Anderson, 10.
5. See Ozment (1986).
6. Febvre, 15–19.
7. Pearson, 206–207.
8. Coryat, 71–74.
9. Ibid., 76.
10. Platter, 32.
11. Ibid., 38.

18

THIRTY YEARS' WAR

In the year 1618, all the troubles of Europe, social, economic, and religious were released in a frenzy of war and atrocities. At no time throughout the long Middle Ages or the Early Modern period did the four horsemen of the Apocalypse (religion, war, famine, and death) ride so brazenly over the European lands.

For much of the population of Germany, the apocalypse, foretold by preachers and laymen, seemed to have arrived. The forces of evil and the forces of good were about to engage each other in a cataclysmic battle. Both Catholics and Protestants considered themselves the force of good. In the Holy Roman Empire, an interwoven population pattern of Catholic and Protestant sects turned to bloody disaster. Townsmen and peasants were often caught in the path of advancing or retreating mercenary armies generally more bent on plunder and rape than on religious ideologies.

The simmering cauldron began to boil over when the Holy Roman Emperor, Rudolf II, transferred his court from Vienna to Prague in 1583 and placed Catholics in the key positions of the provincial administration throughout Bohemia. In 1608 anti-Catholic forces advanced into Bohemia and the following year Rudolf reluctantly issued a charter granting freedom of worship to both Catholics and Protestants. Upon Rudolph's death in 1612, Matthias became emperor, and in 1617 Catholic officials closed Protestant chapels in violation of a religious-liberty guarantee of 1609. At an assembly called by the Protestants, the imperial regents representing the emperor were accused of violating the guarantee and were thrown from a window of the council room of Prague Castle. Only the regents' pride was seriously hurt, but the incident sparked the Bohemian revolt against the emperor.[1]

Soon after the defenestration of Prague, the battle lines were drawn throughout all of Greater Bohemia (Bohemia, Silesia, Lusatia, and Moravia) under a new Catholic emperor, Ferdinand II. On November 8, 1620, imperial forces won a great victory at White Mountain near Prague, and Bohemia soon fell back into the hands of the Catholics. Leaders of the rebellion were executed and others who had participated had their property confiscated. Ferdinand rescinded the declaration of 1609 and began a program, led by the Jesuits, to eradicate Protestants. The League of Evangelical Union. a collection of German Protestant states, was dissolved. and the remnants of the Protestant armies fled north.

DANISH INTERVENTION 1625–1629

Threatened by the recent Catholic military successes, Denmark, a sympathetic Protestant nation under king Christian IV (also king of Norway), feared for its sovereignty and rising Habsburg power. Raising an army he invaded Germany in 1625. The Danish troops were forced to fall back under the combined pressure of two Habsburg armies led by Albrecht von Wallenstein and Count Johannes Tilly. Christian IV signed the Treaty of Lübeck with the Habsburgs dynasty ending Danish intervention in the war.

SWEDISH INTERVENTION 1630–1635

Under Gustavus Adolphus, Sweden entered the war on the side of the Protestants and drove the Catholic armies back regaining Protestant territory. The Swedish army lived off the land, and its invasion of Catholic areas resulted in cruelty and pillage. Gustavus forced loans from Jews and Catholics alike to sustain his army and held religious leaders for ransom. After the death of Gustavus in the Battle of Lützen in 1632, the Protestant armies were soundly defeated in the battle of Nördlingen in Bavaria in 1634.

To appease the nobility of the Baltic regions and to win them over to his side, General Wallenstein exempted them from all taxation and lay the burden for financing his war effort on the peasants and townsmen. Adding insult to injury, the people were forced to attend lectures and sermons by Jesuit clergy.

Protestants who had seen their houses, farms, and businesses taken over by Catholics were also out for blood. When the Swedes invaded Bohemia and took Prague, the Lutherans of the city who had been dispossessed of property and forced to wander around in misery now took back their property, plundered their Catholic overlords and churches, and silenced anyone who resisted.

FRENCH INTERVENTION

France, alarmed by Habsburg power and despite its own Catholic orientation, entered and prolonged the war. The French government had already helped finance Denmark's intervention. French and Swedish armies defeated Emperor Ferdinand III and the imperial army at the Battle of Zusmarshausen in Bavaria in 1648 bringing the conflict to an end.

SOLDIERS

The regions ravaged by war took years to recover. The common people of Germany were overwhelmed with soldiers, some carrying the plague and other diseases.

The majority of soldiers, mostly mercenaries, did not have specific uniforms and dressed the best they could. To identify themselves as friend and not foe they used head or armbands along with passwords. In many cases in Germany, there was little alternative than to become mercenary soldiers when their farms and livelihood were destroyed in battles or by looters. Providing for the many thousands of mercenary soldiers was generally a problem. Sometimes the men were enlisted by the prince of a realm and sometimes through independent organizations of recruiters. Suppliers of the men-at-arms were also private entrepreneurs.

During the course of the Thirty Years' War, the situation for the common soldier deteriorated as clothes and boots wore out and were hard to replace due to shortages in supplies. Food was often slow in coming as the means of production might be far removed from the war zone where crops and animals had been destroyed. Living conditions in battle areas quickly degenerated as masses of men fouled their camps. Ragged and torn tents were difficult to replace. Foraging was too often the only means to stave off hunger and undernourished, weakened troops died more often from contagious diseases than in battle. When pay turned up, there was nothing to buy in a badly devastated area; and when not fighting or scrounging, money was used for gambling or to buy food from a private provider that turned up now and again around army camps to sell produce at an enormously inflated price. Soldiers accompanied by families, as was frequently the case, or by female companions, had to look after their welfare also. Lack of discipline and desertion were always present and commanders resorted to severe military justice.

PLIGHT OF THE COMMON PEOPLE

In some places such as Sweden, men were conscripted for the ranks often resulting in hardships for peasant families who needed their young sons in the fields for planting and harvesting. Many would never return, and others came back maimed, presenting still further adversity.

With the economy in ruins, the common people of Germany suffered the most. They were the ones who supplied the needs of the large armies, willingly or not. Those who had not become totally destitute paid much heavier taxes to the state that in turn paid the soldiers. Workers and peasants lucky enough to escape the great devastation were close to the brink of ruin as larger and larger percentages of their crops or money went to the state in taxes as the war continued on.

When armies loomed on the horizon, the inhabitants fled into the forests trying to survive on berries, wild fruit, bark, and roots. Subject to the elements, many died of exposure. Entire villages and towns were razed to the ground. Many people lost everything.

After months of hiding out in the dark forests of southwest Germany, it takes little imagination to picture men, women, and children, their faces hollow and sunken, ribs protruding, and eyes glazed. With raw fingers tearing at roots to chew on and stripping bark from trees to suck out the few nutrients, picking maggots and worms from decaying plants, they shuffled from place to place moving through the trees in search of anything edible. Stumbling upon a hamlet they would see flames and smoke rising from the houses and withdraw back into the forest to avoid the mercenaries warming themselves by the fires, roasting a cow, and drinking the plundered wines, dead villagers lying at their feet.

Those who had seen their houses and crops destroyed as armies passed through, saw the process repeated as they retreated, and again as another army passed in pursuit. Agriculture all but ceased.

Depredation and misery gripped the land for years. Sieges were particularly difficult for townsmen. In the autumn of 1638, Bernhard of Saxe-Weimar besieged the city of Breisach, cutting it off from provisions for nearly four months. Nearly all the animals including house pets were eaten. Rumors were rife of cannibalism as children disappeared never to be seen again. One contemporary reported cannibalism in the prisons and the eating of kidnapped children.[2]

In the countryside, once cultivated fields returned to shrub and forest land, and wolves stalked the villages and farms in search of food.

In Brandenburg, about half the population were lost, while in some areas about two-thirds of the people perished. The male population of Germany was reduced by almost 50 percent. The Czechs declined by a third; the Swedish armies alone are thought to have destroyed 2,000 castles, 18,000 villages, and 1,500 towns in Germany—one-third of all towns there.

RURAL POPULATIONS

Pitched battles between large armies took place mostly in the countryside with inestimable damage to crops and livestock. Whole areas were depopulated as the peasantry en masse left for safer ground.

When soldiers marched through the villages and towns where people remained, the poor were forced to work for them and hand over their last crumb of bread with no compensation. Horses, always in demand, were commandeered from the farms and ridden away by soldiers not to be seen again. Cattle, pigs, and sheep were slaughtered on the spot and eaten. Civilians were beaten or killed at the slightest resistance to soldiers' demands.

Officers, their servants and often ordinary soldiers quartered in private houses had to be fed along with their horses depleting the last of the owner's supplies and money. Agreements were sometimes made between a military commander and a regional council in which the region paid their conquerors a certain amount of money and provided items such as straw, candles, hay, and salt and the army refrained from plundering.[3]

THE FATE OF CITIES

Leaving their quarters at night Imperial soldiers terrorized the inhabitants of the Baltic coast sacking the surrounding villages and towns. Some towns were forced to lodge and feed soldiers for months and even years. For the peasants and shopkeepers to furnish the beer, wine, meat, bread, or whatever the soldiers demanded, resulted in profound deprivation for lower and middle class families.

German cities and towns were not safe for minority groups whether Catholic or Protestant as the war spread across the empire in the spring of 1625. The Protestant citizens of Ulm suffered nine days of beatings, rape, and murder when at harvest time, a troop of cavalrymen appeared and looted and burned a good part of the town in a rampage.[4]

Magdeburg, a Lutheran city on the Elbe River, rebelled against the emperor, but its inadequate forces were quickly defeated in the field. With Tilly's army camped outside the city's walls, the months came and went. The city vainly tried to entice other Protestant princes to its rescue. By May 1631, the defenses in shambles, Tilly's troops broke in. The rich city was stripped of priceless manuscripts and books, paintings, tapestries, and every other removable treasure. Whoever they encountered, the soldiers slew. Women of all ages were raped; old and young were cut down. The massacre at Magdeburg was the worst slaughter of the Thirty Years' War.[5]

Of the 20,000 or so citizens, the vast majority were slain. In addition, of the numerous peasants who had crowded into the city along with many nobles, only about 1,000 survived the killing according to the then new French weekly newspaper, the *Gazette*.

Heidelberg was looted for three days after which the town was more systematically stripped of its treasures. Books and manuscripts in its famous library were shipped off to the Vatican as a present to the pope.[6]

Some cities fared better than others: the Protestant city of Leipzig, although sacked on a few occasions, remained a valuable trading center. The Catholic city of Regensburg, seat of the elections to the imperial throne, although plundered by Bernhard of Saxe-Weimar, was retaken 10 months later by imperialist troops and quickly rebuilt. A few other cities escaped the devastation of war altogether such as the imperial city of Vienna, and the free imperial city of Hamburg. As a neutral area, Hamburg flourished during the war attracting Catholics, Jews, and Protestants to its lucrative commercial markets.

DISEASE

Pestilence raged throughout the war zones and surrounding areas among both civilians and soldiers spread by troop movements and migrating populations. The overcrowding of refugees from the countryside into walled cities already ridden with vermin, decaying garbage, and unclean water along with shortages of food, further accelerated mortality rates; and untold people perished from typhus, scurvy, and endemic dysentery. Estimates of civilian casualties have ranged up to as high as 30 percent of the population of Germany.

ATROCITIES AND REVENGE

The sack of Magdeburg, the worst atrocity of the war, was far from the only act of senseless cruelty. The imperial armies burned villages, burned churches, and killed indiscriminately. Civilians were diabolically tortured to disclose where their money and valuables were hidden, their houses were burned, and hangings were common. When a man had nothing further to give, soldiers took his life. Neither the old, nor the young were safe.

When 50 Swedish troops were surprised and captured by an army of peasants, they had their feet, hands, noses, and ears severed from their bodies and their eyes poked out. The Swedish army took full revenge for the outrage by burning 200 Catholic villages to the ground. Now it was the Catholics' turn to seek shelter in the forests and hills where many starved or died of exposure.

PRICES

Due to shortages of food and rising prices, landlords of the estates worked their land to capacity, and their peasants toiled longer hours to produce more. Peasants had little choice in the matter since they needed work. The larger profits did not accrue to them, however. Distributors were also in a position to raise prices and did so.

TREATY OF WESTPHALIA

Some four million people lost their lives, and many more returned home to find it in ruins. Another half century would go by before the damage was repaired and the grief and pain of the war began to subside. After 30 years of bloody conflict, the Peace of Westphalia was signed by the warring parties, bringing the conflict to a close.

Christians living in principalities where their denomination was not the established church were guaranteed the right to practice their faith in public during allotted times, and in private at any time. Jews were excluded. Any individual living in an undesirable region had the right to emigrate. The Protestant princes and cities were allowed to keep whatever Church lands they had confiscated up to the year 1624, but they now could take no more land. The document also declared that any Catholics or Protestants who wished to change their religion must "be patiently tolerated and have freedom of conscience in their homes without investigation or disturbance."[7]

The treaty ended the pope's European political power, and Innocent X declared it "null, void, invalid, iniquitous, unjust, damnable, reprobate, inane, and meaningless." European sovereigns, both Catholic and Protestant, ignored his opinion.[8]

NOTES

1. Although the representatives of the emperor fell several storeys, in the Protestant version they landed in a carload of manure; Catholics claimed that angels appeared, and lowered them safely to the ground.

2. For this and other aspects of cannibalism, see Frey, 43.

3. Ibid., 32.

4. Ibid., 30.

5. See Cunningham, 180 ff.

6. Frey, 26–27.

7. Ibid., 48; Cunningham, 323.

8. Information in this chapter was primarily extracted from two excellent sources: Frey, Chapter 2, and Cunningham, 180ff.

19

CATHOLIC PERSPECTIVE AND COUNTER-REFORMATION

Well before the Protestant Reformation, some efforts were made by the Catholic Church itself to reform abuses; but lacking rigorous enforcement, little was accomplished.

A TROUBLED CHURCH

As some members of the Church acknowledged, a regrettable worldliness manifested itself among high ecclesiastics. Apologists admitted that this had diverted many from their primary objective of saving souls, but found numerous reasons as to why the Church was not more effective in its suppression of Protestantism. The Turks were pressing on Hungary and Austria from the southeast threatening Europe, a great concern and preoccupation of the popes; while the French allied themselves with the reformers for political reasons and invaded the German west, annexing some of the bishoprics and aiding heretics. As the Church itself was aware, Catholic religious idealism had failed to a large extent in its primary purpose as an intermediary between God and mankind. Accordingly, intellectual cultivation, previously confined in large measure to the clergy, had become more common among the people, giving rise to a Renaissance and Humanistic pagan morality along with the desire for luxury associated with the revival of Greco-Roman heathenistic traditions. Crass materialism had begun to manifest itself within the upper classes of society including some high ranking clergy, who had sought accumulation of wealth and a sybaritic life style diametrically opposed to the spirit of Christianity and its ascetic virtues.

At first, many bishops and high clerics, paid little heed to the new movement among them. Similarly, the too often poorly educated, lazy, and indifferent village clergy made little effort to preserve the loyalty of their parishioners and restrain their defection. As the Church soon realized, Reformers, on the other hand, displayed a prodigious passion for what was considered in the eyes of the Catholic Church a false cause.

Deceptively feigning adherence to Catholic principals, Reformers retained for a time many of the ceremonies of Catholic worship, but had lied about repudiating only matters pertaining to human invention deceiving the people concerning their real objectives. They had indulged the people by singing popular religious hymns and reading the Bible in the vernacular at divine service.

Protestant tenets that advocated justification by faith alone, giving everyone a share in sacerdotal functions, thus denied the difference between priests and ordinary people along with the virtues of good works. Protestant rejection of free will furnished an excuse for immoral and debauched behavior.

COUNCIL OF TRENT

To thwart the Reformation, the Roman Church initiated a Counter-Reformation (the Protestant name) in 1545 with the Council of Trent that intermittently met in 25 sessions until 1563. In this major reform council, the participants addressed the most serious problems confronting the internal workings of the Church. They reviewed Church doctrines and all were upheld such as the trinity, apostolic succession, good works, veneration of saints, and the celibacy of priests. The seven sacraments remained as they were throughout medieval times, but priests were to be better educated and teach plainly and coherently what was necessary for salvation according to the Catholic principals. The tradition handed down from previous councils was considered of paramount significance, but the plurality of offices was abandoned, and bishops were no longer to be appointed on political grounds. They were now required to preach and live within their bishopric. Theological seminaries were to be created in all dioceses to both address the problems of clerical deficiencies in literacy and to retrain priests on all levels in a manner befitting religious principles of spirituality, focusing on asceticism rather than temporal or earthly preoccupations. By defining doctrine on salvation, the sacraments, and the Biblical canon, the Council of Trent attempted to rebut Protestant dissension. A Roman Inquisition, already established earlier to control heresy within Catholic territories, would continue.

VILLAGE REFORM

In the middle of the sixteenth century, before the reforms of the Council of Trent became effective, life in the villages was conservative in most matters of change; and while some villagers were open to new Protestant ideas, others rejected out of hand both Protestant and Catholic reforms that interfered with established daily patterns of life.[1]

A major problem for the Catholic Church was to be found in the villages and small towns of the countryside where misuse of the sacraments took place, and other sinful activities such as heavy drinking on religious holidays, overindulgent feasting, worship at unauthorized shrines, the failure to attend Mass, and the superstitious allure of witches and black magic.

It was also considered desirable to install schools for catechism classes and primary schools to give the young a better understanding of Catholicism.

Popular culture embedded in the countryside that prevailed at carnivals and local fêtes, especially among the youth, included immoral pagan practices such as parades in bizarre costumes, enormous ugly giants (men on stilts), dancing around the bonfire, allusions to witches and goblins, flirtations, licentious plays, and prodigious drinking, as far as the Church was concerned. The banning of masks at carnival time as well as actors and plays did not set well in town or village and were generally not enforced.

It was also felt that a clear and sharp distinction should be made between Catholicism and Protestantism; but here the Church walked a fine line. To impose discipline, obedience, and morality on the people appeared to imitate the strict principles of Protestantism. If reform were needed, were not the Protestants correct? If the need for reform was denied, most people could see that this was not true.[2]

It was well understood that more often than not parish priests did not try to force on their parishioners reforms that were unpopular and opposed by the congregation. As they also frequently preached in an uninspiring manner, much of the flock nodded off or left before the sermon was over. The Catholic reforms were now to bring a new kind of better educated priest who would encourage conformity through energetic preaching and example.

In some places, extreme unction and confirmation remained nearly unknown as few peasants requested it, especially when the priest charged a fee. Group confession was also the norm in some places although officially not allowed. Priests and villages in some parishes ignored the new marriage ordinances ordered by the Council of Trent concerning mandatory posting of banns and a Church register.

In the diocese of Speyer in the region of the middle Rhine, however, it appears that peasants were mostly content with their priests, favoring reforms that improved local church services; but they firmly resisted those Catholic reforms that interfered with the running of the communal churches over which they had control.

Because Catholic reform had to come from outside and local communities did not welcome foreigners, new problems arose. The local population maintained zealous control of church finances and had a large say in appointing or dismissing the local priest.

The priest they were used to was a member of the community, often lived with a local woman, worked his own fields, and wore peasant dress except when officiating. His duties were to perform Sunday services, baptize children, and preside over marriages and funerals. If he was liked, he stayed; if not, he was sent away. People expected the priest to live according to their rules and standards. Some priests married their women and had children, but such matters were of little importance to the villagers. In the Bishopric of Speyer, attempts by higher church authorities to eradicate such priestly misbehavior alienated Church and peasants.[3] The dictates of the Council of Trent expected priests to be celibate, morally upright, sober, and remain aloof from community conflicts. The villages did not share these impositions. They expected the priest to behave in a similar manner to themselves.

COMPLAINTS AGAINST THE CLERGY

When visited by Church officials in 1583, 12 out of 22 clergymen were living with women. Some priests were prosecuted and imprisoned by officials of the bishop for that reason, but it appears not to have been effective enough to stop the practice. The peasants had no objection. Nor did villagers mind their priest drinking with them even when he overdid it. In general, complaints against a priest were similar to those that might be brought up against a neighbor. One priest allowed his cows to wander through people's fields; another shouted too loudly at his mistress and two sons, disturbing the neighborhood. The fact that Catechism lessons were ordered by the bishop, did not appeal to many, and the local youths did not bother to attend. There was some talk in one of the villages when a priest, in his last will and testament, left all his property to his nine grandchildren.

A BAD EXAMPLE

The case against the cleric of Wiesental embodies the behavior of others that the Council of Trent hoped to correct. Not only was he living with a woman whom he had promised to marry, but he did not teach the catechism and heard confession in groups, not privately. He drank too much, including before Easter services, entered into disputes with neighbors while intoxicated, accepted wine in lieu of his burial fee, and consumed meat during Lent. He also reputedly stole some flour set aside for a hospice.[4]

NEW PRIESTS AND PEASANTS

After about 1580, the Counter-Reformation arrived in the region of the diocese of Speyer with the newly ordained and better educated priests who were very different and more austere than the old traditional peasant priests whom they replaced. The village people found them arrogant, while the priests complained that the peasants did not perform their religious duties.

These men insisted on following to the letter the mandates of the Council of Trent, but local people were not impressed. When fines were issued for not attending church on Sundays or for dancing on that holy day, people became angry and ignored the regulations. Peasants were used to making use of their free time as they wished and were not pleased to be told how to use it.

People were ordered to avoid contact with Protestants with whom they traded in neighboring villages and to allow memberships in their communes only to Catholics. Once again, these measures failed and commerce continued as before.

Fines for hunting and fishing on Sundays, the closing of inns during church services, and rules that allowed dancing only on Saturday afternoons brought on the wrath of the populace. Church leaders complained that more people were in the inn than in the church during vespers and ordered fines to be given to anyone found there.

In one village no one could be married without parental permission and a ceremony had to be held. It was argued that the poor could ill afford it.[5]

JESUITS IN SPEYER

Jesuits arrived in Speyer in the 1560s much to the consternation of the city council and the bishop, all of whom heartily disliked them. The bishop was reported as saying he wished the devil would take them all.[6] One of the arguments against them was that they would arouse serious conflict with Protestant neighbors in nearby villages, which could lead to a breakdown in the so-far peaceful relations. Jesuits were also foreigners in the Catholic villages with no respect for local traditions. Their high degree of education and their moral comportment would also be an affront to the traditional clergy of the region.[7]

PRINTING AND CENSORSHIP

Censorship of reading material was established by the Congregation of the Index that denounced books at variance with the views of the Catholic faith, and it was made a sin to read or possess them. Because the new art of printing made it possible to widely disseminate the works of heretical authors and their Humanistic imitators, immoral poems, romances, satires on ecclesiastical persons and institutions, revolutionary works, and songs were circulated everywhere and wrought incalculable harm, according to the Vatican. The worst kinds of lampoons and libels were disseminated in pamphlets against the pope, the Roman curia, bishops, priests, monks, and nuns who remained true to their Catholic convictions. In vulgar language, Catholic doctrines were ridiculed; while among the lower, uneducated classes, the Church asserted the most base passions were stimulated.

COUNTER-REFORMATION AND THE COMMON PEOPLE

The reaffirmation of Church institutions and procedures helped inspire Catholics to cling to their beliefs. Emphasis on better education for priests, especially those in the villages (many of whom had only the rudiments of Latin, the language of the Church, and a shallow knowledge of scripture), improved relationships between the priest and his flock.

The Counter-Reformation also brought about a steady improvement in popular piety and the foundation of new orders such as the Jesuits who carried the Church's message to the far corners of the globe. The Catholic reformation was not successful in its attempts to recapture many of the converted Protestants of northern Europe.

STRUGGLE FOR SUPREMACY

The Church believed the entire Reformation was based on human rather than divine authority. Controversies, debates, executions, cruelty, wars, and destruction accompanied the Reformation and Counter-Reformation between 1517 and 1648. Catholics saw the Reformation as leading to enslavement under the authority of false prophets. Individual means of salvation associated with the new sects was a sham. Egotistical, power-greedy, land-hungry secular princes and officials found the Protestant movement to their advantage to snap up Church property, buildings, and revenues.

For Catholics, the Protestant Reformation was an unmitigated disaster causing great harm to the social, political, and religious unity of Christian Europe. Freedom of religious belief advocated by reformers did not exist according to the Church, who claimed that Protestantism gave rise to evil tyranny and anarchy in matters of conscience. Catholic sources blamed the Reformation as the cause of indescribable suffering among the people, for civil wars lasting decades, the destruction of countless treasures of art and priceless manuscripts, and rampant hatred between people of the same region and language. Further, Protestants were seen to be responsible for the Thirty Years' War that devastated Germany, and in which the Holy Roman Empire lost the leading position it had held for centuries.

The Reformation, it was believed, promoted absolutist designs of princes and kings repudiating papal authority. For many Catholics, it had led to terrible abuses by twisting and distorting what was good in the eyes of God into a degenerate view of religion and society by encouraging subservience of Church to state, fostering carnal desires through marriage of the clergy and by reckless, gross errors of doctrine.

The Church, in its own view had continued on its benevolent course for many centuries, undertaking prodigious works of education and charity. Hostility that arose toward its holy deeds and compassionate nature was due to impious civil influences and greed. As in all large organizations there were always a few immoral individuals, but the Church was hindered in its own internal reforms in the sixteenth century due to the antagonism of civil and Protestant interference, allowing misguided men to engross themselves in heresy and schism.

The secular leaders of town councils such as in Augsburg, permitted Protestants to take over, allowing them to forbid the celebration of Mass, and all Catholic ecclesiastical ceremonies, while giving Catholic clergy no alternative but to reform or depart the city.

INDULGENCES

According to the Catholic Church the war against the Turks, construction of churches and monasteries, aid to the poor, and numerous other good causes led to the selling of indulgences in the fifteenth century. When secular rulers demanded that a portion of the money collected in their territories be given to them, abuse became flagrant; and in the public mind, indulgences represented another oppressive tax. The use of indulgences for the new Saint Peter's church in Rome gave Luther an opportunity to attack them in general, and this assault brought on the Reformation in Germany. It may not have happened if he had not been protected by the unwise Elector, Frederick the Wise.

Similar motives had led Zwingli to propagate his erroneous teachings, thereby inaugurating the Reformation in German Switzerland. Both he and Luther asserted they were attacking indulgences, but they soon propagated doctrine contrary to that of the Church. Their errors led to rebellion against Church authority and to apostasy and schism. Political considerations played a large role in the development of Zwingli's control in Zürich. Arbitrary decrees, issued by the magistrates, concerned ecclesiastical organization; while members of the city council who remained true to the Catholic faith were expelled. Catholic services were soon forbidden in the city.

FALSE DOCTRINES

Proclaiming the false doctrine of "justification by faith alone," by denying the merit of good works, and the condemnation of monastic vows, Luther obviously intended to subvert the true fundamental institutions of the Church. His doctrine of the Bible as the only guide in religious questions, along with his rejection of Church authority, seduced a large number of priests, monks, and nuns into breaking their vows.

FRENCH SWITZERLAND

French Switzerland developed its own heretical point of view, organized in Geneva by Calvin who regulated all aspects of life of the citizens, supported by the authorities. Calvin's word was law, and he tolerated no contradiction of his views, introduced by means of violence. Catholic priests were banished, and the people oppressed and compelled to attend Calvinistic sermons.

SENSUALITY

The ideas that many reformers advocated, including Christian freedom of thought and the ability of individuals to seek and find their own salvation in the Bible, appealed to the base and morally corrupt. The abolition of religious institutions, which had functioned to constrain sinful human nature (confession, penance, fasting, abstinence, vows), appealed to the carnal desires and to the malleable, superficial, and unlettered. Hostility toward religious orders, to virginity, and to celibacy, attracted many people who preferred to be free from obligation to God and indulge their sensual cravings.

NORTHERN COUNTRIES

In Denmark, Norway, and Sweden, the Reformation found approval due to royal influence when King Christian II of Denmark welcomed it as an instrument to weaken the clergy and confiscate their extensive property. The barons and prelates deposed him, however, and elected his uncle, duke Frederick of Schleswig and Holstein to the throne. A secret follower of Luther, Frederick deceived the bishops and nobility when he swore at his coronation in 1523 to maintain the Catholic religion. Once on the throne, he granted the reformers freedom of belief, permitted the clergy to marry, and reserved for the king the confirmation of numerous, eventually Episcopal, appointments. His son, Christian III, who had already reformed Holstein, threw the Danish bishops into prison where they agreed to resign and to refrain from opposing the new doctrine.

Priests who opposed the Reformation were expelled, monasteries were closed, and the new Church introduced everywhere by force. At the Diet of Copenhagen in 1546 all rights of Catholics were nullified including the right of inheritance and eligibility for office. Catholic priests were forbidden to reside in the country under pain of death. Christian III also introduced the Reformation into Norway and Iceland by violent means.

The Reformation in Sweden was launched for political reasons by Gustavus Vasa. The Catholic faith proved difficult to overcome, but Gustavus appointed to high positions Lutherans who won over many adherents, including the archdeacon, Lorenz Anderson, whom the king made his chancellor. In his dealings with legates of Pope Adrian VI, the king pretended fidelity to the Church while giving support to heretics. He confiscated ecclesiastical property, compelled clergymen to accept the new doctrine, and a popular rebellion gave him an excuse to execute two Catholic bishops in 1527 for high treason.

The king assumed the right to decide Church appointments and removals while nobles found it beneficial to support the king when they were granted the right to take back all donations to the Church made by their ancestors since 1453. Clerical celibacy was abolished, and the vernacular introduced into divine service. Like Henry VIII of England, the king made himself supreme authority in religious matters, severing ties with the Vatican.

POLAND AND HUNGARY

Elsewhere, as in Poland, heresy was not deeply rooted. Protestantism had filtered in from neighboring countries, but the Catholic faith was supported by the people and Jesuit colleges. The king and many nobles, although tolerant, could not be drawn into changing their religious views. The different reformed sects fought bitterly among one another: but nevertheless, in 1573, they secured the religious Peace of Warsaw, gaining rights for Protestants equal to those of the Catholics. The Reformation achieved no further progress in Poland.

In Hungary, the reform movement made more rapid progress than in Poland and ironically was aided by the Turks who wiped out the Hungarian army at the battle of Mohács along with the king, Louis II Jagellon, and a half-dozen bishops, leaving reformers pretty much a free hand in the war devastated country.

For many Catholics the fundamental doctrine of justification by faith alone produced a deplorable shallowness in religious life. Ardor and devotion for good works vanished, asceticism that the Church had practiced from its earliest days became despised, charitable and supernatural interests ceased, and devotion to the merely mundane became widespread. Denial of the divinely instituted Church, both in religious doctrine and organization, encouraged perpetual divisions into sects and disputes characteristic of Protestantism. Freedom of belief was a fraud; only tyranny in matters of faith was displayed by the reformers. The various Protestant churches were entirely discordant with the Christian universalism of the Catholic Church and depended for their faith on the will of the secular ruler. Wherever the Reformation found fertile ground, it enslaved the people.

ENGLAND AND SCOTLAND

England, where the observance of the faith was deeply entrenched, once seemed the least likely of any Catholic country to embrace Protestantism. The king, Henry VIII, was emphatically on the side of the Church until the appearance at court of Anne Boleyn. Then it was found that the absolute power of the sovereign, at least in England, overrode the spiritual power of the pope.

Catholic theologians past and present find in Henry VIII's daughter, Mary Tudor, a sterling example of a Catholic monarch who tried to restore the "true faith" to that island. That Catholicism was the preference of the people was clear to Rome since when Mary gained the throne, she had little difficulty restoring the old religious order; and the Marian establishment, from the Church's perspective, proved itself more stable in light of Elizabeth's subsequent persecutions. At the close of the period, the Puritans were renewing Elizabeth's cruelties, and priests' blood was still flowing.

Though the oppression never ceased, and some 60 people were martyred during the reign of Elizabeth, the Counter-Reformation made great progress, and there were moments when it seemed about to triumph. Oliver Cromwell, Lord Protector of England, Scotland, and Ireland, and his anti-Catholic views, blotted out all the good that had been accomplished, however.

In Scotland, bloody and continuous feuds sadly demoralized monastic life, where barons placed their illegitimate children into the abbacies and episcopal sees, making Church government difficult. Yet the Scots resisted the Protestant Reformation for a generation although Henry VIII and his son Edward strove to impose it upon the people. Catholic Mary, Queen of Scots, relied upon French arms for royal and religious authority, but the nobility considered this an insult to those on whom the government of Scotland should naturally fall. Further, the Calvinists in France had won over many young Scottish soldiers and students.

The revolution took place with little doubt as to the issue. Elizabeth I actively supported the rebels with money, men, and ships. The ninth clause of the Treaty of Edinburgh (July 6, 1560) stipulated that "the matter of religion be passed over in silence," which in effect left to the Scottish

Protestants, the power to do as they pleased. The Treaty was drawn up by the parliament of Scotland in an attempt to end the old alliance with France, although it was not ratified by Mary, Queen of Scots, it led to the withdrawal of French troops from Scotland and the eventual fall of the Catholic Church there. Church estates were seized, and (except in the inaccessible north) every vestige of Catholic observance was forcibly thrown off in this last national revolt against the Church.

OTHER EUROPEAN COUNTRIES

By the energetic introduction of true ecclesiastical reform in the sentiment of the Council of Trent through the activity of many saintly people with the vigilance of the bishops and the diligence of the Inquisition, the Reformation did not take hold in Italy, Spain, Portugal, or much of France.

Events in Spain and Portugal (the latter under the Spanish crown) were similar to those in Italy. Despite attempts to disseminate anti-Church books and pamphlets in Spain, the Reformation gained little success, thanks to the zeal of the Spanish Inquisition, public authorities, and the absolutism of the crown that prevented the spread of the heretical movement. The few Spaniards who accepted the new doctrines were unable to mount any significant reforming movement. Similarly, in France, in spite of much unrest and civil wars, the monarchy, in large measure along with true, dedicated Catholics, assured the continuance of the Catholic faith.[8]

BATTLE FOR CONVERTS

The battle for converts worldwide is far from over. The reader will note that in once solidly Catholic Central and South America, although the majority of the population remains Roman Catholic, in the last few decades evangelists have made a rapid and deep incision into the Catholic numbers. The battle for hearts, minds, and especially souls continues today.

NOTES

1. Another school of thought presupposes that the pre-Tridentine Church in the villages was morally corrupt, financially bankrupt, and administered by ignorant clergy. Efforts to reform the Church were thus welcomed. See Forster, 19.

2. Hillerbrand (2007), 270.

3. Forster, 21–27.

4. Ibid., 80.

5. Ibid., 94–116 a detailed examination of some of the villages in the Bishopric of Speyer and their involvement and resistance to reform.

6. Ibid., 48.

7. Ibid., 47.

8. For much of the Church's view presented here, and for further detail, see Kevin Knight. "The Counter-Reformation" in *The Catholic Encyclopedia*. John Hungerford Pollen (New York: Robert Appleton Company, 1908), http://www.newadvent.org/cathen/04437a.htm (accessed March 16, 2010).

APPENDICES

The Holy Sacraments of the Catholic Church

The seven sacraments of the Catholic Church are ceremonies indicating what is sacred and significant and purport to be occasions for experiencing God's saving presence.

1. Baptism to remove the stain of original sin
2. Holy Eucharist. The body and blood of Christ in the wafer and wine of the Mass
3. Penance of confession
4. Confirmation the act admitting a baptized person to full church privileges.
5. Matrimony. No marriage was valid performed outside the Church
6. Holy Orders or ordination, the process that set priests apart form ordinary Christians.
7. Extreme Unction, the last blessing performed on the death bed

Only an ordained clergyman of the Church could perform the above functions.

APPENDIX 2

Rulers of the Countries Most Affected during the Time of Reformation and Counter-Reformation

Emperors of the Holy Roman Empire.

Maximilian I	14931519
Charles V	1519–1558
Ferdinand I	1558–1564
Maximilian II	1564–1576
Rudolf II	1576–1612
Matthias	1612–1619
Ferdinand II	1619–1637
Ferdinand III	1637–1657

Kings of France

François I	1515–1547
Henri II	1547–1559
François II	1559–1560
Charles IX	1560–1574
Henri III	1574–1589
Henri IV	1589–1610
Louis XIII	1610–1643
Louis XIV	1643–1715

Monarchs of England

Henry VIII	1509–1547
Edward VI	1547–1553
Mary I	1553–1558
Elizabeth I	1558–1603
James I	1603–1625
Charles I	1625–1649

Monarchs of Scotland

James V	1513–1542
Mary (queen)	1542–1567
James VI	1567–1625
Charles I	1625–1649 (also king of England)

Rulers of the United Provinces after 1572

William I	1572–1584
Maurice	1585–1625
Frederick Henry	1625–1647
William II	1647–1650

Kingdom of Denmark

Christian II	1513–1523
Frederick I	1523–1533
Christian III	1534–1559
Frederick II	1559–1588
Christian IV	1598–1648

Kingdom of Sweden

Gustavus I	1523–1560
Eric XIV	1560–1568
John III	1568–1592
Sigismund	1592–1599
Charles IX	1599–1611
Gustavus II	1611–1632
Christina	1632–1654

Popes

Leo X	1513–1521
Adrian VI	1522–1423
Clement VII	1523–1534
Paul III	1534–1549
Julius III	1550–1555
Marcellus II	1555
Paul IV	1555–1559
Pius IV	1559–1565
St. Pius V	1566–1572
Gregory XIII	1572–1585
Sixtus V	1585–1590
Urban VII	1590
Gregory XIV	1590–1591
Innocent IX	1591
Clement VIII	1592–1605
Leo XI	1605
Paul V	1605–1621
Gregory XV	1621–1623
Urban VIII	1623–1644
Innocent X	1644–1655

APPENDIX 3

Summary of the Articles of the Peasant Revolt of 1525

The Peasants justified their revolt that was as much political and social as religious, through Scripture and offered to withdraw any of their demands if they were proved contrary to the word of God.

They demanded:

1. To have the right to choose, appoint and dismiss their own local priests.
2. That the grain tithe be used to pay their local priest and to supplement the poor, inasmuch as it is commanded in Scripture. The tithe on cattle should be withdrawn since it was man's creation.
3. That serfdom be abolished since Christian men are free men in the eyes of God.
4. That they should be allowed to hunt and fish on lands that do not by right belong to overlords.
5. The poor should have the right to collect firewood and lumber for carpentry from the forests.
6. There should be no excessive services required by the peasants for the landlord.
7. There should be remuneration for services not previously agreed upon by tenant and lord.
8. Excessive rents should be reexamined allowing peasants to collect some benefit from their labors.
9. Judgments should be made according to the old written laws and not in accordance with laws recently imposed.
10. Previous communal fields, now owned by individuals, should be given back to the community with remuneration if purchased legally.
11. The death tax, that places an undue burden on widows and orphans, must be abolished.
12. Peasants should have future rights to add stipulations that are in line with scripture.

GLOSSARY

Ales A local church fête held in spring or summer involving food, drink, and entertainment, to raise money for the Church.

Anabaptist A radical, religious group heavily persecuted by both Catholics and Protestants for their views opposing infant baptism.

Annates Also known as "first fruits," this was the entire first year's profits of a benefice that accrued to the pope.

Apocalypse Cataclysmic events heralding the approaching end of the world when God would destroy all evil and raise the righteous to paradise.

Arminianism The Dutch theologian Arminius, rejecting Calvinism, asserted a belief in free grace in place of predestination and maintained the importance of the sacraments in worship.

Benefice Once a gift of land as a reward for services, it came to signify a permanent right administered by the Church giving ecclesiastical revenues to a cleric for the performance of some holy service.

Bull Official document issued by the pope for public communication. After the fifteenth century, these were issued only for formal occasions such as excommunication, beatification, or canonization of a saint.

Canon A clergyman belonging to the chapter or staff of a cathedral or collegiate church.

Canon law The body of laws and regulations for the government of a Christian church and its members.

Chapter The body of canons of a cathedral.

Curia (Roman) Tribunals and offices (the administration) by which the pope governed the Roman Catholic Church.

Drinckgeld Literally drinking money—a tip.

Ecumenical Representing the entire body of churches in matter of faith.

Elect Those chosen for salvation by divine mercy.

Free City A city of the Holy Roman Empire that owed its allegiance directly to the emperor.

Heresy Deliberate deviation from the official religious belief of a baptized member. When religious authorities thought a belief was heretical, they made efforts to eradicate the offending believers by excommunication, banishment, or death.

Humanism Doctrine centered around human secular concerns and interests, rejecting mysticism and the supernatural. It proclaimed the dignity and value of individuals and their capacity for betterment through reason.

Iconoclasm Destruction of religious symbols and icons.

Justification The act that deems a person justified or righteous before God.

Landgrave German *Landgraf*, comparable to a count, who owed feudal duty directly to the Holy Roman Emperor. His jurisdiction might cover a considerable territory.

Landsknechts Literally "servant of the country," applied to the mercenary soldiers of the Holy Roman Empire. They swore their allegiance to the emperor and his cause.

Margrave A *Markgraf*, or margrave, originally a nobleman and a military governor of a border province who maintained military forces and fortifications. A Margrave might conquer neighboring territory acquiring more power and wealth.

Palatinate A province, controlled by a count palatine (of the palace), which was at first the representative of a sovereign and later, the ruler of a territory subject to the crown but with rights of transfer to offspring.

Pluralism Holding several eccliastical offices at the same time.

Politique Used in the sixteenth and seventeenth centuries in France to describe moderate Huguenots and Catholics. The term often had a derogatory meaning of moral or religious indifference.

Prebend Portion of the cathedral revenues set aside for clerical support and regarded as a benefice. The right of a member of a chapter to his share in the revenues of the cathedral.

Predestination God's predetermination of the selected for salvation.

Schmalkaldic League An alliance of Lutheran princes within the Holy Roman Empire during the mid-sixteenth century deriving its name from the German town of Schmalkalden. It had a sizable military to bolster its political and religious values.

Sabbat A midnight assembly of witches and warlocks on certain days of the year, believed to renew allegiance to the devil through mystic and licentious rites.

Swabian League Catholic association of twenty-six Swabian cities in south western Germany united for the protection of trade and peace. Supported by the Holy Roman Emperor, by nobles, knights, and prelates. It had its own court, army, and constitution.

Synod Council convened to decide an issue of Church doctrine or administration. An ecumenical council is a synod of the whole Church.

Tithe A 10 percent levy by the landlord, secular or ecclesiastical, on farm produce or income.

Waldensians A heretical, severely persecuted Christian spiritual movement, seemingly begun by Peter Waldo in twelfth-century Italy, which joined the Reformation toward the end of the sixteenth century.

BIBLIOGRAPHY

PRINT SOURCES

Anderson, James M. *Daily Life during the Spanish Inquisition*. Westport, Connecticut: Greenwood Press (2002).

Ariès, Philippe. *Centuries of Childhood*. Transl. Robert Baldick. New York: Alfred A. Knopf (1962).

Bainton, Roland H. *The Reformation of the Sixteenth Century*. Boston: Beacon Press (1952).

Bainton, Roland H. *Women of the Reformation in Germany and Italy*. Minneapolis: Augsburg Publishing (1971).

Bainton, Roland H. *Women of the Reformation in France and England*. Minneapolis: Augsburg Publishing (1973).

Baumgartner, Frederic J. *France in the Sixteenth Century*. New York: St. Martin's Press (1995)

Bideleux, Robert and Ian Jeffries. *A History of Eastern Europe*. London: Routledge (1998).

Braudel, Fernand. *The Structures of Everyday Life*. Vol. I. Transl. by Siân Reynolds. New York: Harper & Row (1979).

Brears, Peter. *Food and Cooking in 16th Century Britain*. English Heritage (1985).

Brockliss, L. W. B. and Colin Jones. *The Medical World of Early Modern France*. Oxford and New York: Clarendon Press (1997).

Brooks, Peter Newman, ed. *Reformation Principle and Practice. Essays in Honour of Arthur Geoffrey Dickens*. London: Scolar Press (1980).

Cantor, Norman F. *Civilization of the Middle Ages*. New York: Harper Collins (1994).

Carlson, Eric Josef. *Marriage and the English Reformation*. Oxford: Blackwell (1994).

Chadwick, Owen. *The Reformation*. Harmondsworth: Penguin (1964).

Chaunu, Pierre. *L'Aventure de la Réform*. PARIS: Hermé (1986).

Clark, George. *Early Modern Europe*. New York: Galaxy (1960).

Constant, Jean-Marie. *La Vie Quotidienne de la Noblesse Française aux XVI et XVII Siècles*. Hachette Littérature (1985).

Coryat, Thomas. *Coryat's Crudities*. Vol II. Glasgow: James MacLehose and Sons (1905).

Couchman, Jane and Ann Crabb, eds. *Women's Letters Across Europe, 1400–1700*. Burlington, VT: Ashgate Publishing (2005).

Couliano, Ioan P. *Eros and Magic in the Renaissance*. Transl. By Margaret Cook. Chicago and London: University of Chicago Press (1987).

Coulton, G. G. *Art and the Reformation*. Oxford: Blackwell (1928).

Cowan, Ian B. *The Scottish Reformation*. London: Weidenfeld and Nicolson (1982).

Crowder, Michael and Paul Richards, eds. *A Social History of Western Europe 1450–1720*. London: Hutchinson University Library (1984).

Darnton, Robert. *The Great Cat Massacre*. New York: Basic Books (1999)

Dickens, A. G. *Reformation and Society*. London: Thames and Hudson (1966).

Dickens, A. G. *The English Reformation*. Collins/Fontana (1972).

Duke, Alastair. *Reformation and Revolt in the Low Countries*. London and Ronceverte: The Hambledon Press (1990).

Elliott, J. H. *Europe Divided 1559–1598*. London: Fontana Press (1968).

Elton, G. R. *Reformation Europe 1517–1559*. Glasgow: Collins Sons (1963).

Elton, G. R., ed. *The New Cambridge Modern History*. Vol II. Cambridge University Press (1965).

Erlanger, Philippe. *La Vie Quotidienne sous Henri IV*. Hachette (1958).

Erlanger, Philippe. *The Age of Courts and Kings. Manners and Morals 1558–1715*. London: Weidenfeld and Nicolson (1967).

Febvre, Lucien and Henri-Jean Martin. *The coming of the Book. The Impact of Printing 1450–1800*. Transl. by David Gerard. Thetford, Norfolk: Lowe and Brydon (1976).

Febvre, Lucien and Henri-Jean Martin. *Life in Renaissance France*. Transl. by Marian Rothstein. Cambridge: Harvard University Press (1977).

Febvre, Lucien and Henri-Jean Martin. *The Problem of Unbelief in the Sixteenth Century. The Religion of Rabelais* Transl. by Beatrice Gottlieb. Cambridge: Harvard University Press (1982).

Ferro, Marc. *Le Siècle de Luther et de Christophe Colomb*. Paris: Plon (2008).

Flandrin, Jean-Louis. *Families in Former Times. Kinship, Household and Sexuality*. Transl. by Richard Southern, Cambridge University Press (1979).

Forster, Marc. R. *The Counter Reformation in the Villages*. Cornell University Press (1992).

Frey, Linda S. and Marsha L. Frey, eds. *Daily Lives of Civilians in Wartime Europe, 1618-1900*. Westport, Connecticut: Greenwood Press (2007).

Fudge, John D. *Commerce and Print in the Early Reformation*. Leiden/Boston: Brill (2007).

Garrisson, Janine. *A History of Sixteenth-Century France, 1483–1598*. Transl. by Richard Rex. Basingstoke and London: Macmillan (1995).

Gies, Frances and Joseph. *Marriage and the Family in the Middle Ages*. New York: Harper & Row (1987).

Graham, Roderick. *John Knox Democrat*. London: Robert Hall (2001).

Greaves, Richard L. *Theology and Revolution in the Scottish Reformation*. Grand Rapids, Michigan: Christian University Press (1980).

Hampe, Theodore. *Crime and Punishment in Germany as illustrated by the Nuremberg Malefactors' Books*. Transl. by Malcolm Letts, based on Wm Smith's 'Breeff Description of the famouse and Bewtifull Cittie of Norenberg' (1594). London: Routledge (1929).

Harrison, Molly. *The Kitchen in History*. New York: Charles Scribner's Sons (1972).

Hillerbrand, Hans J., ed. *The Reformation in its own Words*. London: SCM Press Ltd. (1964).

Hillerbrand, Hans J., ed. *The World of the Reformation*. New York: Charles Scribner's Sons (1973).

Hillerbrand, Hans J., ed. *The Division of Christendom*. Louisville, Kentucky: Westminister John Knox Press (2007).

Johnston, Andrew. *The Protestant Reformation in Europe*. London and New York: Longman (1991).

Jones, John. *The Early Modern World 1450-1700*. Basingstoke: Macmillan Education Ltd. (1987).

Kamen, Henry. *The Iron Century. Social Change in Europe 1550–1660*. New York: Praeger (1971).

Kamen, Henry. *Early Modern European Society*. London and New York: Routledge (2000).

Knecht, R. J. *The French Wars of Religion*. London and New York: Longman (1989).

Klein, Ernest. *A Comprehensive Etymological Dictionary of the English Language*. Amsterdam. Elsevier (1971).

Lace, William W. *Elizabethan England*. San Diego: Lucent Books (1995).

Ladurie, Emmanuel le Roy. *The Beggar and the Professor. A Sixteenth Century Family Saga*. Transl. by Arthur Goldhammer. University of Chicago Press (1997).

Luther, Martin. *Table Talk*. Edited and transl. by William Hazlittle. Philadelphia: Bridge-Logos (2004).

MacDonald Fraser, George. *The Steel Bonnets*. London: Collins Harvill (1971).

Mahoney, Irene. *Madame Catherine*. New York: Coward, McCann & Geoghegan, Inc. (1975).

Markham, Gervase. *The English Housewife*. Michael R. Best, ed. Kingston and Montreal: McGill-Queen's University Press (1986).

Markwald, Rudolf and Marilynn Morris Markwald. *Katharina Von Bora. A Reformation Life*. St. Louis: Concordia Publishing House (2002).

Michalski, Sergiusz. *The Reformation and the Visual Arts*. London and New York: Routledge (1993).

Moryson, Fynes, Gent. *An Itinerary*. Vols. i–iv. Glasgow: J. MacLehose and Sons; Reprinted in New York: The Macmillan co. (1907).

Moryson, Fynes, Gent. *Shakespeare's Europe (1617)*. New York: Benjamin Blom (1967).

Oberman, Heiko A. *The Roots of Anti-Semitism in the Age of Renaissance and Reformation*. Transl. by James I. Porter. Philadelphia: Fortress Press (1984).

Ozment, Steven. *When Fathers Ruled*. Cambridge: Harvard University Press (1983).

Ozment, Steven. *Magdalena and Balthasar*. New York: Simon and Schuster (1986).

Ozment, Steven. *Three Behaím Boys*. New Haven: Yale University Press (1990).

Ozment, Steven. *Protestants: The Birth of a Revolution*. New York: Doubleday (1992).

Ozment, Steven. *Scandal in a Sixteenth Century German Town*. New York: St. Martin's Press (1996).

Ozment, Steven. *Flesh and Spirit. Private Life in Early Modern Germany*. New York: Viking Penguin Group (1999).

Ozment, Steven. *Ancestors. The Loving Family in Old Europe*. Cambridge: Harvard University Press (2001).

Parish, Helen and William G. Naphy, eds. *Religion and Superstition in Reformation Europe*. Manchester University Press (2002).

Parish, Helen and William G. *Monks, Miracles and Magic: Reformation representations of the Medieval Church*. London and New York: Routledge (2005).

Parish, Helen and William G. *Clerical Marriage and The English Reformation: Precedent Policy and Practice*. Burlington, Vermont: Ashgate Publishing (2000).

Parker, Geoffrey. *The Dutch Revolt*. Rev. Cornell University Press (1985).

Payne, Joseph. *Lectures on the History of Education with a Visit to German Schools*. London: Longmans, Green and Co. (1892).

Pearson, Lu Emily. *Elizabethans at Home*. Stanford University Press (1957).

Platter, Felix. *The Journal of Felix Platter a medical student in Montpellier in the Sixteenth Century*. Seán Jennett, ed. London: Frederick Muller Ltd. (1961).

Poortvliet, Rien. *Daily Life in Holland in the Year 1566*. Transl. by Karin H. Ford. New York: Harry N. Abrams Inc. (1992).

Rank, J., "Latin School," in *Fass, Paula S. J. Encyclopedia of Children and Childhood in History and Society. New York: Macmillan Reference USA (2004)*.

Richardson, Catherine. *Clothing Culture, 1350-1650*. Burlington, Vermont: Ashgate Publishing (2004).

Roper, Lyndal. *The Holy Household. Women and Morals in Reformation Augsburg*. Oxford: Clarendon Press (1989).

Rosman, Doreen. *From Catholic to Protestant. Religion and the People in Tudor England*. London: UCL Press (1996).

Salzman, L. F. *England in Tudor Times*. New York: Russell and Russell (1969).

Sanderson, Margaret H. B. *A Kindly Place? Living in Sixteenth-Century Scotland*. East Linton: Tuckwell Press (2002).

Sass, Lorna J. *To the Queen's taste* (Elizabethan Feasts and recipes). New York: Metropolitan Museum of Art (1976).

Sax, Boria. *Crow*. London: Reaktion Books (2003).

Scott, Tom and Bob Scribner. *The German Peasants' War. A History in Documents*. London: Humanities Press (1991).

Scribner, R. W. *Popular Culture and Popular Movements in Reformation Germany*. London and Ronceverte: The Hambledon Press (1987).

Seccombe, Wally. *A Millennium of Family Change. Feudalism to Capitalism in Northwestern Europe*. London and New York: Verso (1992).

Simon, Edith. *The Reformation*. Time–Life Inc. (1968).

Smith, L. Pearsall, ed. *The Life and Letters of Sir Henry Wotton 1568-1639*. Oxford: Clarendon Press (1907).

Thorndike, Lynn. *A History of Magic and Experimental Science*. New York: Macmillan (1929).

Turner-Wilcox, R. *The Mode in Costume*. New York: Charles Scribner's Sons (1958).

Vecellio. Cesare. *Vecellio's Renaissance Costume Book*. New York: Dover Publications (1977).

Von Greyerz, Kaspar. *The Late City Reformation in Germany. The Case of Colmar 1522-1628*. Wiesbaden: Franz Steiner Verlag (1980).

Walker, Williston. *A History of the Christian Church*. New York: Charles Scribner's Sons (1959).

Warrack, John. *Domestic Life in Scotland, 1488-1688*. London: Methuen & Co. Ltd. (1920).

Watts, Sheldon, J. *A Social History of Western Europe 1450-1720. Tensions and Solidarities among Rural People*. London: Hutchinson University Library for Africa (1984).

Weiditz, Christoph. *Authentic Everyday Dress of the Renaissance*. New York: Dover Publications (1994).

Wiesner, Merry E. *Women in Reformation and Counter Reformation Europe*. Sherrin Marshall, ed., Indiana University Press (1989).

Wiesner-Hanks, Merry. *Convents Confront the Reformation: Catholic and Protestant Nuns in Germany*. Milwaukee: Marquette University Press (1998)

WEB SITES

Andrew Pettegree. "The English Reformation" British Broadcasting Corporation. http://www.bbc.co.uk/history/british/tudors/english_reformation_01.shtml (accessed March 15, 2010).

Gail Fineberg. "Tyndale and the English Bible." Library of Congress. http://www.loc.gov/loc/lcib/9707/tyndale.html (accessed March 16, 2010).

Presence Switzerland. "Two Reformers: Zwingli and Calvin." Federal Department of Foreign Affairs, General Secretariat, Presence Switzerland, http://www.swissworld.org/en/history/the_reformation/zwingli_and_calvin/ (accessed March 16, 2010).

Scott Eric Atkins. "Reformation Puritans and Pilgrims." University of Virginia, http://xroads.virginia.edu/~CAP/Puritan/purhist.html (accessed March 16, 2010)

Frederick Engels. "The Peasant War in Germany." Marx and Engels Internet Archive. http://www.marxists.org/archive/marx/works/1850/peasant-war-germany/index.htm (accessed March 15, 2010).

J. P. Sommerville. "Elizabeth I." Department of History, University of Wisconsin-Madison, http://history.wisc.edu/sommerville/361/361-14.htm (accessed March 15, 2010).

Virtual Museum of French Protestantism. "The Reformation in France" Virtual Museum of French Protestantism, http://www.museeprotestant.org/Pages/Salles.php?scatid=3&Lget=EN (accessed March 15, 2010).

Saxon State Library. "The Reformation in Germany." Library of Congress, http://www.loc.gov/exhibits/dres/dres3.html (accessed March 15, 2010).

Carrie. "The Counter-Reformation." European University Institute, http://vlib.iue.it/carrie/exts/carrie_books/gilbert/19.html (accessed March 15, 2010).

Luther, Martin, "Disputation of Doctor Martin Luther on the Power and Efficacy of Indulgences." *Project Wittenberg*, http://www.iclnet.org/pub/

resources/text/wittenberg/luther/web/ninetyfive.html (accessed August 17, 2010).

Jacob Isidor Mombert. "Tyndale's Letter from Prison" *Bible Research*, http://www.bible-researcher.com/tyndale3.html (accessed March 16, 2010).

J. Rank. "Latin School," in *Encyclopedia of Children and Childhood in History and Society*, http://www.faqs.org/childhood/Ke-Me/Latin-School.html (accessed March 16. 2010).

Kevin Knight, "The Counter-Reformation," in *The Catholic Encyclopedia*. John Hungerford Pollen (New York: Robert Appleton Company, 1908), http://www.newadvent.org/cathen/04437a.htm (accessed March 16, 2010).

INDEX

About the Author

Dr. JAMES M. ANDERSON is Professor Emeritus at the University of Calgary, Canada. He has spent many years in western Europe including Spain, Portugal, and France, both as a Fulbright Scholar and as the recipient of multiple Canada Council and SSHRC grants, contributing numerous articles and books to the field of European studies. He is the author of 14 books including *Daily Life during the French Revolution* (Greenwood 2007), *The Spanish Civil War* (Greenwood 2003), *Daily Life during the Spanish Inquisition* (Greenwood 2002), and *The History of Portugal* (Greenwood 2000).